FICTION AS FACT

FICTION

The Horse Soldiers and Popular Memory

AS FACT

Neil Longley York

THE KENT STATE UNIVERSITY PRESS

Kent, Ohio, & London

© 2001 by The Kent State University Press,

Kent, Ohio 44242

ALL RIGHTS RESERVED

Library of Congress Catalog Card Number 00-062021

ISBN 0-87338-685-X

ISBN 0-87338-688-4 (pbk.)

Manufactured in the United States of America

06 05 04 03 02 01   5 4 3 2 1

Library of Congress Cataloging-in-Publication Data

York, Neil Longley.

Fiction as fact : The horse soldiers and popular memory /
Neil Longley York.

p.   cm.

Includes bibliographical references and index.

ISBN 0-87338-685-X (alk. paper) ∞

ISBN 0-87338-688-4 (pbk. : alk. paper) ∞

1. Grierson's Cavalry Raid, 1863.   2. Horse soldiers.
3. Grierson, Benjamin Henry, 1826–1911.   4. United States—
History—Civil War, 1861–1865—Cavalry operations.
5. United States—History—Civil War, 1861–1865—Literature
and the war.   6. United States—History—Civil War, 1861–1865—
Motion pictures and the war.   7. Historical fiction, American—
History and criticism.   8. Historical fiction, American—Film
and video adaptations.   I. Title.

E475.23 .Y67 2001

973.7'3—dc21   00-062021

British Library Cataloging-in-Publication data are available.

FOR FRED

departmental horse soldier

CONTENTS

Illustrations   ix

Preface   xi

Acknowledgments   xv

1 The Inspiration: Grierson's Raid   1

2 The Story as History   25

3 The Story as Novel   52

4 The Story as Film   78

5 The Story Not Told   105

6 The Truth—Ever Elusive   127

Notes   146

Bibliographic Essay   171

Index   175

ILLUSTRATIONS

Map of Grierson's raid   3

Grierson's raiders at the Pearl River bridge   11

The raiders parading in Baton Rouge   17

Benjamin Henry Grierson   23

Dee Brown   27

Stephen Forbes   36

Henry Forbes   40

Grierson as cavalier   49

Harold Sinclair   54

Jacket art for *The Horse Soldiers*   58

John Ford   80

Opening scene from *The Horse Soldiers*   84

Cadets advancing in *The Horse Soldiers*   97

Harold Sinclair receiving award   103

Historical markers in Newton, Mississippi   131

Cover to the Dell paperback of *The Horse Soldiers*   140

Grierson family grave marker   143

PREFACE

The seed of this book was sown over twenty-five years ago, when I was an undergraduate. In a course that started with Herodotus and Thucydides, I was obliged to think deeply about the nature of historical inquiry, more deeply than I had ever imagined I would or could. At the end of the semester my classmates and I turned in papers attempting to answer the question of whether history is an art or a science. I learned the hard way the meaning of the phrase "false dichotomy"; I had been set up and did not realize it until too late.

Other issues discussed in that same course, ranging from the possibility of objectivity to the existence of historical truth, have stayed with me over the years. Like most historians, I concentrate on research and writing, not on exploring, in any systematic fashion, the big questions in the philosophy of history. And yet those questions are always there, not quite buried in the back of my mind. Every lecture I give, every essay I write, is a reminder of their importance. I find excuses to slip the big questions into my courses, though I do so carefully. Many of my students are history majors, but they are rarely interested in the abstractions that fascinate philosophers. Few have read serious historical works even if they are considering a career in history teaching. More than a few had their understanding of the American past shaped in movie theaters or in front of the television—something that professional historians often lament. Perhaps it is lamentable, but such is life, and it is a development that is not entirely bad. If nothing else, the popularity of certain films and television programs is proof that curiosity about the past still exists, that there is still an audience for historians to try to reach.

I have spent almost all my academic career studying Revolutionary America. At one point, well over a decade ago, I combined my interests in that period with an inquiry into the nature of history and commentary on how elements of the past as we know it are formed by popular culture.

Using a half-dozen honors students as guinea pigs, I taught a course on the Declaration of Independence that began with the film version of the Broadway musical *1776*. Sherman Edwards, who conceived the idea for the play, had been a history major at New York University and taught high school history for a time. He and collaborator Peter Stone were convinced that they had written something of historical merit (their exercise of dramatic license notwithstanding), something that in its own way told the truth. "In historical drama, a number of small licenses are almost always taken with the strictest fact," and *1776*, they conceded, was no exception. "But," they asserted, "none" of the changes they made, "either separately or in accumulation, has done anything to alter the historical truth of the characters, the time, or the events of American independence."[1] No small claim, this.

My students watched *1776* cold, with no explanatory comments from me. I wanted them to see it as if they were members of a general audience; evaluating it as budding historians came later. Each member of the seminar took one character to compare what Edwards and Stone did with what we know from the surviving documents. Essays by Carl Becker, Dominick LaCapra, John Lukacs, and Hayden White got them thinking about some deeper considerations. Not surprisingly, opinions of *1776* as history varied, depending on how many liberties the playwrights took with the persons the students had researched. Though all agreed that fictionalizing the past can be a valuable learning and teaching tool, they disagreed on whether *1776* is a good example of how that tool should be used.

It was quite by accident that I returned to the issues addressed in that seminar and began the research leading to this book. Walking down the aisle of a video store to buy a copy of *Emma* for my daughters, I passed a display featuring John Wayne films, and one of them, *The Horse Soldiers*, caught my eye. It is a Civil War adventure about Yankee cavalrymen who swept through Mississippi in the spring of 1863 and did not stop until they had ridden all the way to Baton Rouge, Louisiana. I remembered that my parents took me to see this film at one of the many drive-in movies sprinkled around the northern California of my youth; I had probably watched it as a late-night television offering two or three times since.

That triggered yet another memory, of a firsthand account of the raid dramatized in the film. I had read excerpts from that account years before, when my department was smaller, my colleagues and I were stretched thinner, and I taught our Civil War course. In fact, for a time as an undergraduate I had thought that I would be a Civil War specialist. Frank W.

Fox, the professor who did more than anyone else to keep me in history instead of veering off toward law, studied under David Potter, the great Civil War historian then teaching at Stanford. His enthusiasm sparked my own. He and I eventually moved into other fields, yet the Civil War still beckons—"the great single event of our history,"[2] as Robert Penn Warren called it.

So I bought *The Horse Soldiers* and read the credits carefully as they flashed by. I saw that the film had been inspired by a novel of the same title by Harold Sinclair. Curious to know what historians have done with the raid, I pulled down one of my Civil War histories from the shelf and found a reference to an account by Dee Brown. I read Brown's book first because it was published first—in 1954—before turning to Sinclair, whose novel appeared two years later. The film was released in 1959.

Two things struck me after I read both books and viewed the movie again. One was that they had come out so close to each other in time. The other was that I had examples in each of three major categories—film, fiction, and history—that routinely mine the past, with practitioners who claim to be telling the "truth." I could stop here with a bad pun and say "the rest is history." That might leave the impression that I wrote what follows with tongue firmly in cheek, which I have not. Most of us, I am convinced, learn about our past from a mishmash of sources and without giving much thought as to how the national memory is formed. Films, novels, and histories play a part in this formation for almost all of us. I have not in these pages set up any straw men to knock down, citing the virtues of historical writing and the vices of fiction and film. There is already enough of that to go around. Besides, I do not believe that history as it is often written is superior to or necessarily that different from novels and movies. Read on and I will explain why. But first there are stories to retell.

ACKNOWLEDGMENTS

Just as no man was an island in John Donne's world, no author works alone in mine. I must thank Kendall Brown, my past department chair (he who controlled the money), and department secretary Julie Radle (she who knows how much can be spent) for giving me the funds I needed to travel and do research at this place and that. Colleagues Fred Gowans and Mark Grandstaff were kind enough to read my first draft and tactful enough to keep their criticisms friendly.

One of the great joys—if not ironies—of studying the past is that it so often brings together the living in their pursuit of the dead, people scattered across the map who would otherwise never meet. Dee Brown was unfailingly kind in responding to my many queries about a book that he had written over forty years before. Dan Ford was likewise a great help as I delved into his grandfather's film work. Bill Weber, whose efforts on behalf of a better historical record are recounted briefly in the final chapter, generously sent me material, as did newspaper editor Keith Justice of Newton, Mississippi. The staff at the Lilly Library, Indiana University—most especially Sue Presnell—proved to be both efficient and congenial. Teresa Thomason at the Milner Library, Illinois State University, turned up uncatalogued Harold Sinclair papers. At the Illinois State Historical Library, E. Cheryl Schnirring tracked down passages that had eluded me in the Grierson papers. John Hoffman and Bryon Andreasen of the Illinois Historical Survey at the University of Illinois Library provided a relaxed and yet professional setting that is becoming all too rare. Harold L. Miller of the State Historical Society of Wisconsin assisted me with the Walter Mirisch and United Artists collections there. Carlene Mathis-Kull, then of the *Pantagraph*, aided from afar and, when I arrived in Bloomington, arranged for me to meet with her reading group, which included a few local residents who had known Harold Sinclair. John T. Hubbell, who in his role as editor of *Civil War History* first expressed an interest in what I was doing, showed that he is scholarly gentility personified as director of the Kent State University Press. The two reviewers that he sent the manuscript to were most helpful; their recommendations, along with the skillful work of managing editor Erin Holman and copyeditor Trudie Calvert, made the finished product just that much better. To them and to all of the others, named here or not, I offer heartfelt thanks for kindnesses received.

Finally, to my wife, Carole, and our daughters, Jennifer and Caitlin, I apologize for replaying the videotape version of *The Horse Soldiers* with every excuse I could make, and humming the tune to "I Left My Love" over and over. I am not promising, however, that I will stop any time soon.

FICTION AS FACT

1

THE INSPIRATION: GRIERSON'S RAID

With Grierson for our leader
We'll chase the dastard foe,
'Till our horses bathe their fetlocks
In the Gulf of Mexico.

—"Song of the First Brigade,"
in R. W. Surby, *Grierson Raids*

By the spring of 1863, war had been raging for two years with no end in sight. Both North and South showed signs of weariness. In Washington leading Republicans fretted over their tenuous control of Congress and wondered about their ability to at least maintain the appearance of unity within their own ranks. Their president could not be certain that he would win a second term because he had done almost nothing to bring over Democrats and not enough to satisfy the disgruntled in his own party. For all the millions of dollars spent and thousands of lives lost, the war to preserve the Union, now expanded to end slavery, had accomplished little. The Army of the Potomac seemed incapable of winning campaigns in the East. Its attempt to take Richmond by a flanking movement the year before had failed; the Confederate counterattack was turned back in Maryland, but at horrific cost.

If in the eastern theater Union and Confederate forces contested the same ground as they had at the beginning of the conflict, in the West there had been more movement, a hint of real Northern progress. Union troops were inching their way down the Mississippi, hoping to combine with units pushing upriver from New Orleans, which had fallen the previous spring. But that hope was mixed with uncertainty. The move north had ground to a halt not far above Baton Rouge because Confederate defenses around Port Hudson proved too strong for Union land and naval forces to take. The men in blue marching south would likely have to meet their comrades where they were, and that could not be done until Vicksburg fell.

Well over two hundred thousand Union troops were scattered in an arc from Baton Rouge to Nashville, bivouacked in large groups and smaller clusters. William S. Rosecrans, commander of the Union troops in central Tennessee, had some eighty thousand men under him, but nearly half were stationed along supply and communication routes while the rest were gathered around Nashville. The largest Union force, the Army of the Tennessee headquartered in Memphis, was sprinkled from Corinth in northeastern Mississippi to positions just northwest of Vicksburg, a total of nearly one hundred thousand men but with no more than twenty thousand concentrated in any one place. To the south in Louisiana were thirty thousand in yet another independent military district. Although orders came from Washington, local cooperation was essential for these armies to be effective. Opposing were Rebels arrayed in the same fashion, with perhaps forty-five thousand under Braxton Bragg in eastern Tennessee and thirty-five thousand or so under John C. Pemberton in Mississippi. Pemberton set up headquarters in Jackson, where he could stay close to Vicksburg on the west and still be ready to meet a threat from the north. Like their Northern counterparts, coordination between these groups could be called for from the national capital, but success depended on their willingness to cooperate, a state of mind that Richmond could not impose.

Washington looked to Maj. Gen. Ulysses S. Grant for victory in the West. Grant, who had taken overall command of the Army of the Tennessee in October 1862, knew that "so long as . . . [Vicksburg] was held by the enemy, free navigation of the river was prevented."[1] Grant well understood that Vicksburg was a vital logistical link, through which men and matériel from the western Confederacy flowed east. Rail lines converging in Shreveport carried goods to the edge of the Mississippi, where they were taken across and put back on rails, to roll from Vicksburg to Jackson and points farther east. Union warships had proved that they could steam past Vicksburg's guns back in the summer, and troops were positioned along the river above the city, but Vicksburg had not been cut off from its western sources or eastern connections.

Initially Grant thought that he could take Vicksburg by marching overland straight into Mississippi from Memphis, with the river to his right, the Mobile and Ohio Railroad off to his left, and the Mississippi Central Railroad, its terminus in Jackson, bisecting his line of march. That

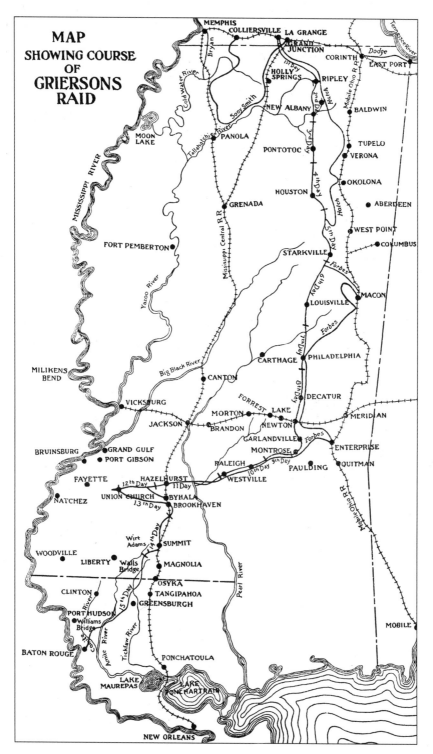

This detailed and quite accurate map is in the Stephen Alfred Forbes
Collection, 4 D 2.2. Courtesy of the Illinois Historical Survey, University of
Illinois, Urbana-Champaign.

assumption changed at the end of 1862. All along he had feared that Confederate forces would tear up bridges and rail lines in his front while enemy cavalry operating out of central Tennessee, especially the resourceful, unpredictable Nathan Bedford Forrest, threatened his rear. Riding too quickly for his more numerous but sluggish Yankee opponents, in December, Forrest, with fewer than two thousand men, wreaked havoc on the Mobile and Ohio Railroad, Grant's lifeline to stockpiles in Columbus, Kentucky. When three to four thousand Rebel troopers under Earl Van Dorn dashed into Grant's Holly Springs supply depot in northern Mississippi and torched the stores there, Grant reconsidered his strategy. He did not pull all of his troops out of northern Mississippi, but he did decide to find another approach to Vicksburg. As a Chicago newspaper correspondent who passed through Holly Springs and saw the utter destruction there put it, the "wily" Van Dorn "had accomplished his purpose, which was to show Gen. Grant the impossibility of maintaining such a long line of communication."[2]

Using soldiers already in place near Vicksburg, William Tecumseh Sherman made a direct assault from the marshy, broken terrain above the city not long after the Holly Springs raid; it failed. Grant's various attempts in February and March to find a more indirect route also failed. Grant therefore decided to take the bulk of his river forces—perhaps forty thousand men—march them down the west bank of the Mississippi, combine them with the fleet assembled by Adm. David D. Porter, which first had to run the gauntlet at Vicksburg, and take their objective from below. Grant was naturally inclined to participate in this risky operation, and the politics of command reinforced his inclination. If he were not on the scene, the ranking general along the river would be John A. McClernand, not Sherman. Grant despised McClernand and thought him incompetent. Moreover, Sherman was skeptical about the new strategy, despite his relatively smooth working relationship with Grant. "It is not a good plan," he surmised, and told Grant as much.[3] He would just as soon keep his smaller, independent force to the northwest of Vicksburg, then strike the city from that direction after the main army worked its way overland down to a point between Vicksburg and Jackson, approaching Vicksburg from the east. Sending troops south along the Louisiana side of the Mississippi, like the earlier attempt to dig a canal circumventing Vicksburg, struck Sherman as wasted effort.

But Grant had made up his mind, and Sherman, still grumbling, fell into line. In the meantime, Gen. Joseph E. Johnston, sent by Jefferson Davis to Tennessee as a link between Pemberton and Bragg, became convinced that some of the Union forces Grant pulled back after his unsuccessful maneuvering around Vicksburg would be transferred for a campaign against Confederates in central Tennessee. He consequently detached Van Dorn's Mississippians for service there, taking the largest and best cavalry unit away from an aggrieved Pemberton. Van Dorn rode northeast with nearly twice the number of men he had led into Holly Springs. His departure all but stripped Mississippi above Jackson of regular cavalry, with the exception of a few depleted regiments in the Okolona area below Corinth. Johnston wanted to use Van Dorn's men "to hold the country" where the larger Confederate army under Bragg obtained its supplies.[4] Pemberton asked that Van Dorn be sent back in mid-March when it became clear that Grant was still determined to take Vicksburg. Johnston delayed, thereby opening the door for Grierson's raid.

Skirmishing between cavalry units along the Tennessee-Mississippi border had become common by the end of 1862. Holly Springs had been seized in November by a Yankee column, and Van Dorn's raid, which carried into southern Tennessee before the Rebels wheeled right and looped back into Mississippi, was repayment in kind. Union and Confederate cavalrymen often crisscrossed each other's paths. In one near miss a Yankee column headed back to base came within sight of Van Dorn's rear guard as the Mississippians rode toward Holly Springs. If the two columns had become engaged then or if the Union troopers had dogged Van Dorn's tail, the fiasco at Holly Springs might have been averted.

Col. Benjamin Henry Grierson, who commanded an understrength cavalry brigade composed of the 6th and 7th Illinois regiments and the 2d Iowa, was one of those many horse soldiers involved in this intermittent hit-and-run warfare. Operating out of La Grange, Tennessee, just over the Mississippi border, from January through the end of March 1863, Grierson had led little forays into eastern Tennessee and down into northern Mississippi as far south as the Tallahatchie River. Grierson and his men spent most of their time in search of quarry, riding more than shooting and engaging their counterparts in small actions that in one sense did not amount to much. But in another they mattered a great deal. Union cavalrymen had not won the respect of their enemy and had no one to match the exploits of Forrest or John Hunt Morgan. Though Grierson had fought nothing but small unit engagements, sometimes against regular Confederate cavalry, sometimes against partisan raiders, he had never been beaten and, as Sherman noted in recommending him for promotion to brigadier general, his unit was becoming known as Grierson's Cavalry—an eponymous identity more common among Rebels than Yankees.[5]

General Stephen A. Hurlbut, commander of Union forces in Memphis, looked for a chance to do more than jab at the enemy, and Grierson's brigade figured prominently in his plans. After determining that northern and central Mississippi were lightly defended, he and Grant concurred that Union columns should attack Rebel positions and divert attention away from the operation to take place along the river. Hurlbut proposed sending one force south from Memphis, to fall in with a detachment marching out of La Grange, another to swing out from Corinth, and a fourth—the most important—to strike from La Grange deep into enemy territory, perhaps as far south as Meridian, to disrupt the rail services of the Southern and the Mobile and Ohio Railroads that converged there. He proposed using Grierson and the men of the 6th Illinois for this raid. Grant was sympathetic, responding to Hurlbut in mid-February that "Grierson, with about 500 picked men, might succeed in making his way south, and cut the railroad east of Jackson," which was two hundred miles inside Mississippi. "The undertaking would be a hazardous one," the general conceded, and he would not order anyone to do it. Still, "it would pay well if carried out," and he could be sure that Grierson would not turn down this chance to prove his mettle.[6] Grant, like Hurlbut, had great respect for Grierson; both were convinced that if anyone could pull off such a daring maneuver, he could. Hurlbut had begun talking to Grierson about a raid of some sort very early in February. All they waited for was news of when Grant wanted them to act and more information on Confederate troop dispositions in Mississippi. Eventually it was decided to send the entire brigade.

Grierson was lucky that Hurlbut and not Charles Hamilton, Hurlbut's predecessor, headed the Memphis district. Hamilton considered a raid advisable, but he thought that Edward Hatch's 2d Iowa should be detached from Grierson's brigade to carry it off, or perhaps another cavalry outfit should be chosen.[7] Hamilton had gone to La Grange after Hurlbut relieved him in Memphis. He and Grierson did not get along. "Hamilton was the most disagreeable man I had served under," Grierson recalled later; he "was tyrannical, dogmatic and repulsive in his manner and seemed to arrogate to himself the assumption of being one of the great men of the age."[8] Hurlbut put Grierson under his personal command until Hamilton's transfer out of Tennessee solved the problem. Hamilton's successor, William Sooy Smith, got along with Grierson and ardently supported a cavalry dash into Mississippi. Even so, command of the coming raid almost devolved on Hatch by default because Grierson was back home in Jacksonville, Illinois, on a brief leave when the brigade received its marching orders. Grierson rushed back to camp and arrived by train just hours before he would swing into the saddle at the head of his troops.

Grierson's seventeen hundred men filed out of La Grange at dawn on Friday, April 17, in fair weather and "buoyant spirits."[9] Grierson's old regiment, the 6th Illinois, led out, followed by the 7th Illinois, Hatch's 2d Iowa, and a six-gun battery of two-pounders from the 1st Illinois Artillery that brought up the rear. Although the brigade had been resupplied for the expedition and many of the men had new equipment and rode new mounts, there were still shortages. Some soldiers left camp riding mules normally hitched to supply wagons with the hope that horses for them would be requisitioned along the way. Only Grierson and his adjutant, Lieutenant Samuel Woodward, knew the precise nature of the mission. The rest, officers included, knew only that they were pushing deep into enemy territory. The troops were ordered to carry sabers, forty rounds of ammunition for their single-shot Sharps carbines, apparently more if they carried Colt repeaters, and rations for five days that could be stretched to ten.[10] Some had guessed that they were going farther than ever before, possibly even to disrupt rail communications east of Jackson. Private property with no military use and civilians were to be left undisturbed; these men were not to be mistaken for a band of marauding partisans.

Sooy Smith turned out to wish Grierson luck as the column, some two miles long, started down the road to Mississippi. He would himself be setting out in a few hours to act as a diversion for Grierson, just as Grierson was to divert attention from Grant's river operations following Porter's run past Vicksburg, accomplished the night before. Sooy Smith led three infantry regiments and a gun battery southwest out of La Grange, above the Tallahatchie and below Holly Springs, before turning north toward the Coldwater River. This group was to cooperate with a similarly composed column dropping south out of Memphis to pinch whatever resistance they encountered between them. The day before, a much larger force under Gen. Grenville Dodge—nearly five thousand men—had marched east from Corinth to turn attention toward northern Alabama. "These various movements along our length of line," Hurlbut informed Grant, would so distract the enemy "that Grierson's party will get a fair start and be well down to their destination before they can be resisted by adequate force."[11] Hurlbut did not expect to hear anything for two, perhaps three weeks, unless he chanced to read about Grierson in Mississippi newspapers. He and Sooy Smith sent Grierson forward with virtually no written orders, allowing him the freedom to perform effectively. The brigade would embark "upon an expedition so mysterious," reminisced Grierson's adjutant, Samuel Woodward, "that even the commanding officer did not know, beyond a certain objective, where it was going, or when, if ever, it would return."[12] It was up to Grierson to work out his line of march, his targets, and his route to safety—whether back along his original tracks or east into Alabama and to La Grange by a circuitous northern route, or southwest to join with Grant's river command, or even farther south to Baton Rouge. "God speed him, for he has started gallantly on a long and perilous ride," Hurlbut added thoughtfully as he closed his letter to Grant.[13]

The first twenty-four hours of what would be a sixteen-day, nearly five-hundred-mile trek was auspiciously uneventful. Union cavalry in north-central Mississippi was not an unusual sight, and it would take time for the locals to comprehend that the seemingly ordinary was actually extra-ordinary, especially with Sooy Smith causing a commotion to the west and Dodge to the east. Upon leaving Tennessee, Grierson divided his brigade into three columns that traveled along parallel lines the first two days. Each crossed the Tallahatchie at a different point. A battalion of the 7th Illinois quickly chased off some Confederates who tried to burn a bridge before the Union troopers could reach it. The rest of the 7th and the 6th Illinois and 2d Iowa, crossing at fords upstream, encountered no opposition. The two Illinois regiments spent the second night together on a plantation below New Albany, with the 2d Iowa a few miles away. They were now forty miles into Mississippi and had encountered no significant resistance or suffered any casualties.

Grierson began practices that he would continue throughout the expedition. He sent out small parties to cut telegraph lines, take prisoners, disperse any gathering opposition, and confuse those along the route about his real intentions. His men soon learned to live off the land, a necessity after they emptied their haversacks of what they had brought from La Grange. They commandeered the contents of smokehouses and barns and exchanged worn-out horses and mules for fresh remounts whenever they could—hardly a fair or voluntary exchange for the owners, but something short of theft.

The weather had turned for the worse by the end of the second day, with rain falling in "torrents," as it would off and on for the next week and a half.[14] On the third day the entire brigade moved together toward

Pontotoc. There the advance companies brushed aside some light resistance by irregulars and the local citizenry and destroyed what little contraband could be found. Grierson brought the column to a halt south of town and culled from the ranks men he deemed too disabled to continue. Some of the two hundred or so singled out to return begged to continue on with the brigade. Grierson relented, and "they made the long journey all right."[15] Those destined for La Grange, later to be known as the "quinine brigade," also traveled safely, though in the opposite direction. Ever concerned about throwing the enemy off his tracks, Grierson had the men returning to La Grange leave in the middle of the night in a column of fours to give the impression by their hoof prints that the entire force had faced about. They took a gun from the battery to strengthen the illusion.

Grierson's three regiments continued on through April 21, when, south of Houston and ninety miles into Mississippi—not quite halfway to their prime objective, the east-west running Southern Railroad—Grierson detached the 2d Iowa and another gun from his battery. Hatch's men trotted east toward Columbus, then doubled back north along the Mobile and Ohio Railroad. Grierson, now pointed toward Starkville, wanted them to destroy what they could as they rode along; more important, he wanted them to draw off whatever Confederate forces had been converging in his rear. The ruse worked splendidly. Hatch was not able to do much to the Mobile and Ohio, but he was pursued by Confederates who assumed that his regiment was the entire brigade. They did not realize their mistake until Grierson was another one hundred miles away, beyond their reach. Hatch pushed through to La Grange, arriving on April 26. The 2d Iowa saw sharper action than Grierson would with the main column but ended up no more bloodied than it had been in the earlier skirmishing around La Grange.[16]

By April 26 much had happened to Grierson and his 950 remaining troopers. They had reached the Southern Railroad at Newton Station two days before, did what they came to do, then rode south before shifting to the southwest. It had taken them three days to cover the one hundred miles from where they left Hatch to where they swept into Newton Station. Sometimes the column stayed on the muddy main road leading from Starkville to Louisville and on through Philadelphia and Decatur. More often the raiders traveled off the road, occasionally in the dark, through uninhabited pine barrens and areas turned swampy by the heavy rains and swollen creeks and rivers. Along the way Grierson temporarily detached

some men from the 7th Illinois to ransack a tannery. That they decided to
burn the boots and shoes they found there rather than exchange them for
what they were wearing was testament to how much better equipped they
were than their Confederate foes.

On April 22, near Louisville, Grierson had detached Company B of the
7th Illinois for a diversionary move east toward Macon to cut telegraph
lines, disrupt the Mobile and Ohio Railroad, and mislead the enemy. Company commander Capt. Henry Forbes knew as well as Grierson that
the odds of making it back to the main column were slim. He and his
troopers were, as Forbes later wrote, sent out as a "forlorn hope" to sacrifice themselves, if need be, for the larger mission.[17] The men of Company B, a mere thirty-six in all, were unable to reach Macon or carry
out their charge, but not for lack of trying. Amazingly, they eluded capture, tricked potential pursuers into thinking they were the advance party
of the full brigade, and caught up with the main column five days later.
Theirs was a narrow escape, as astounding as anything else accomplished
on the expedition.

The day before Forbes rode away toward Macon, Grierson authorized the formation of a special scouting party of nine men, who, by their
peculiar attire, became known as the "Butternut Guerillas." Dressed in a
hodgepodge of clothes that they had expropriated along the line of march,
they looked like local militia, irregulars, or down-at-the-heels Confederate cavalrymen. Led by the clever and enterprising Sgt. Richard Surby,
they fooled dozens along the line of march. If caught, they ran the risk of
being hanged as spies, which they well knew and which is why they were
all volunteers.[18] Riding a mile or two ahead of the main column they were
able to gather information from unsuspecting locals, grab those they
thought should be interrogated at length, and, at the Pearl River crossing
between Louisville and Philadelphia, secure a bridge before the militiamen there could burn it. The raiders had already lost some horses, drowned
in the overflowing creeks and swamps. The Pearl was so swollen by spring
rains that it might not have been fordable, and Grierson would have been
stopped short of his goal.

As it was, neither the obstacles of nature nor of man seemed to stop
him. Anxious that word of his coming preceded him, when he was on
the outskirts of Decatur he sent a contingent ahead to Newton Station to
secure it until the rest of the raiders could arrive. By this point they were
so caked with dust and dirt that it was hard to tell which army they were
in, and they passed people who had no idea they had just seen Yankee cav-

Grierson's raiders seizing the Pearl River bridge between Louisville and
Philadelphia, Mississippi. A dramatic but inaccurate scene from
Harper's New Monthly Magazine (February 1865).

alrymen in their own neighborhood. Some even mistook them for Van
Dorn's troopers, presumably coming home from Alabama or Tennessee.
Still, Grierson could not be sure that his tricks fooled everyone so it was
with some relief that he finally cantered into Newton Station. The Butternut Guerillas and the advance force, two battalions of the 7th Illinois
under Lt. Col. William Blackburn, had reached the town around dawn
and seized it with virtually no opposition. Grierson and the rest arrived an
hour later, in time to help Blackburn's men burn the depot, sundry supplies, and two locomotives and three dozen boxcars filled with munitions, machinery, and lumber. The raiders had hidden themselves while
the trains, one from the east, one from the west, chugged unsuspectingly
into their grasp. Parties sent both directions from town tore up ties and
tracks, toppled telegraph poles, snipped wires, and burned bridges.[19]

By now Mississippians were thoroughly confused. Rumors swept the
state, putting Grierson's strength at five thousand, or, in more frantic
reports, twenty thousand men. As the Yankees departed Newton Station
they encountered civilians fleeing them. The refugees, intent on escaping

with whatever they could carry, were surprised that the raiders left them alone. Outside Garlandville the local home guard put up a show of resistance and wounded one trooper and one horse. Grierson disarmed them, lectured them "on the folly of their actions, and released them," as he had many others, including one hundred or so Confederate invalids whom he paroled at a hospital in Newton Station.[20] He did, however, keep some prisoners in tow, and escaped slaves were beginning to attach themselves to the column.

Grierson temporarily slackened the pace after leaving Newton Station—temporarily because he knew that speed and the ability to change direction were his best weapons. He and his raiders were eight days and well past two hundred miles into enemy territory. Most of the men had not slept in nearly forty hours; they and their mounts were in desperate need of food and rest. Though the region Grierson traversed was thinly populated and relatively poor, he foraged enough provisions and remounts to keep the column going—but on what course, he had to decide. Hurlbut and Sooy Smith assumed that he would attempt to return to La Grange by the most direct route north. In fact, they turned around Hatch's 2d Iowa three days after its return, reinforced with an Illinois regiment and mounted Iowa infantry, and sent them all to the edge of northern Mississippi in anticipation of helping Grierson cut his way to safety.[21]

Grierson had no intention of doing that. He guessed that the opening he had passed through a week before had long since closed behind him and that it was wiser to press on, either east into Alabama and then north or, instead, to angle southwest toward the Mississippi. Camped at a plantation on the outskirts of Raleigh he made his decision.

> From information received through my scouts who were kept out in all directions and from other sources I found that Jackson and the stations east as far as Lake Station had been re-enforced by Infantry and Artillery and hearing that a fight was momentarily expected at Grand Gulf I decided to make a rapid march, cross the Pearl River again and strike the New Orleans, Jackson and Great Northern Railroad at Hazlehurst and after destroying as much of the road as possible to endeavor to get upon the flank of the enemy and co-operate with our forces and join them if practicable should they be successful in the attack upon Grand Gulf and Port Gibson.[22]

That Grierson had shown great skill to this point cannot be doubted; that he had been and would continue to be very lucky is equally true. At the very moment that he determined his course, a Butternut Guerilla ser-endipitously saved the column from having to fight for its life. Sent to cut telegraph wires and perhaps find and set fire to a trestle on the Southern Railroad, now to their north, this scout ran smack into a regiment of Confederate cavalry coming from the west in search of the Yankee raiders. The Rebels—in the dark he could not tell how many, but there may have been several hundred—traveled a route that would take them into the raiders' camp. He fooled them completely, and, following his misdirections, they hurried down a road that led them east and away from the column. He returned without having cut the wires and yet more successful than Grierson could ever have hoped.[23]

The column's recrossing of the Pearl River on April 27 is yet another example of Grierson's luck. Two battalions of the 7th Illinois under Col. Edward Prince pressed ahead to secure the crossing and intercepted a courier carrying instructions to destroy the ferry. The Pearl, much wider and swifter here than it had been farther upstream, appeared unfordable for many miles in either direction. One trooper who volunteered to swim his horse across the river and bring back the ferryboat nearly drowned. Hailed from the far shore by the ferryman shortly after, Prince did his best to feign a Southern accent and asked that the boat be sent across. The ferryman, thinking that he was aiding his own, did so readily. Grierson brought up the main column just as Prince finished getting his men across. All the while the ferryman did not catch on, nor did the residents of a house where Grierson and his staff were invited to breakfast "until some blunderhead of a soldier" entered and "blurted out" something about the 6th Illinois.[24] Their true identities revealed, the Yankees exited quickly.

Hazlehurst lay ten miles ahead. Grierson dispatched the Butternut Guerillas, by then masters of dissimulation and deception, to survey the town. At the telegraph office they sent a phony dispatch to Jackson claiming that the Yankees had been stopped at the Pearl, reversed their march, and were now retreating to the northeast. Shortly after, the wires were cut, preventing the telegrapher from disclosing that the lead battlion of Yankees was actually trotting down the streets of Hazlehurst. The raiders quickly set to work as they had in Newton Station, destroying munitions and commissary stores. They chose not to torch the depot because it was so close to other buildings but soon became fire fighters when burning boxcars set adjoining structures alight. Exploding munitions and the fear that a major fight was under way caused Grierson and the rest of the column to enter town at a gallop; meanwhile, a train coming in from

Jackson screeched to a halt and backed up the track when the engineer saw what was happening.[25]

After heartily eating food confiscated from Confederate supplies, the full column rode west on the road to Port Gibson. The raiders were passing dangerously close to Jackson, thirty miles to the north, a long day's gallop or short train ride away. Some Rebel units stationed in the area were even closer. Back in the saddle after a night's rest at a plantation west of Hazlehurst, Grierson resolved to press on and assist Grant; he was sure he "could hear the great guns of the fleet and the rebel strongholds on the Mississippi."[26] But as the Yankees neared Union Church, they ran into their first significant opposition, skirmishers from Wirt Adams's Mississippi cavalry regiment. Adams's men were pushed back through Union Church, which the raiders then occupied. Adams had positioned a handful of his Mississippians east of Union Church, hoping they would direct whatever troops were coming to assist him. Instead, they were captured or chased off by a returning detachment that Grierson had sent to disrupt rail communications at Bahala. But Adams now stood between Grierson and the river. Grierson could assume that word of his location was spreading fast and that Adams, who had an artillery battery that more than matched the four pieces he had kept with him, would be reinforced by troops from Port Gibson and possibly even Jackson if he tried to shove his way through. Though he had only a small pocket map with him, the one map he carried on the expedition, he consulted it once more and changed direction yet again.[27] Port Gibson was out, at least for the moment, but the raiders could always swing west again, even as they moved farther south.

Grierson's column slipped off to the southeast early in the morning of April 29 but only after elements of the 6th Illinois made a feint toward the Confederates. When Adams realized that he would not be attacked, it was already early afternoon and the Yankees were swooping down on Brookhaven. They easily dispersed a mix of home guardsmen and recent conscripts that had assembled to protect the town and put into practice what they had learned at Newton Station and Hazlehurst. Now able to devote full attention to the task his small detachment began at Bahala, Grierson turned his men loose on the New Orleans and Jackson Railroad: rails bent, ties burned, rolling stock destroyed, stores sacked. They did the same in Summit the following day. It was here, on the twenty-mile stretch from Brookhaven through Summit, not at Newton Station, that the raiders were at their destructive best. "We thus effectively broke up the railroad connection between Port Hudson and Vicksburg" so completely, Grierson recalled proudly, "that it was not repaired till long after the war was over."[28] He could not know that Grant's quick movement from the river and Pemberton's subsequent withdrawal toward Vicksburg would sever that tie even more dramatically, nor did he realize that just as he finally decided he had to press on to Baton Rouge he could have struck off to the west; Grant's big push had begun. But the raiders would not be part of it. They were destined to cover another seventy miles of enemy territory, leaving the sound of the big guns behind.

Many of the troopers rode fresh mounts. They had eaten well and enjoyed their first good rest since Hazlehurst, and the weather on this first day in May was beautiful. Nevertheless, they were wearing down—in "poor trim for fighting," as Sergeant Surby put it, "and it was not the intention of Colonel Grierson to engage the enemy, but rather to avoid him."[29] Therefore, Grierson took the column west off the main route running through Magnolia and Osyka to travel south through "woods, lanes, and by-lanes."[30] A local resident, thinking that they were Rebels, guided them. As they approached the Tickfaw River, the Butternut Guerillas, as always screening the main force, encountered enemy pickets just above Wall's Bridge. They were part of a small force of Louisianans, no more than a hundred men, hiding along the road on the south bank.

Poor timing and miscues led to the bloodiest skirmish of the entire journey. Gunfire erupted between Rebels and Yankees who stumbled into each other at a house not far from the crossing, just as the surprised pickets were being safely disarmed. Instead of waiting for Grierson to bring up the column, Lieutenant Colonel Blackburn and the scouts tried to shoot their way over the bridge. They were driven back, and a dozen troopers who followed them were also stopped. Grierson began deploying his soldiers—mounted troopers to charge across the fifty-foot-wide stream on either side of the bridge, dismounted troopers to provide covering fire, one gun unlimbered to lob shells into the woods, several companies on horseback to charge over the little plank bridge itself. The Louisianans fled, and the fighting was over in minutes. One raider lay dead; Blackburn sprawled mortally wounded, pinned by a leg under his horse; Surby took a bullet in the thigh; two others suffered serious wounds. Grierson reluctantly left them all behind, in the care of the 2d Iowa surgeon, who had stayed with the column and volunteered to remain, as did two troopers. They understood that they would be captured and could expect to become prisoners of war.[31]

His fears that the enemy was closing in now confirmed, Grierson determined not to stop until he had put Mississippi behind him and crossed the Amite and Comite Rivers in Louisiana, the last obstacles between his men and Baton Rouge. Having read intercepted dispatches, he knew that Rebel troops from Port Hudson were on their way to cut him off at the Amite; he also knew that Wirt Adams was only hours behind. He had no choice but to push his men forward. The raiders quickly dispersed a company of Confederate cavalry encountered on the road and pushed on to the Amite. They did not arrive until midnight, but to Grierson's great relief the bridge still stood. Here the Amite was deep and some six hundred feet wide—absolutely unfordable. The exhausted riders clattered across in a column of twos well ahead of Confederate cavalry sent east from Port Hudson to intercept them, who did not arrive until after dawn.[32]

The raiders were now so fatigued that some dozed off in their saddles. Upon learning that a Rebel encampment lay just ahead, they shook themselves of their lethargy, readied for action, and at daylight stormed through before the Rebels could react. Most of the troops assembled there had left the day before, crossing the Amite in search of the very men now pulling down their tents, ransacking their supplies, and taking their comrades prisoner. At the north bank of the Comite the raiders hemmed in and surprised a last company of Rebel cavalrymen. Only the captain escaped, by hiding in the low-hanging Spanish moss of a tree. After taking another forty prisoners, the raiders located a ford not far from the destroyed bridge, "and in due time the entire command reached the opposite side of the stream, where knowing that no enemy in sufficient force could possibly be between us and Baton Rouge," Grierson told his men to dismount for a long-needed, much appreciated rest.[33]

The Illinoisans had halted a scant six miles outside Baton Rouge. One of Grierson's orderlies, lulled to sleep by his horse's rhythmic gait, continued on for another four miles until stopped and awakened by Union pickets. Knowing nothing of Grierson's mission, they listened to his tale skeptically. Two companies of cavalry dispatched from Baton Rouge went out to investigate and could scarcely believe what they saw; the lone rider had told the truth. Excitement spread with the word of these horsemen who seemingly appeared from nowhere. Crowds formed as Grierson's column entered the city in an impromptu parade, Grierson at the head of the 6th Illinois, followed by the four-gun battery and Rebel prisoners, then the 7th Illinois, and, bringing up the rear of this "strange cavalcade," hundreds of escaped slaves in wagons and carts, on foot, or riding a va-

The victorious raiders on parade in Baton Rouge, Louisiana, as depicted in
Harper's New Monthly Magazine (February 1865).

riety of animals. Dirty, hungry, bone-weary, the troopers pulled themselves erect as they "marched in triumph through the city," all the way to
a park of blooming magnolias. There they "laid down to sleep amid flow-
ers and perfume, beside the deep waters of the great Mississippi River,
without guard and without danger."[34]

Grierson estimated that they had killed or wounded one hundred of
the enemy, taken twice that number prisoner, and paroled well over five
times as many along the way. More important, they had destroyed some
sixty miles of rails, ties, trestles, bridges, and telegraph lines and millions
of dollars in locomotives, rolling stock, and military stores. By his rough
computations, they had ridden six hundred miles. It was actually closer
to five hundred, still no mean feat. Over seventy of those miles had been
covered in the last twenty-four hours and with virtually no food or rest.
Company B of the 7th Illinois earned brigade bragging rights by riding the
farthest—quite possibly the six hundred miles Grierson claimed for the
full column—and being exposed to the gravest danger. Capt. Henry Forbes
called it "our dare-devil expedition" straight "through the heart of Dixie,"
an unmatched accomplishment. "I was once 48 hours without tasting
food, and we rode at one time 52 miles without feeding" their mounts, he

added.[35] No wonder that he and the other raiders felt so proud. And the cost was only three killed, seven wounded, five left behind because they were too ill to continue, three who offered to stay with those wounded at the Tickfaw, and another nine "supposed to have straggled."[36] The 6th and 7th Illinois had suffered higher casulaties in small actions within a day's ride of La Grange during the previous months.

"This raid is the most successful the Yankees have yet made, and a disgrace to our State," wrote one disgusted Mississippian.[37] Grierson even won the grudging respect of his pursuers. Wirt Adams, who blocked his move toward Port Gibson, set off after the Yankees once he learned that they had veered southeast. Adams guessed, incorrectly, that they would turn toward Natchez. When he was certain they were riding instead toward Baton Rouge, he sent men ahead to burn the bridge over the Amite. They arrived too late. "I found it impossible, to my great mortification and regret, to overhaul them," he reported apologetically to Pemberton.[38] Col. Robert Richardson of the 1st Tennessee Partisan Rangers expressed the same frustration. Richardson's men had gone against Grierson's in various skirmishes around La Grange in February. Grierson suffered losses, but Richardson's were worse and his command had come apart. In Jackson, when news of Grierson's movement southwest out of Newton arrived, Richardson was authorized to give chase. Ultimately he gathered nearly five hundred mounted infantry as he attempted to catch up, but Grierson left him confounded and in the dust. "We had forces enough to have captured and destroyed him, but his movements were so rapid and uncertain of aim that we could not concentrate our scattered forces or put them in concert of action," he explained to Pemberton. Grierson's exploits, Richardson groused, "will exhilarate for a short time the fighting spirits of the Northern war party."[39]

The exhilaration was real enough. Benjamin Henry Grierson, onetime music teacher, understandably became the North's military hero of the hour. News of his exploits sped by wire around the country. From his headquarters in Memphis, General Hurlbut called the raid "unequaled."[40] Gen. Nathaniel Banks, commander of the Louisiana district, considered it "the most brilliant expedition of the war."[41] A relieved General Grant told Admiral Porter that "Grierson of the cavalry has taken the heart out of Mississippi."[42] Grant, fighting inland from Port Gibson as Grierson's men paraded through Baton Rouge, was perhaps the most satisfied of all. He had wanted a diversion and he got it. At one time or another perhaps ten thousand Confederate troops had been deployed in a futile attempt to catch and stop the Yankee raiders. "Colonel Grierson's raid from La Grange through Mississippi has been the most successful thing of the kind since the breaking out of the rebellion," Grant reported to Halleck. "The Southern papers and Southern people regard it as one of the most daring exploits of the war," he added.[43] Halleck in turn reported to Secretary of War Edwin M. Stanton that "this expedition was most successfully conducted."[44]

Feted by admirers from Baton Rouge to New Orleans, caught up in the congratulatory excitement greeting him at every turn, Grierson was convinced that the Confederacy would soon fall and expressed those sentiments to a large audience jammed into a New Orleans hotel auditorium to hear of his exploits. The Confederacy, he proclaimed, was "nothing but a shell." It had neither the resources nor the manpower to fight much longer. Unionists, he predicted, would "rally round the old flag" as Northern armies advanced to victory. "Under the circumstances," he jotted in his memoir a quarter-century later, "I trust I may be pardoned" for "underestimating the strength of the enemy and the time it would take to conquer the rebellion."[45]

Whatever unionist sentiment he detected on the expedition—and it did exist—was more than matched by the steadfastness of Southern nationalists. The Mississippi press tried to minimize the impact of Grierson's raid. First reports had predicted that "the whole pack will yet be hemmed in and destroyed, or be taken prisoners."[46] When it became clear that Grierson would elude his pursuers, the local papers claimed that he had not really accomplished much anyway. He was no Morgan, no J.E.B. Stuart; rather, he led murderers and robbers on a villainous binge— sentiments echoed around the Confederacy. "In the Mississippi raid, we must admit" that the Yankees "showed daring worthy of a better cause" the *Macon (Georgia) Daily Telegraph* editorialized in a backhanded compliment. "While such raids are mortifying to our pride, they do us really but little injury," the paper scoffed, "and in some respects are a positive benefit. These thieving, plundering expeditions carried on in the midst of our country, give our people striking illustrations of Yankee meanness and rascality, and strengthen the universal sentiment of our people that there can be no affiliation with a people who war upon women, and plunder unoffending private citizens."[47] This certainly was no admission of defeat and no indication that Grierson's raid had changed any "Secesh" minds.

Grierson was indeed overly optimistic, and he was not alone. Supporters of the unionist cause had looked desperately for some sign of success, some proof that the enemy could be beaten; thus the focus on Grierson. Printing reports from correspondents, paraphrasing columns from the Confederate press, and drawing on official dispatches, the *New York Times* lavished praise on the raiders. Emphasizing that Grierson rode the length of Mississippi with but slight opposition, almost "at his leisure," the *Times* gave credence to the empty shell notion. Reviewing the column's movement day by day, the paper waxed eloquent about the "noble band" whose "triumphal entry created a furor of joyful excitement that will not cease till it has thrilled every loyal heart upon this continent—aye, every heart that loves liberty and human bravery through the civilized world."[48] Surely, it opined, there were no more men to replace Rebels who fell in the field. Once they were beaten, victory would be inevitable.

But defeating the Rebels already under arms was no easy task. Col. Abel Streight's failed raid, which came close on the heels of Grierson's success, demonstrated that sobering fact all too clearly. Streight proposed to sweep across northern Alabama into western Georgia, disrupting rail lines and supply routes as he went, and destroying the cannon foundry in Rome at the end of his ride. Rosecrans approved, and Streight set out with a polyglot force of two thousand mounted infantry on April 22. He entered Rome on May 3, not in triumph but in humiliation, the prisoner of Nathan Bedford Forrest. With a force half the size of Streight's, Forrest had pursued the Yankees across Alabama. Streight possessed neither Grierson's luck nor skill, and Forrest took him with relative ease, ending a poorly planned, poorly executed enterprise.[49]

Obviously, putting soldiers on horses did not automatically turn them into cavalrymen. Even those trained as cavalry found it difficult to duplicate Grierson's exploits. One of the more notable disappointments came about a year later, this time in Virginia. Brig. Gen. Judson Kilpatrick concocted a harebrained scheme to free the Union prisoners being held at Belle Isle and Richmond's Libby Prison that was approved by both Secretary of War Stanton and President Abraham Lincoln. Kilpatrick intended to set out from his encampment sixty miles north of Richmond with four thousand men. They would sweep around the flank of Gen. Robert E. Lee's army, shoot their way through home guardsmen defending the Confederate capital, liberate the prisoners, and whisk them away to safety behind the Union lines above Williamsburg, roughly forty-five miles to the east.

Nothing worked as planned. Kilpatrick divided his force into two columns, the larger one under his command, a smaller one under Col. Ulric

Dahlgren. Neither got to Richmond. Kilpatrick encountered stiffer resistance than he expected and withdrew; Dahlgren ran into even heavier opposition. He was killed, and many of his men were taken captive as they attempted to flee. Confederates claimed that Dahlgren carried papers instructing his men to leave Richmond in flames and kill Jefferson Davis and his cabinet. An indignant Lee sent the papers to Gen. George G. Meade, commander of the Army of the Potomac. Though Meade denied that any such order had been given, the incident proved most embarrassing to him and the Lincoln administration.[50]

These failures, however, do not mean that Yankee cavalry never proved its worth or that Grierson's raid was its one shining moment. Still, it did not seem to have men capable of matching Forrest and Morgan in the West or J. E. B. Stuart and Jubal Early in the East until very late in the war, when attrition had taken its toll on the Confederacy. James Wilson's famous raid through Alabama in the spring of 1865 is a case in point. Wilson, like Grierson an Illinoisan, but, unlike Grierson, a West Point graduate, had been on Grant's staff during the Vicksburg campaign. He fought hard as a cavalryman around Richmond the next year, distinguished himself thereafter in fighting below Nashville, and, as a reward, was given command of a force numbering over twenty-five thousand troopers. On March 22, 1865, Wilson, now a major general, took over half of his command on a romp through Alabama, starting in the northwest corner, riding to and taking Selma, thence across to Montgomery and into Georgia through Columbus and Macon. Wilson covered about the same distance as Grierson but he took nearly a full month—until April 20—and moved through a region almost stripped of regular Confederate troops. True, Wilson's men beat back Forrest, but this was not the Forrest of old. Except for the defenders of Selma, there was essentially no one to stop Wilson from going where he wanted, a far different situation from that Grierson faced in Mississippi two years before. Whereas Grierson had to keep moving to survive, Wilson could take his time, spending nearly a week in Selma after it fell. Whereas Grierson had to worry about the outcome of the larger campaign, Wilson could be confident that he would win because the South finally had been reduced to an empty shell. By the end of his mission, Lee and Johnston had surrendered their armies, and it was Wilson's men, after all, who captured a fleeing Jefferson Davis.[51]

No cavalryman, no matter how talented, was invincible, and even the best could make wrong choices, for example, Stuart in the Gettysburg campaign and Morgan at almost the same moment in the western theater.

Morgan's audacious plunge across the Ohio River into Indiana and Ohio gained precious little for the Confederate cause. Most of Morgan's two thousand horsemen were chased down, and Morgan himself was captured outside Steubenville, Ohio. These were men the South could ill afford to lose.[52]

By contrast, Grierson, finally promoted to brigadier general a month after—and because of—the raid, never experienced such a disaster. Though his claim in spring 1863 to have been undefeated could no longer stand by the end of the war, he did not get himself into any inextricable messes. And at the end of 1864 he pulled off another successful long ride. He led three brigades in a serpentine loop from La Grange into eastern Mississippi and then back toward the center of the state at Grenada before angling south for Vicksburg. They destroyed rails, ties, and rolling stock. Although Grierson passed over the line of march of his earlier raid, his primary target was the Mobile and Ohio Railroad, which had been just beyond his reach in 1863. There was more fighting this time, and he suffered more casualties. Even so, he showed the same combination of skill and luck that had served him so well before. Once again, his opponents— including Wirt Adams—failed to concentrate effectively and he threw them off with feints and rapid marches.[53]

Grierson, then, did nothing later in the war to tarnish his earlier sterling reputation. And yet memory of him would fade, despite efforts to keep it alive. Richard Surby, the onetime Butternut Guerilla leader, wrote a journal during the 1863 raid and had it published soon after the war ended. He depicted Grierson as a decisive leader, a good man who deserved to be remembered. John Abbott, author of a series of essays called "Heroic Deeds of Heroic Men" for *Harper's,* also sought to preserve Grierson's fame. "Among all the thrilling stories of the war there is not one which can surpass, in wild and perilous adventure, the tale of Colonel Grierson's cavalry raid through the State of Mississippi," he opened dramatically. "Poetry in years to come will claim the chivalrous record as her own" and sing the praise of those "bold raiders."[54]

Such was not to be. Grierson never had the real or symbolic stature of a Grant or Sherman, and his exploits in the spring of 1863 were eclipsed by the larger Northern victory in the Vicksburg campaign. A Union veteran who thought sure that his having seen Grierson, Grant, and Sherman on the same streetcar in St. Louis before the war was somehow an omen of cosmic significance erred.[55] Grierson would not be remembered as one of the great men of the Civil War. He did not rise to high command, he

The successful raider promoted: Brig. Gen. Benjamin Henry Grierson,
photographed in Chicago sometime during the fall of 1863. Courtesy of the
Fort Davis National Historic Site, Fort Davis, Texas.

had not been a mighty survivor of battlefield slaughter, and there was no lost cause to link him with, in the way that Southern cavalrymen had their memories enshrined as gallant cavaliers. After the war he came to see his raid as a precursor to Sherman's famous March to the Sea, though hardly anyone else made the same connection. Eventually Benjamin Henry Grierson would be all but forgotten, not only in Illinois but to a large extent even in Mississippi, becoming just one more Yankee in a war whose details blurred with the passage of time. But he, like others, would be resurrected, his importance rediscovered, his fame reinvented. This shaping and reshaping of historical memory recurs constantly. For Grierson it began in 1954 with a book by Dee Brown.

The Story as History

Here I must pay homage to the historians on whom writers like me base so much of their writing. The differences between a historian and someone like me is that the former must pay close attention to a host of important and sometimes difficult themes, whereas I can evade the difficult problems; however, I try never to abuse facts or invent situations contrary to known conditions. The historian's task is many times more difficult than mine, and I know it.

—James Michener,
The World Is My Home

Dee Brown was born in Louisiana and raised in Arkansas. He attended Arkansas State Teachers College before moving on to George Washington University, where in 1937 he earned a bachelor's degree in library science. He had already begun working for the U.S. Department of Agriculture as a library assistant before finishing school and remained there into the early days of World War II. After a stint in the army, he became a technical librarian at the army's Aberdeen Proving Grounds in Maryland. In 1948 he accepted a position as a librarian at the University of Illinois and remained there until his retirement a quarter-century later. He then returned to Arkansas and sank his roots in Little Rock, which is still his home.

"If I had to do it over again, by all means, I would have still chosen to be a librarian rather than a historian," Brown once told an interviewer. "I would have never gotten the material I did if I hadn't been a librarian. Librarians know the secrets, not historians."[1] As a college student in Arkansas, Brown had taken a job in the school library to be close to books, his imagination fired by what he found on the shelves. From those early days through the rest of his career he has allowed himself to be guided by serendipity—the chance discovery taking him into unknown worlds.[2] His interest does not end there; since he was a teenager he has wanted to share his discoveries with others, as a writer. In high school he had thought he would be a journalist. Little did he then know that he would someday make his mark as both a historian and a novelist.

He began his writing career before he left Washington for Urbana, most notably with a trilogy that he produced with Martin Schmitt, a friend from his army days. Though Schmitt moved to the University of Oregon while Brown was beginning his duties at Illinois, they continued the collaboration long distance. The foundation of their work was laid with photographs they had cataloged in the National Archives. First came *Fighting Indians of the West,* then *Trail Driving Days,* followed by *The Settlers' West,* each published by Charles Scribner. Scribner himself took an interest in the project after Brown wrote and told him what he proposed to do. All three volumes have the same basic structure: a brief introductory essay followed by chapters organized around photographs. Oversize format and pictorial cornucopia notwithstanding, these are not simple coffee table fare. A concern with major themes, even hints of mythbusting, can be found. *Fighting Indians,* for example, touched on a variety of important areas, such as the tragic fate of Plains tribes. Brown would return to this and other subjects in future books, notably in the one that made him internationally famous, *Bury My Heart at Wounded Knee.*

Though Brown liked his job and the university, his librarian's pay was typically low. "To supplement my income I wrote several Western novels, all based on actual incidents in the West," he reminisced. "In the middle of this pleasant and slightly profitable avocation I stumbled upon the unpublished letters of two brothers who had served in the Union Army during the Civil War."[3] The brothers were Henry and Stephen Forbes. They had ridden with Grierson through Mississippi to Baton Rouge. Henry, the older brother, commanded Company B of the 7th Illinois, which had been sent off on the daring and dangerous mission toward Macon while the main column pressed on to Newton Station. Stephen was a sergeant in that same company.

Brown had found the perfect story. Long fascinated by the Civil War as well as the West, he could remember tales about frontier living told to him by his grandmother. One was about her husband, a Confederate cavalryman captured in Tennessee and sent to prison in Illinois. He returned home after the war wearing what looked like part of a Yankee uniform. Had he become a "Galvanized Yankee," a Southerner recruited for western duty by Washington, not Richmond? This was an intriguing mystery,

Author Dee Brown. Photograph by Linda Brown. Courtesy of Dee Brown.

one that would eventually lead Brown to write another book.[4] But for now here were the Forbes brothers, their papers close at hand in the University of Illinois library. Stephen Forbes had become a respected entomologist and distinguished professor at the university; his daughter still lived in Urbana and had pounded out a typescript of her father's letters and reminiscences. Richard Surby's published account of the raid and a multivolume collection of official documents drawn from Union and Confederate materials, *The War of the Rebellion,* were both in the university library. Grierson's papers were close by, less than a two-hour drive away, at the state historical library in Springfield. "While going through the letters, diaries, and memoirs of participants in Grierson's raid," Brown recalled, "I felt as if I knew well the men on both sides."[5] He was hooked. "Only bits and pieces of this dramatic adventure had been published, and so I resolved to write the complete history."[6] The University of Illinois Press published *Grierson's Raid* in 1954.

The attractiveness of the volume accentuated Brown's fast-paced narrative. A mounted Grierson, adapted from the cover of *Harper's,* adorns the jacket cover. The title and Brown's name are superimposed over horsemen battling in the background; in the lower left is a statement attributed to William Tecumseh Sherman calling the raid "the most brilliant expedition of the Civil War."[7] A synopsis written for the jacket flaps emphasizes the singularity of Grierson's accomplishment, the depth of Brown's

research, and the verve with which the story is told. Endpapers feature a
map of Mississippi copied from one drawn for Stephen Forbes and preserved in his papers. This map shows the brigade's progress through
the state, with Hatch's return route to La Grange and Company B's independent venture clearly set apart from the movements of the larger body.
Towns are located; rail lines are laid out and labeled. Slashes through the
line of march mark the distance covered on each of the sixteen days, and
off to the side are one-sentence synopses for each major occurrence of the
raid. Contemporaneous etchings of Union cavalrymen dot the endpapers
and are inserted at the beginning of each chapter, seventeen chapters in
all—one for each day of the raid—with an epilogue. Eight photographs,
including one of Grierson, one each of the Forbes brothers, and the raiders' camp at Baton Rouge are placed in the text.

The text follows an outline suggested by Richard Surby's 1865 printed
account, which told the tale day by day, as originally recorded in Surby's
diary. "I have carefully perused the manuscript," Grierson attested in December 1864, "and I pronounce it correct in every particular"—an endorsement that invites a heavy reliance on what the sergeant wrote.[8] This
is not to say, however, that Brown slavishly imitated Surby or that his
book in any sense wrote itself. He did not snip a little from Surby here, a
little from Grierson and the Forbes brothers there, in a simple scissors and
paste exercise. Brown has always felt that history at its best is a form of
storytelling. Thus, even though the outline was provided for him by actual
events as well as the participants' rendition of them, he imposed his own
order on the past and emphasized the human element first and foremost.
In his subtitle he called *Grierson's Raid* "A Cavalry Adventure of the Civil
War" and it was the sense of adventure that he coaxed from the documents that he wanted to inject into his readers. He was not above creating
conversations and stretching inferences, practices which most professional
historians avoid and look askance at when they see it in others. But Brown
the storyteller has never felt bound by traditional orthodoxies, nor has he
been intimidated by the raised eyebrows of his academic critics.

He opens his narrative with Grierson's troopers leaving La Grange
at dawn, "the column of twos coiling down into the shortleaf pine forest
away from the town that had seen no fighting, yet was dying in the back-
wash of raids and counter-raids of two years of war."[9] Here and else-
where Brown showed that he could turn a phrase, but by and large he kept
his prose crisp and lean so that language did not intrude on the story. He
often quoted from Surby, Grierson, and the Forbes brothers, all of whom

were thoughtful and articulate. Within each chapter the scene could shift from Yankee action to Rebel reaction, a literary device that helps engage the reader by heightening anticipation and stimulating a sense of excitement over the enterprise.

Brown of course notes the raid's importance to Grant's Vicksburg victory, but he does not overstate his case. After sending Grierson's column down the road from La Grange in the first chapter, he shifts to grand strategy just long enough to set the stage for what follows. "Bogged down in the marshy bottomlands west of the Confederacy's Gibraltar," Brown writes, "Grant spent the winter laying plans for an 1863 campaign that would either win the war in the west or lose an army" (8). Grant, we are told, is gambling. Sending Grierson deep into danger is just one of the many risks he is taking, and there are other diversions to be staged. Even so, Brown emphasizes with good reason that Grant "considered Grierson's raid the main thrust, the feint with the punch" (38).

Grant appears rarely in *Grierson's Raid*—enough to remind readers of the stakes involved and yet not so much that attention shifts from the troopers in the saddle to the generals behind their desks. Brown gives us a Grant who is determined and careful, a man who knew that his reputation was on the line, a general who understood that Vicksburg was the key to unlocking the Mississippi basin. He had failed seven times to take his objective; the eighth attempt could very well be his last, given the politics of command. Whereas Grant is depicted as decisive, his opponent, John C. Pemberton, appears just the opposite. But then, that has usually been Pemberton's historiographical fate. Grant served with Pemberton in the Mexican War; Brown bestows him with insight into Pemberton's limits as a leader who "liked his fighting to be neat and tidy, with well-defined lines" so he "would be thoroughly fretted by enemy cavalry disarranging his rear" (106).[10]

Not surprisingly, then, Pemberton acts as a foil to Grant. His failure to intercept Grierson presages his failure to prevent Grant from landing below Vicksburg. Grant soon after drives Pemberton from Jackson, pens him in Vicksburg, lays siege to the city, and ultimately forces the hapless Confederate general's surrender, an outcome that even those few historians sympathetic to Pemberton cannot change.

At the same time, Brown is not insensitive to Pemberton's plight. The Pennsylvania-born Pemberton, a "Yankee turned Southerner," as Brown put it, was caught in a precarious position (59).[11] Brown uses him as he does others to show the complexity of the military situation and the variety of

personalities involved. Pemberton was not the only transplanted North-
erner who became attached to the Confederate cause, and he, like the
other actors in this drama, was not always able to comprehend, much less
control, events. He complained endlessly about insufficient men and matériel and tended to feel slighted too easily, but his complaints were hardly
groundless. Van Dorn's transfer to Tennessee had weakened his army, and
neither Jefferson Davis nor Joseph Johnston seemed to appreciate his difficulties. It took him a few days to sort through the conflicting reports he
was getting about Grierson's raiders—who they were and where they were
going—but once he knew their direction, he issued orders to stop them,
realizing all along that they were a diversion from more important matters
on the river.

Reading through the dispatches that Pemberton received from officers
in the field and his orders in response, most of which were published in the
Official Records, Brown could see that Pemberton had to make tough
choices based on sketchy, conflicting information. Nonetheless, Brown
holds Pemberton and those reporting to him from northern Mississippi
accountable primarily for a failure of the imagination. Even by April 22,
the sixth day of the raid, after Hatch had turned north and Company B
had been detached, "nowhere in all the day's official messages of the
Confederate command does there appear to be any intimation of what
Grierson's real objective was, any comprehension of the grave danger facing Vicksburg's vital rail line" (92).

Inaction was not Pemberton's greatest failing; it was guessing poorly
and making the wrong countermoves. Thus when he concentrated troops
around Meridian to protect the Mobile and Ohio Railroad, he further
exposed the Southern line at Newton Station. Poor guesses and bad
choices would hinder Pemberton throughout the days of Grierson's raid,
and those failures became a prominent theme in Brown's tale. Pemberton
thought the raiders would retreat to the east through Alabama after they
left Newton Station. Then, when they turned up in Hazlehurst, he was
convinced that their real mission was to cut Jackson off from Vicksburg
by destroying a bridge over the Big Black River. Learning that Grierson
had backed away from Wirt Adams at Union Church, he decided that the
raiders were merely groping their way toward Natchez. "His intense
concern with the petty details of his command, details which hourly increased in number as the enemy prepared for the big strike, was beginning
to tell on Pemberton" (127). By the time Grierson broke through to safety
in Baton Rouge, Pemberton was thoroughly frazzled. But again, in fair-

ness to Pemberton, Brown shows that his poor judgment was exacerbated by the failure of others to act decisively, and Grierson, after all, shifted his intentions as well as his direction as he rode. Even if Pemberton was increasingly "frantic," on April 27 he had ordered the commander of Rebel forces at Port Hudson to send troops "to block a possible southern flight by Grierson's raiders" (156).[12] That those troops did not arrive in time to stop the Yankees from crossing the Amite cannot be blamed on Pemberton.

Even more interesting are Brown's thumbnail sketches of Grierson's adversaries in the field. At various places in the book readers learn tidbits about Mississippi cavalry commander Wirt Adams and Tennessee partisan leader Robert Richardson. Both men had engaged Grierson in skirmishing around northern Mississippi, so both had a score to settle. And both serve to personalize the conflict, infusing the story with yet another dramatic edge.

Adams comes off fairly well. He did not catch the raiders before they could slip away to the south, but he did halt their progress toward Port Gibson. That he was outmanuevered is treated more as the result of Grierson's combination of luck and skill than as owing to inadequacies on his part. Indeed, Brown presents the "hot-blooded" Adams and his "wild riders" as second only to Nathan Bedford Forrest in the respect accorded them by their Yankee opponents (82, 164).

Richardson, by contrast, is more "enigmatic" (169). Not only had Grierson bested him in the fighting around La Grange before the raid, but Richardson had gotten in trouble with his superiors. Richardson left Tennessee and crossed into Mississippi when Joseph Johnston sought to arrest him for "his unorthodox actions," and Hurlbut let it be known that if his men captured him he "would bring the freebooting colonel to a drumhead court-martial" (170). Pemberton too had wanted him removed, and yet when he turned up in Jackson "with all the bland innocence of an erring schoolboy," Pemberton sent him off to intercept Grierson. Though he picked up men as he went, he could never quite run down his old adversary. "An impetuous but tenacious hound after a clever fox" (177), Richardson came tantalizingly close to his intended prey as he spurred on from Hazlehurst to Brookhaven to Summit, sometimes on the right road, sometimes not, but seemingly always a half day and twenty miles behind. Richardson pressed on to Magnolia and Osyka, sure that he would finally catch Grierson on May 1. But Grierson had swung to the southwest, crossing the Tickfaw at Wall's Bridge. "Even the stubborn Richardson was now discouraged," his inability to overtake the raiders a case study of the larger Confederate failure to stop an embarrassingly elusive foe (190).

Brown juxtaposed Lt. Col. Clark Barteau of the 2d Tennessee with Col. Edward Hatch of the 2d Iowa as a variation on that theme. The poorly equipped men of Barteau's regiment were still recovering from disasters at Shiloh and Corinth. Barteau himself was trying to make sense of a Confederate chain of command that divided him between Tennessee and Mississippi and between national and state duties. The first commander of a significant force to learn of Grierson's incursion, he mustered his troops at Verona and went in search of the enemy late on April 18. It was his job to protect the Mobile and Ohio Railroad, so off he rode to stop the intruders. "Even so patient a man as Barteau must certainly have cursed the rain, the Yankees, and the hopeless disorder of his command" (36).

Barteau, like Pemberton, was a Southerner by adoption, not birth. Perhaps this intrinsically interesting phenomenon was particularly intriguing to Brown, himself a Southerner then living in the "land of Lincoln." A native Ohioan and graduate of Ohio Wesleyan, Barteau migrated to Tennessee in search of opportunity. He tried his hand at running a boys' academy and editing a newspaper before turning to law. He married a local woman and came out in favor of states' rights and against abolition. "By 1861 the Ohio Yankee was beyond compromise," Brown observed; consequently "he would fight for the South" (46). Barteau's choices gave Brown the chance to comment on one of the war's many ironies:

> Barteau could not have speculated upon the ironies of the contest in which he was involved, being too close to the scenes and the actions. But irony was there in his own history. It was there in the person of Grant whose wife was a slaveholder when the war began, while he was fighting now to end slavery. And in the record of Sherman who hated war, and had tried to stop his Southern friends from war by detailing its horrors, redbearded Sherman who was head of a Louisiana military school and often boasted that he had more friends in the South than in the North, who wept when Louisiana seceded. Sherman, the warhater, now before Vicksburg preparing to make his name the epitome of war and the scourge of the South. (51–52)

Barteau gathered his Tennesseans and a ragtag bunch of Mississippi state troops. Combined, they made almost a full regiment. Trying to sort through what his scouts told him about the size and intentions of the enemy force, confused by the small parties that Grierson had sent out for that purpose as soon as he entered Mississippi, Barteau took up a position to the east of Grierson's presumed line of march to interpose himself between the raiders and the Mobile and Ohio Railroad. The Yankees slipped by to the west without ever seeing him. He began a cautious pursuit, passed through Pontotoc, saw the tracks of the "quinine brigade" headed north, and correctly deduced that the main column had continued south. Not fooled by Grierson's first ruse, he fell for the second below Houston. Coming upon the trail of Hatch's 2d Iowa leading east, he and his officers "were quickly convinced that the main column of the Yankee raid had finally turned toward their valued railroad." Because he succumbed to the same failure of imagination as Pemberton, "it never entered Barteau's mind that any Yankee cavalry force would dare to ride the hundred perilous miles south to that other railroad—the idea was a fantastic one" (67). He had something else in common with the general in Jackson: bad luck compounded the problems brought by poor choices.

Although Brown had only official reports and the reminiscences of Sgt. Lyman Pierce of the 2d Iowa as his sources, he told an exciting story-within-a-story. Grierson had ordered Hatch to ride all the way to the Mobile and Ohio, the very target that Barteau feared the Yankees were aiming at all along—hence he took the bait Grierson dangled before him. If Barteau's scouts had ridden just a bit farther, they would have seen the tracks of the 6th and 7th Illinois going south. Instead, they rushed in headlong pursuit of Hatch, making it impossible for him to concentrate on his target—at least they accomplished that much. Barteau's troopers caught up with Hatch just hours after the brigade had been divided. In the hectic running fight that ensued, Hatch's rear guard was overrun, but the Iowans drove off their attackers before they could envelop the regiment. Most of those captured by the first Rebel rush were freed by their comrades. The Tennesseans and Mississippians lost a score or so killed and wounded while, according to Sergeant Pierce, "not a drop of Yankee blood was shed."[13] Troopers from the 2d Alabama who had been dispatched from Columbus to help Barteau did not arrive in time, so Hatch escaped for the moment.

If the Alabamans had come sooner, "Hatch's predicament would have been grave indeed," and the 2d Iowa was by no means safe yet (69). Hatch would have everything he could do just to get his regiment back to La Grange in one piece. One twist in all this Confederate chasing to and fro is that Hatch passed through Okolona virtually unopposed because the town "had been left undefended by the Confederates pursuing vainly in his rear" (89). The Iowans demolished military stores and began driving a herd of horses and mules that would swell to over five hundred by the time they crossed back into Tennessee. Hatch had pushed his men to ride all night, off the main roads and passing through swamps, at times guided—as Grierson would be on his trek—by local blacks risking their lives to assist the Yankees.

The Alabamans, exhausted, gave up the chase on April 23. Barteau, however, would not let the raiders go without taking one more crack at them. The next day he struck Hatch, who stopped the retreat and stood his ground. With some troopers on horseback and others dismounted and formed into line, the Iowans beat back their pursuers. "The gallant Barteau and his Tennesseans could do no more," wrote Brown sympathetically. "Their ammunition was all gone. With ten more rounds they might have won the day, ten rounds being all that Hatch's men had left in their deadly revolving rifles" (118). Again, Hatch did not lose a man. His luck held; Barteau never had any.

The ride of the 2d Iowa adds to the drama of an already exciting tale. Much of that excitement arose from the escapades of the 7th Illinois's Company B, the "forlorn hope" whose safe return to the main column was little short of miraculous. Both Henry and Stephen Forbes wrote thoughtful reminiscences that Brown in turn used deftly in shaping his larger story. Henry Forbes, the thirty-year-old company commander, is introduced as a man of conscience, the patriotic American everyman serving his country. "Captain Henry Forbes was a sensitive, well-read farming man who usually carried a copy of Emerson's *Conduct of Life* in his saddlebag, a man subject to shifting moods of elation and despair, and who regarded the war as a great personal tragedy," Brown tells us. "He disliked military life intensely but had a high sense of duty and a sincere belief in the precepts of his time" (79).

Henry and his brother Stephen had left the farm in northern Illinois to join the cavalry after the firing on Fort Sumter and Lincoln's call for volunteers. Henry, by virtue of his age and bearing, was elected company captain, his experience replicating that of many other citizen-soldiers, North and South. By April 1863 the Forbes brothers had seen plenty, perhaps too much, of war. Stephen had been captured by the Rebels outside Corinth the year before. Imprisoned, he fell ill and then was paroled and set free. Soon after that he was part of a prisoner exchange, which meant that he was eligible to rejoin the fight—and he did. Captain Forbes could be sure that his brother Stephen and the rest of his "boys" were "ready to follow him through hellfire with the fierce loyalty of a blood clan" (80). And yet, Brown suggests, he must have paused that April 22 when, on the road south of Houston, Col. Edward Prince of the 7th Illinois asked him to lead his little band on a diversion toward Macon and the Mobile and Ohio Railroad.

> He was thinking of his younger brother, Stephen, nineteen years old—Stephen to whom he had been a father figure since the boy was ten—of the bitter irony of Stephen's being caught in this wild mission on his first field duty after seven months' absence, four in rebel prisons, three in that Rhode Island hospital where Henry had gone all the long way from Illinois to see him. (The difficulties of obtaining the furlough had seemed insurmountable, but he had been bound to see if the boy was all right.) Stephen was a quiet one, but Henry had heard him say he would prefer death to being captured again. (81)

Forbes steeled himself and set off on a mission to tear up rails, pull down telegraph lines, and cause general confusion and consternation. Prince could not tell him where the column would be after it reached Newton Station; Grierson did not know himself which way he would go after that. Forbes was on his own, deep in enemy territory with just enough men to stir up resistance but not enough to fight their way out of anything more than a scrape. But then the very smallness of the company could be turned to advantage, provided its real numbers were not known. It was much easier to move three dozen riders undetected through broken fields and backcountry lanes than it would have been for two regiments.

While halted at a plantation just three miles outside Macon, Forbes plied a captured Rebel scout with coffee and tobacco to learn what he could. The news was not good: the Yankees were expected. Brown quotes Forbes: "We thought it best to consider Macon too large a prize to be captured by thirty-six men" because the enemy "would have swallowed us up as a half mouthful" (85).[14] Forbes picked his way carefully around Macon. He decided to strike the Mobile and Ohio below town, at a bridge over the Noxubee River. A Rebel artilleryman, happy to be captured and then paroled by the captain, agreed to act as guide. But once again Forbes was thwarted. More guards stood watch at the bridge than he had troopers in

Stephen Forbes, trooper in the 7th Illinois Cavalry.
Courtesy of the University of Illinois Archives.

his entire company. "We were now entitled to overtake the brigade if we could," Forbes later explained, so the company turned southwest and just above Philadelphia struck the road traveled by Grierson (98).[15]

Company B had its first close call soon after. Grierson's column had passed through the day before, and the locals were ready for trouble. Forbes halted the company for a brief rest north of town and sent three men ahead to scout. Two had been selected as Butternut Guerillas before the company left the column and still wore their disguises; the third trooper dressed to match them. They stopped at a house, only to be accosted by three Rebel soldiers not fooled by their attire. Revolvers were whipped from holsters, and a gunfight erupted. William Buffington, one of the former Butternut Guerillas, was shot dead; Charles Martin was hit in the arm before he could take cover in some bushes. He and an unwounded Isaac Robinson were saved only by the arrival of the full company. As it came charging down the road in response to the gunfire, the Confederates ran. The company then rode through Philadelphia proper, guns blazing. No more men were hit, and the home guardsmen who resisted were disarmed, paroled, and several had their horses drafted as Yankee remounts. For an interesting sidelight, Brown again quoted Forbes. We learn that William Buffington, slain in that first exchange outside town, was "stretched on a Southern porch, under the solemn promise from the householder that he would decently bury him—a pledge which I had afterwards the satisfaction to learn was honorably fulfilled" (117).[16]

At the same moment that Forbes readied his company to move out of Philadelphia, Grierson's men were finishing what they had started at Newton Station that morning, some thirty miles to the south. Though they had had little sleep in the past couple of days, Forbes kept his men in the saddle through the night with the hope that he would catch Grierson before the column left Newton Station. But he was too late. "The raiders' rear guard," paroled Confederates convalescing at Newton's makeshift hospital told him truthfully, "had departed late yesterday afternoon, about fifteen hours past" (128). They reportedly passed through Garlandville, then turned east. Forbes weighed the possibilities and concluded to move that way too. "Thus," ironically and dangerously, Brown commented, "did Colonel Grierson's carefully planned deception mislead one of his own company commanders" (129).

Forbes decided to intercept the column at an angle. Instead of marching to Garlandville, he would slice southeast and link up with Grierson at Enterprise, on the Mobile and Ohio line. Little did he realize that "every hoofbeat" took him and his men "in the opposite direction from their comrades" (129). Continued good luck and quick thinking, combined with one of the greatest bluffs of the war, saved B Company. The tired but wary troopers were just outside Enterprise when they passed over a rise and came within sight of a Rebel post. A half dozen of the raiders, Forbes and his lieutenant in the lead, rode forward under a white flag. A few shots were fired at them, but they kept on, at a walk. The firing then ceased and three mounted Confederate officers came forward under their own flag of truce. What followed was later described by Captain Forbes and retold with little embellishment by Brown. It is a truly fine example of the old adage that facts can be stranger than fiction.

The Confederate carrying the white kerchief wore a gold sash around his waist; his horse pranced nervously to within a few feet of Captain Forbes. The man glanced once at the company drawn up in a column of fours on the slope beyond. His voice came firmly, yet disinterestedly courteous, soft and Southern, the words stilted in the old chivalric form: "To whom are we indebted for the honor of this visit?"

"I come from Major-General Grierson," replied Captain Forbes sternly. "To demand the surrender of Enterprise."

Betraying no surprise, the Confederate officers held their horses steady, the eyes of all three fixed on Captain Forbes's austere face, as if waiting for a limiting clause to follow the blunt request. After a moment of silence, the spokesman replied: "Will the Captain put the demand in writing?"

"Certainly," replied Forbes quickly. "To whom shall I address it?"

"To Colonel Edwin Goodwin, commanding the post."

"Very well. I shall give the Colonel one hour to consider the demand for surrender."

My informants were either lying or mistaken, Captain Forbes was thinking. *This town is garrisoned.*

He finished scribbling the surrender demand. "One hour only for consideration, after which further delay will be at your peril." Glancing up, he saw that the rebel carrying the white flag had also written a message. Their horses came closer, the notes were exchanged.

"Will the captain await a reply here?" asked the Southerner.

"We shall fall back to the main body," replied Captain Forbes, "and there await the reply."

The Confederates swept off their hats in a gesture of farewell, turned their mounts about, and galloped back toward the town. Captain Forbes nodded to Lieutenant McCausland. "Right about gentlemen! And let's pray that we find the main body." They rode at a slow canter back to the company, the captain unfolding the Confederate officer's note and reading it hurriedly: "Colonel Goodwin's compliments to General Grierson, commanding United States forces, and asks permission to consider his demand for one hour."

Forbes slipped the paper inside his saddlebag. He hoped he would be lucky enough to pass it on to Grierson; the colonel would appreciate his promotion in rank. (130–31)[17]

After the raid Forbes chuckled when reading Southern newspaper accounts stating that two thousand Rebel infantry had later marched cautiously out of Enterprise, fully expecting to do battle with fifteen hundred Yankee raiders. But at the time his smiles at his own cleverness and the relief of his men faded quickly. Once they had ridden a safe distance toward Garlandville, where the column was last seen, Forbes paused. Brown inserted a note here, telling readers that according to Stephen Forbes's recollection the captain gave his men the option of splitting up into small groups to escape on their own or staying together as a company to try to catch the column. To a man they chose to stick together (132n).

They did not reach Garlandville until dusk, but they found the trail. Forbes selected three men—his brother Stephen one of them—to take the fastest horses and get to Grierson. Forbes feared that the three might be shot by snipers or be picked up as stragglers, but the alternative for all of them was to be so far behind that they would be separated from the column by bridges burned in its wake. His gambit paid off; the riders reached the column as it was crossing the Strong River. Grierson was indeed going to burn the bridge after he crossed it. As Stephen Forbes told it, in words repeated by Brown, he good-naturedly greeted Grierson: "Captain Forbes presents his compliments, and begs to be allowed to burn his bridges for himself!" Brown adds that "it is easy to picture that dramatic moment—the drenched and mud-stained nineteen-year-old sergeant sitting erect upon his spent horse, the colonel grinning at him through his black, spade-shaped beard" (142).[18] And Brown wisely uses Henry Forbes's own summary to review what B Company had done.

We had been absent five days and four nights; we had marched fully three hundred miles in ten different counties, had captured and

Henry Forbes, after he was promoted to colonel of the
7th Illinois Cavalry. Courtesy of the Illinois Historical
Survey, University of Illinois.

paroled forty prisoners, confronted and evaded several thousand of the Confederate troops at Macon and Enterprise; slipped through the home guards of six county towns, been twice misled and once lost; had had but eighteen hours of sleep, while rations for man and horse had been for the most part conspicuous by their absence. We simply had not had time to eat. The men who did this work *were a year and a half from the plow-tail*, and their chief claim to consideration is that they were representative men—fair types of our American citizen-soldier. (150)[19]

The high drama and close calls of Company B were matched by the exploits of the Butternut Guerillas, yet another reason why Brown's book is such good reading. Virtually all of Brown's information about the Butternut Guerillas and even much of what occurred with the main column came from Richard Surby's narrative, published soon after the war's end. Indeed, without Surby's account Brown would not have been able to write the sort of book that he did. The sense of adventure that had taken the Canadian-born Surby from home in his teenage years and into Illinois by the outbreak of war comes through vividly in his account of the raid. Surby provides anecdotal color that makes Grierson's autobiography appear rather pale by comparison. The Forbes brothers had a dramatic flair closer to Surby than to Grierson, but they did not see much of what Surby described, both because of their five-day escapade and because of Surby's role as scout ahead of the column.

Surby enters Brown's narrative on the fifth day of the expedition, April 21, when the Butternut Guerillas were formed. A sergeant in the 7th Illinois, Surby was friendly with Lieutenant Colonel Blackburn. Together they selected the other eight men, all of them from that same regiment, who joined Surby as scouts. Brown explained how their irregular attire— pants, coats, and hats that did not match, weapons that were often not military issue—would enable them to pass themselves off as Rebel cavalrymen. "Butternut" referred to the brownish, home-dyed uniforms that clothing-starved Confederates often wore instead of regulation gray.

Riding ahead of the column, which would be moving along, unseen, a mile or so behind, Surby and his men acted as Grierson's eyes and ears. They were, as Brown noted, "to report back regularly what they could learn of the roads' destinations, distances and conditions, the number of streams and whether bridged or fordable, and before noon and nightfall of each day they were to search out favorable camping sites near forage and water" (74–75). They were not to disclose their real identities to the people they met along the way. Rather, they were to say that they were Tennessee cavalrymen. Residents of the towns they passed through would ask them if they had spotted the Yankees rumored to be about; as often as not they would reply, no, they were out looking for them. Amazingly, their deceit was rarely detected until too late, and Surby filled his account with examples of how easily the enemy could be fooled. Brown had only to choose which tales to tell.

Surby and his companions rarely resorted to force. Subterfuge worked well, and when it failed they almost always got the drop on those they encountered before shots could be fired. Brown included various instances of this repeated occurrence. One came from the day after the scouts took on their new persona. They met up with two Rebel soldiers at a plantation set back from the line of march. "In their Secesh clothing the scouts were immediately accepted as comrades," and the unsuspecting Confederates "invited them into the house." Surby warned them that Yankees were in the neighborhood so the men decided to leave. Brown let Surby take the story from there.

> Having told them that we would accompany them some distance [Surby wrote], the demijohn was brought out, glasses placed upon the table, and a cordial invitation given to help ourselves to some "old rye," which invitation a soldier never refuses. . . . We started out, the young men armed with shotguns, eight negroes following with fourteen mules and six fine horses. It was about one and a half miles to the road, upon which the column was advancing, and in the direction that we were going; when about half way I had a curiosity to examine their guns, which they seemed proud to exhibit; making a motion to one of my men he followed suit, thus we had them disarmed. (87)[20]

The next day Surby and his compatriots approached an all-important bridge over the swollen Pearl River, a few miles above Philadelphia. The Pearl was spilling out of its normal channel and into the lowlands and moving so swiftly that it could not have been crossed anywhere for miles except over the bridge. The scouts stopped an old man riding a mule down the road through the thickly wooded area on their side of the river. Surby inquired about the bridge and asked if it was guarded. Before becoming suspicious, the man told him that five others, his son included, were acting as pickets. They were prepared to burn the bridge if necessary to keep the raiders from crossing it. Finally realizing that Surby was in fact one of those very Yankees, he did not want to say anything more. Determined "to frighten the old man into an unconditional surrender of the bridge," Surby advised him that "it lies in your power to save your buildings from the torch, to save your own life, and probably that of your son, by saving the bridge" (95).[21] Threatening that if the bridge were set alight he would see that the old man's house and barn were burned, Surby let him go reason with the guards at the bridge, who had not observed what just transpired. Surby and the other scouts watched nervously through the trees as the old man passed onto the bridge and began talking to the shotgun-toting militiamen. The Illinoisans could not hear what was said; no matter. All six men on the bridge suddenly fled toward town, the scouts replaced some planks that had been taken up and removed combustibles gathered to make sure the bridge burned if fires were set, and the column passed safely over.

And so it went, again and again. For nearly two weeks and four hundred miles the Butternut Guerillas gathered information and passed it back to Grierson. They gave the lay of the land, the direction of roads, the location of food for men and forage for horses, and fair warning if trouble were likely. Without these scouts Grierson might not have gotten south of the Pearl; he certainly would not have been as successful as he was at Newton Station. Only because the Butternut Guerillas slipped unobtrusively into town and asked seemingly innocent questions did the advance group under Blackburn know to rush ahead and arrive before the trains. True, the scouts became adept at the game they played, but they were aided greatly by the openness, even gullibility of the local whites and willingness to help of so many blacks along their route.

This is not to say that Surby's men were off on a lark. They never knew what to expect, and on rainy, moonless nights, when tensions were high and visibility low, they had to be careful not to shoot each other. They had numerous close calls, the closest coming at Hazlehurst. Ordered by Colonel Prince to send two men into town to plant a fabricated telegraph dispatch on the column's whereabouts, Surby picked George Steadman and Lycurgus Kelly for the job. "Under a blackening sky that threatened a thunderstorm," Brown wrote ominously, "Steadman and Kelly rode slowly into town. Hazlehurst's false-fronted, unpainted pine-board buildings clung in a narrow strip along the single line of rail track, resembling a western frontier town rather than a southern village," and "few people were moving in the muddy street or along the planked sidewalks" (152).

With a practiced air of nonchalance, the two Yankees ambled into the train station past lounging Confederates and handed their message to the telegraph operator, who tapped it off excitedly to Jackson. "Thunder was rumbling" as Steadman and Kelly left the train station and then decided to cross the street to a hotel where they could "trade some of their Secesh money for some Secesh food before riding back to inform Surby he could cut the wires." Then they walked into trouble.

> They were half way across the street, skirting the deeper mudholes, when a horseman came galloping around the corner of the hotel. Steadman lifted one hand in a casual greeting. His arm froze in mid-air. The horseman had pulled up sharply, staring at the scouts, his face flushing in sudden anger.
>
> The rider was the deputy sheriff who eighteen hours ago had been captured by them only to escape later during the night from Williams' Plantation. He was riding the horse stolen from Grierson's orderly, and now began to brandish a saber stolen at the same time.
>
> "Help! Stop the Yankees!" the sheriff shouted in a voice high-pitched from sudden excitement. He shifted the saber awkwardly to his left hand, withdrawing a pistol from his belt with his right. His horse, feeling the bridle loosen, began to twist and stamp in the mud.
>
> The scouts drew their revolvers and began backing toward the station. Standing in his stirrups now, the sheriff continued bellowing: "Help! Help! Stop the Yankees!" He did not fire his pistol, and the scouts guessed it was empty.
>
> But his urgent clamor brought the Confederate soldiers out of the station just as Steadman and Kelly reached their horses and began jerking the hitches loose. The scouts were mounting when several Confederates came pounding around the depot.
>
> Steadman fired his revolver above the rebels' heads and sent them scurrying to cover, while he and Kelly lashed their horses into a gallop, using the line of side-tracked freight cars for a screen as they sped out of town. (153)[22]

They made it back to Surby, who ordered the wire cut, sent one man to bring on Colonel Prince at the run, then leaped into his saddle and with the other scouts charged into town, fully expecting a fight. Instead, the streets were empty, the depot nearly deserted. "Only two old men re-mained, sitting quietly on a bench in the waiting room" (154).[23]

Surby finally got his fight, not in Hazlehurst but at Wall's Bridge over the Tickfaw. There his luck ran out and he was wounded in the thigh, not while acting as a scout but while caught up in Lieutenant Colonel Black-burn's impetuous dash across the bridge. Surby could no longer ride and knew that he had to be left behind. If caught dressed as a Butternut Gue-rilla he ran the risk of being shot as a spy, so before his friends departed they helped him back into his uniform, which a member of his old com-pany had carried in his saddlebag. With that reluctant parting of comrades in arms one element of Brown's story, an essential component in the ac-tual raid, effectively came to an end, one day and fifty miles short of safety.[24]

Surby was daring, the Forbes brothers brave, but arguably the most interesting and most crucial character in Brown's narrative is Benjamin Henry Grierson. What makes Grierson so intriguing is that he is an un-likely hero. He personified much that Americans have found appealing over the years: the common man of uncommon valor, the quiet citizen forced to lead men into war, the underdog who defies skeptics and beats the odds. Nothing in his background had hinted at the greatness that lay ahead. It is this combination of characteristics that Brown exploits so adroitly. He actually says little about Grierson's life before the war, and what little he says he saves for the second chapter, when the raiders are al-ready on the road. But it is enough to whet the reader's appetite.

The thirty-six-year-old Grierson, we learn as the column moves south, was the son of Scots-Irish immigrants, born in Pittsburgh and raised in Youngstown, Ohio. Of average height and slight build, he was anything but physically imposing. Music was his first love, and in his mid-twenties he moved to Illinois and tried to make a living teaching it. "He set him-self up as a music teacher in the pleasant little village of Jacksonville, and began organizing amateur bands there and in neighboring towns." Cir-cumstances conspired to bring Alice Kirk, "his childhood sweetheart," to nearby Springfield (24).[25] They married, and Grierson decided that he needed to try his hand at something else to earn the money he would need to support a family. He became partners with an old friend, and they opened a general store in neighboring Meredosia. Though it did well early on, it failed after a couple of years. Humiliated, Grierson went back to teaching music.

His involvement in Republican politics would change his future. "An active partisan" for Abraham Lincoln, he made friends in the state party

organization and at the outbreak of the war was rewarded with a
commission—a common occurrence at the time. Still, his prospects did
not seem particularly bright. "For five months he lived on borrowed
funds," Brown observes, "awaiting a permanent assignment, only to be
offered at last a major's rank in the only service he wished to avoid—the
cavalry." The cavalry was unappealing because when he was eight years
old "a supposedly friendly pony had kicked him in the face, splitting his
forehead and mangling one cheek. For two months he was blinded and he
carried the scars to his grave" (25). But his was not to reason why; a horse
soldier he became, and a fine one at that.

Grierson rose to colonel and was put in command of his own brigade
in the fall of 1862. He worked hard to form the men into a cohesive unit;
naturally he became the glue for Brown's book. In a very real sense everything revolved around Grierson. The raid's success was owing to a combination of great skill and good luck, both of which are found in the historical Grierson and in Brown's depiction of him. He planned carefully, he
tried to anticipate what his opponents would do, and as a result he did not
have to outfight them because he outthought them. But he was also astute
enough to know that chance could never be eliminated. There would be
occasions when he would have to guess and hope that he guessed right.
Never a martinet, untainted by delusions of grandeur, he knew that he
was not infallible. The tables were turned on him once during the raid,
Brown points out, when he was tricked into believing that Osyka was
heavily garrisoned. And it was roughly at this same time, Brown contends,
that Grierson became momentarily hesitant, indecisive, not able to choose
whether he should turn west or go south. But Grierson's fallibility makes
him all the more sympathetic, and, ironically, his decision to avoid Osyka
and ride more directly for the Tickfaw crossing may have given him the
time he needed to outpace Adams and Richardson—once again, "Grierson's luck" came to the rescue.

All of this good fortune became clear only after the fact. For the sixteen days and five hundred miles that Grierson was in enemy territory he
could never be sure that he would bring his men back to safety. It is this
sense of uncertainty that Brown keeps implanted in the reader's mind.
Like other good writers, he was able to heighten anxiety and build a sense
of expectation, even though the outcome is known in advance. Chapter 14, "The Trap Begins to Close," is a fine case in point. It is April 30
and the raiders have passed through Summit, turning away from Osyka
and making camp not far above the Tickfaw, which they expected to cross

after sunrise. Grierson now wanted only to ride through to Baton Rouge, and yet he must have wondered if he would make it. Somewhere out there, he knew, Wirt Adams was in furious pursuit; so was Richardson, which he did not know. "Thus, while the raiders slept peacefully on Spurlark's Plantation, five miles to their west Wirt Adams was resting his regiment for the night, and fifteen miles to the east Richardson's forces were cautiously surrounding the town of Summit" (188). To the southwest, troops from Port Hudson were preparing to cut Grierson off at the Amite. If all of those forces converged, a bloody battle was inevitable. Was Grierson's luck about to run out? So Brown left the scene as he ended the chapter and the day, thus subtly nudging the reader into the next chapter, the next day. Anxiety for those readers hoping that Grierson will run the gauntlet and come out alive ends as it did for Grierson himself, when he crosssed the Comite and his men dropped exhausted from their saddles. Grierson was too tense to sit and relax. Instead, the former music teacher sought another way to unwind, which Brown, with Grierson's help, turned into this dramatically satisfying scene:

"So tired they were," observed Grierson, "they scarcely waited for food, before every man save two or three was in a profound slumber." To keep himself awake Grierson entered the plantation house, wandered into the parlor and began playing upon a piano which he found there. "I astonished the occupants by sitting down and playing upon a piano which I found in the parlor and in that manner I managed to keep awake, while my soldiers were enjoying themselves by relaxation, sleep and quiet rest."

What music did Grierson play at his moment of triumph? Might it have been *Life Let Us Cherish*, the first piece of music he had learned—when he was twelve years old—worked out laboriously on a large yellow box-wood flute while he sat upright in the middle of the bed? Or was it, as one of his friends back in Jacksonville, Illinois, suggested later, *The Bold Soldier Boy?*

He did tell of his thoughts while he was there, playing the piano: "Only six miles from Baton Rouge and four miles would bring us inside the lines guarded by the soldiers of the Union. Think of the great relief to the overtaxed mind and nerves. I felt that we had nobly accomplished the work assigned to us and no wonder that I felt musical; who would not under like circumstances?" (215)[26]

Grierson's long ride was over at last. The spontaneous victory parade through Baton Rouge ended the raid and all but closed the sixteenth chapter of the book. An epilogue, "Heroes to the Union," follows that assesses the raid's significance and reveals what happened to some of the leading characters. It serves as a fit conclusion to the stirring saga—drama accentuated, not created, by Dee Brown. He had told an engaging story, a literary feat appreciated by reviewers and readers alike. No doubt the enthusiastic jacket blurb by Pulitzer Prize–winning Civil War historian Bruce Catton helped sales. Catton called the book "a real contribution to the story of the Civil War," adding, "I'm glad it was done so ably." Perhaps Catton's endorsement would be enough for general readers, but serious Civil War students would likely hold their opinions open and their wallets closed until they heard from the academic historians. If anything, some academicians were more effusive in their praise than Catton. One wrote that "Civil War fact has hardly been so imaginatively handled since the days of Stephen Vincent Benet."[27] Another concluded that Brown "has proved himself a dexterous writer" and his "book bids fair to become a minor classic of its kind."[28] Sure enough, prophecy has been fulfilled. To this day Brown's rendition remains the most quoted, most respected account of Grierson's raid.

Brown has had his critics, then and since, however. One historian, Thomas Belser of Jacksonville State College, was not so charmed by *Grierson's Raid*. Overall he thought Brown had written a good book, and he recommended it to readers. He noted that Brown made some "minor" errors in his citations and that he should have stated more clearly that Pemberton's lack of cavalry "made Grierson's task considerably easier"— comments that are fairly typical for reviews of this sort. Direct quotations with no citations whatsoever disturbed Belser a bit more. What worried him most of all was that "some readers may object to the invention of conversations which are calculated to enliven an already lively narrative."[29] Without becoming too caustic or going into much detail, Belser had leveled a serious charge: that, primary sources consulted and endnotes citing them notwithstanding, Brown had violated the basic rules of historical writing. Possibly some of those other historians who had waxed so enthusiastic over the book would have felt differently had they read it as closely as Belser.

Undeniably, Brown did engage in literary inventions. Sometimes he informed the reader of what he had done, sometimes he did not. For instance, at one point in chapter 6 he included, in quotation marks, orders

COLONEL GRIERSON, SIXTH ILLINOIS CAVALRY.—From a Photograph by Jacobs, of New Orleans.—[See Page 304.]

Harper's Weekly engraving of Col. Benjamin Henry Grierson as dashing cavalier (June 6, 1863). Courtesy of Special Collections, Brigham Young University, Provo, Utah.

issued by Grierson to one of his officers. In the endnotes he tells readers, cryptically, that the "Grierson quotation" was "based" on what he found in the *Official Records* (247). In another instance, he applied a statement made by Henry Forbes in 1862 to the situation on the raid in 1863 (77, 246). In yet another, while writing about the skirmishing between Grierson's troopers and Adams's Mississippians at Union Church, he included a quotation that appears to describe that moment in place and time. Once again in the endnote he tells the reader that actually he used an 1864 entry in Stephen Forbes's journal. "Forbes left no account of the Union Church attack. These descriptions of a similar surprise attack on the Seventh Illinois Regiment are inserted here for dramatic effect" Brown explained (249). There are numerous other instances, and many of those give no warning to the reader in the text or the notes, where he turned his inference into what appeared to be a fact.[30]

For some, perhaps even most historians such applications of literary license make Brown's work suspect. Brown has not let their complaints about this book or ones written later bother him. He is convinced that it is possible to be true to the spirit of the past even while violating some of the conventions of traditional historical writing. From the beginning of his career Brown has produced novels as well as historical works, and he does not consider them to be fundamentally different as literature. His next book after *Grierson's Raid* was indeed a piece of fiction, called *Yellowhorse* and published in 1956. Here Brown uses a novel to tell his truths about the settlement and unsettlement of the West. Stock characters perform their symbolic function: Capt. Thomas Jefferson Easterwood, that supposedly rare cavalry officer who respected native ways; Col. Matthew Quill, a Custer-like figure, too full of bombast, too lacking in wisdom or understanding; Spotted Wolf, the aging Sioux chief trying desperately to preserve what he could as whites violated treaties and encroached on Indian lands; Young Elk, the stripling warrior determined to stop the injustice; Alison Stuart, the good white woman whose love salves the growing bitterness in Tom Easterwood. It is a passable tale but thin by comparison with *Grierson's Raid,* thinner still when compared with Grierson's actual raid.[31]

That same year Brown endorsed the latest work of another novelist, Harold Sinclair. Sinclair had fictionalized Grierson's raid as *The Horse Soldiers.* Col. Benjamin Henry Grierson is metamorphosed into Col. John Francis Marlowe; Capt. Henry Forbes becomes Capt. Asa Bryce; Andy Bullen takes the place of Richard Surby; real events are altered or deleted and new events created. Brown did not have a problem with any of this. "An honest historian would be the first to admit that historical writing at best never more than approximates truth, that it is impossible to reconstruct the true past from documents," intoned Brown in the foreword he wrote for Sinclair's book. Sinclair had invented much, Brown concedes, "yet nowhere has the author departed from essential truth in telling his version of the story."[32] Dee Brown believed that *The Horse Soldiers* was good history then; he believes it still.[33]

3

THE STORY AS NOVEL

Have you ever been tempted to have a go at fiction? You read fiction; have you ever been tempted to write fiction?

Oh, I've been tempted, but never given into the temptation because I don't think that I have the imaginative power. Frankly, I regard good fiction as being a higher form of creation than writing good history. Writing *bad* fiction is obviously not as high a creative act, but in general I think writing fiction is a higher form of creation.

—Edmund S. Morgan, 1987

The Horse Soldiers was the eighth of nine books Harold Sinclair saw published in his lifetime. A tenth, though completed well before he died, appeared posthumously.[1] Sinclair had enjoyed a modest reputation as a writer until *The Horse Soldiers,* when he gained some of the fame and fortune that proved so elusive before, and then but momentarily. It was something he shared in common with others who try to make their living by the pen.

Chicago-born, Sinclair was sent by his mother to live with relatives in Bloomington, over one hundred miles to the south, because his father, a railroad man, had abandoned the family when Sinclair was still a boy. The young Sinclair delivered newspapers to help earn money and tried to think of Bloomington as home. What was always difficult eventually became impossible. He dropped out of high school in his junior year when he was accused—wrongly, he always maintained—of stealing a musical instrument. He became a Western Union telegrapher for a time, and then, in 1926, not yet twenty years old, he gave in to his wanderlust and hit the road. His travels took him to Florida and New Orleans and ultimately back to Chicago before he moved on to Texas. He played honky-tonk piano and Dixieland jazz on trumpet or saxophone at nightclubs and sold hardware during regular business hours.[2]

His *Journey Home,* published in 1936, drew on these years in a loosely autobiographical way. James David Hall, the character who tells the tale, starts life in small-town Illinois and bounces from a brokerage firm in New York to bohemianism in Chicago to shady associates in New Orleans before following the sun to California. He marries and settles down in the Santa Clara Valley, still searching for the meaning of life. "I have made the journey home," Hall tells us, as much as anyone ever can. He would always long to find his true self, his rightful place in the world, but now he could continue the quest spiritually, not geographically. "I know no more of the inward meaning of these things which are past than I did before," he sighs, a caution to readers seeking simple solutions and formulaic advice.[3]

Sinclair had returned to Bloomington and married a local woman a few years before writing *Journey Home.* He was very much like his fictional James David Hall, the displaced, restless American, respecting tradition and yet keeping it at arm's length, in search of community and yet fearful of being stifled by convention. "I am not a very social person and have very few close friends, but those few are most excellent ones," he said. "I think of myself as being about one-third incurable romanticist, one-third cynical realist, and one-third somewhat vague blank." He sold hardware for Sears and Roebuck by day and wrote at night. "I've read more books than I can remember," he noted, "and have wanted to be a writer since I was first able to read."[4] He finished five books in six years, with *Journey Home* the first and *The Port of New Orleans* the fifth, in 1942. During World War II he worked as a machinist and wrote less.

Three of his prewar books were connected as a single story, a trilogy about the fictitious town of Everton, actually a thinly disguised Bloomington. It was, as Sinclair's biographer Robert Bray put it, Sinclair's "anytown that could be everytown."[5] The Everton saga opened with *American Years* and continued through *The Years of Growth,* ending with the bittersweet *Years of Illusion.* There is a life cycle of sorts here, a passage, through each successive volume, from birth to maturation to decay. Sinclair does not, however, reduce everything to a gloomy Spenglerian chronicle of inevitable rise, decline, and fall. He was more interested in personalities than in the power of vast, impersonal forces. Sinclair mixes his imaginary characters with real figures from the past, including, in the first volume, an up-and-coming politician from Springfield named Abraham Lincoln. Some of his characters are composites, a blend of his conjuring and actual people from Bloomington's past who would be easily recognizable to local readers.[6]

Author Harold Sinclair.
Courtesy of the *Pantagraph*
and Michael Sinclair.

Sinclair made his preferences obvious throughout. He lionized common Americans, those men and women of quiet dignity, sure integrity,
and a willingness to work hard who cleared the land and built the towns.
Here in the Illinois soil of Sinclair's imagination were played out the most
primal human dramas. "It had been, and was, an earth of fruitfulness and
promise, of bloodshed and toil and endless hardship, and, sometimes, rich
reward."[7] That Sinclair had no patience for party hacks, boosterish blow-
hards, or puffery became clear in his vignettes of Everton's leading citizens. His discussion of town-building men in the Ransom clan and their
Civil War service even took him into Mississippi, though there was no
hint that he would eventually return south with *The Horse Soldiers*.

Sinclair was aided immensely by a Guggenheim fellowship in 1939, a
$2,000 stipend that enabled him to quit selling hardware and devote more
of his time to writing and to finishing the trilogy. Members of the award
committee had read both *Journey Home* and *American Years*. They thought
Sinclair showed great promise.[8] And for a time it looked as if Sinclair
would indeed be able to write without distraction. Doubleday, his publisher, made *American Years* a Literary Guild selection with the expectation that Sinclair would become as successful as Kenneth Roberts had been
with *Northwest Passage*. It did not turn out as planned. *American Years*

sold perhaps six thousand copies before being relegated to Doubleday's Dollar Club, and the other two volumes fell far short of that mark. Sinclair went back to work during the war years and returned to writing full-time only in 1948 because his wife, who had taught school before they were married, took a job as librarian at Bloomington's newspaper, the *Pantagraph*. Ward, the oldest of their six children, recalled that out of necessity his mother—"a tower of strength who believed abidingly" in his father's "potential as a writer"—became a master at scrimping and saving.[9]

Throughout his career Sinclair sought to combine the historical with the fictional. Doubleday in fact promoted *American Years* as a new type of novel, "an extraordinary departure in the field of historical fiction." Sinclair, readers are told, captured the essence of the frontier experience. His characters are archetypes, and "their lives are fused and focused perfectly into the life of Everton itself, till at the last the reader has an impression of the growth of an American frontier town far more vivid than that which any historian who deals only in facts could hope to give."[10] Sinclair may have smiled inwardly at the gushing tone of this claim, but at heart he believed it to be true. It was a conviction he carried through the Everton trilogy and into *Westward the Tide,* a fictionalized account of George Rogers Clark's Illinois country exploits that he wrote at about the same time.[11] It was a conviction he carried into *The Horse Soldiers* as well.

Sinclair signed a contract for that book with Harper & Brothers in the spring of 1955. It appeared roughly six months later. He and Dee Brown did not meet until after Sinclair finished his manuscript, although they lived within fifty miles of each other. It took Sinclair's publisher to bring them together. Evan Thomas, the Harper & Brothers editor working with Sinclair, had been told about *Grierson's Raid* by a colleague, a Civil War aficionado who thought highly of Brown's book. Thomas contacted Brown and sent him a copy of Sinclair's manuscript. Brown responded with the flattering assessment that Thomas inserted eagerly as a foreword.[12] Sinclair told Brown that he had heard of his "solid historical version," but "frankly I didn't want to read it at the time because I was on the last lap of my own book."[13] Even if he had not read *Grierson's Raid* by this point he must have at least browsed through it before the manuscript went to press. He used the same chapter title, "Fox and Hounds," for the movement that took the column away from Union Church. Brown's chapter ends with the thirteenth day of the raid, just south of Brookhaven; Sinclair's carries all the way through the fighting at Wall's Bridge.

Sinclair had apparently puttered with his story off and on for a dozen years. What first attracted Sinclair to the raid remains unclear. Background research on the Everton trilogy could have caused his path to cross Grierson's, as could his never-finished biography of Stephen A. Douglas or his longtime interest in Mississippi steamboats, the city of New Orleans, or still other possibilities. Somewhere along the line it appears that he had perused the *Official Records,* Surby's account, and perhaps even some of the Forbes material.

In a note to readers he wrote that *"The Horse Soldiers* is fiction, not history, but students of the American Civil War will recognize that it is based on the episode in that conflict generally known as Grierson's Raid." [14] Originally he had included a passage stipulating that "the portrait of Colonel Marlowe is *not* in any sense that of Colonel Benjamin H. Grierson." [15] He dropped that sentence in favor of one stating more generically that the characters "are fictional, although their actions are based on the historical record." Only the names of the men in Grierson's column are changed. Hurlbut and Sooy Smith appear as themselves, as do all the Confederate commanders from Pemberton to Wirt Adams; likewise towns that the raiders passed through and rivers they crossed. Sinclair emphasized that a true sense of the past had been preserved—"place names, elapsed time, the route of the brigade—and its several offshoots—are in general faithful to the original." [16]

Sinclair was an experienced writer who knew how to evoke an image in clean and confident prose. His touch was light, his style occasionally breezy—perhaps too breezy. The sarcastic, profane banter in his dialogue seems almost too familiar, his Civil War cavalrymen talking like Hollywood marines in the Pacific during World War II, as if they had jumped off the screen from *Gung Ho* or *Sands of Iwo Jima.* Anachronistic or not, inspired more by film fiction than by real experience, it was what general readers expected their fighting men to sound like, and critics did not notice.

Like Brown's book, Sinclair's included a map of Mississippi on the endpapers. It is simpler than Brown's map, which had been based on one in Stephen Forbes's papers. Apparently Harper & Brothers adapted it from a printed map that Sinclair marked by hand. As Sinclair recommended, almost all the topographical details not related to the raid are excluded. Jacket art featured a full-color, wraparound scene. In the foreground a blue-coated officer sits astride his horse and looks pensively off into the distance. Behind him is a bustle of activity: a rider coming up fast, another officer waving toward troopers in a column of twos who are weaving their way toward the reader from a bridge in the background. Ominous dark clouds streak the sky, lending a sense of foreboding to the setting. A promotional blurb on the jacket flaps underscores the drama. "This novel is based on one of the most daring cavalry operations of all time," it opens, a "seventeen-day raid by a Union brigade through the heart of Confederate Mississippi." The reader is assured that this is no staid chronicle of that mission. "By all accounts the raid was staggering in effect upon enemy morale and strategy, but so closely does the reader associate himself with the men in the saddle that it is not until the book is finished that he realizes the really continental importance of what has transpired." What is more, "in the glimpses of the men and women of the South, we are made very much aware of the essential tragedy of all this—for these were Americans, fighting each other."[17] Hyperbole aside, the image generated is not so different from that sold on the jacket flap of *Grierson's Raid*. The claims made for Sinclair's Marlowe echo those made for Brown's Grierson; the fictional and the historical are at once different and the same.

Sinclair, like Brown, did not need to come up with an exciting tale on his own; rather, he shaped his dramatic narrative within the framework provided by actual events. Freed by a literary license denied Brown, Sinclair was also able to make his story more compelling by filling in blanks that Brown left open, despite his willingness to bend many of the rules of historical writing. Grierson had sometimes revealed his thoughts about various aspects of the expedition; more often he did not. Brown drew inferences and yet stayed clear of psychohistorical explanation. He did not pretend to know Grierson's innermost feelings, nor did he speculate about what drove the man. Sinclair would not be so constrained with Marlowe, the figment of his imagination. No less important, Sinclair could use Marlowe—could use all of his characters—as surrogates. Through them he could comment on whatever he thought significant and with fewer restrictions than those imposed on Brown.

Even so, Sinclair's story begins and ends in essentially the same place as Brown's, with the same outcome. Both writers allowed the raid's basic chronology and sequential development to dictate the narrative flow. Sinclair's text is longer and divided into nearly twice as many chapters— thirty-three to Brown's seventeen—but these differences should not obscure their overarching similarity. Both writers kept their readers moving briskly, almost as if they were the raiders themselves. On average Sinclair's chapters were only a few thousand words long, with a couple under a

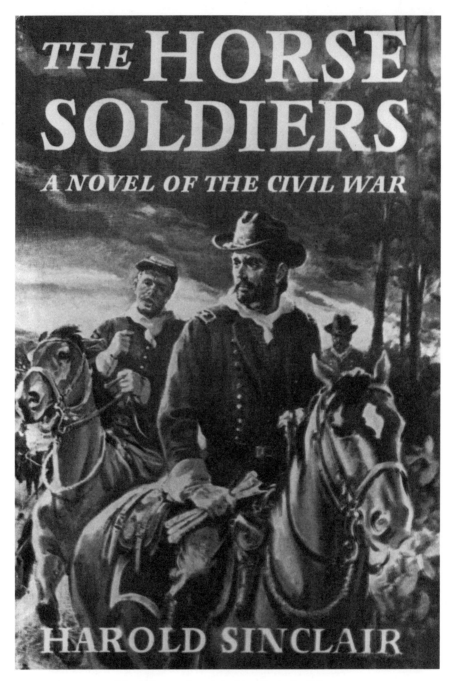

THE HORSE SOLDIERS

A NOVEL OF THE CIVIL WAR

HAROLD SINCLAIR

The jacket to the original hardbound edition.
Courtesy of HarperCollins.

thousand. Brown's chapters were longer but divided into sections that maintained the rapid pace. Although Sinclair did not adopt the Surby-inspired, day-by-day chapter approach taken by Brown, he did keep the same complex components: the main column under Grierson, now Marlowe, renumbered as the 1st and 2d Illinois; the 2d Iowa turning back to La Grange, led by Colonel Blaney rather than Colonel Hatch; and Captain Forbes's Company B of the 7th Illinois now transformed into Company A of the 1st Illinois, under Capt. Asa Bryce. Col. Frank Secord, commander of the 2d Illinois, who plays a relatively minor role in the book, replaces Col. Edward Prince, real-life commander of the 7th Illinois. Sinclair eliminated the battery from the 1st Illinois Artillery entirely "because the part it played was not significant" to the story he wanted to tell. Moreover, he inserted "Pursuit" segments at the end of four chapters and an excerpt from a Mississippi newspaper in one other to apprise readers of what the Confederates were doing to stop the raiders.[18] These literary devices varied from Brown's, but their intent was the same.

The crucial differences come primarily with individual portrayals, not background settings. Col. John Marlowe is if anything more critical to the success of Sinclair's story than Grierson was to Brown's. Marlowe is akin to Grierson in certain ways. He is the same age and a man of unquestionable integrity, a civilian whose military greatness would be thrust upon him. Like Grierson, he had earned the trust of the generals who sent him forth as well as of the troopers who followed him into Mississippi, but in other ways the two men were quite distinct. Marlowe—"Jack" to his friends among the officers—is grittier, tougher, profane. Brown discussed Grierson's background briefly in his second chapter; Sinclair gives Grierson's fictional counterpart a full chapter, titled simply "Marlowe" (20–26). Here we learn that the colonel is a very complex fellow, a complexity that Sinclair could invent for Marlowe but Brown did not explore with Grierson.

Sinclair remains true to historical circumstance in many basic matters, beginning with the character of the raiders. Marlowe and the men of his command are volunteers, not regular soldiers. "The war was an interruption of their normal lives," Sinclair tells us, "something from which they momentarily turned aside, as though to put out a fire in the house of a neighbor" (21). Marlowe had been a successful grain dealer, and "through his acquaintance in state political circles, his former business associates, and his financial standing, he had received his colonelcy with a minimum of effort." The outbreak of war had caught him at a personal crossroads.

His wife of ten years died just before it erupted. "The doctors—he'd had a whole bevy of the best available—had been baffled, and a couple of them had gone so far as to admit it—well, almost." Told that "a complete change of climate and scenery" alone could save his beloved Elaine, Marlowe sold everything—business, house, personal property. She died before they could leave. "Marlowe overnight was set almost completely adrift as a man can be," with no children to care for, no business to tend, no real purpose to life.

> So for John Marlowe, the outbreak of the war, in the limited personal sense, had been providential. It was possible, indeed even probable, that he would have been drawn into it anyway—many another man with an invalid wife was, but in his case that was beside the point. Of course he was hardly so unrealistic as to see the war, even to the smallest degree, as something arranged for his private benefit, and more than most he was aware of the war's larger implications. Certainly the war was not of his personal making or even choice—he had always felt that the North-South dissension should have been settled long since by means of the intelligence nature had provided. But since the war was an inescapable fact, and his own circumstances were what the spin of the wheel had decreed, he had entered the war somewhat in the way a man might emigrate to a new country to make a fresh start. (22–23)

Marlowe did not seek power and glory. He cared deeply for his men and did not consider himself their better because of his rank. "These were good men, he thought." Most were veterans; none were conscripts. "They were no longer innocently enthusiastic—which was really no bad thing, but the one-time eagerness had been replaced by a largely silent determination to see this business through to the bitter end, whatever it might prove to be" (51). These were men essentially like Marlowe himself. Marlowe was tough but fair, a leader true to his word. The troops in his command were consequently devoted to him and would have ridden "to hell if the orders read that way—or even to West Texas" (25). They knew he would not squander their lives in the pursuit of fame. "To him the sole purpose of an army in wartime was to win with the greatest possible dispatch, and within his own personal area of control he acted accordingly and with as little foofaraw as possible" (24). He liked his cigar and whiskey but not so addictively that he lost himself in them, and during quieter moments, when he was "stricken with an almost savage depression of the spirit," they offered some solace (25).

With Marlowe, Sinclair gives us the patriot as realist, the man who knows his duty and does it, but with no illusions. Gone are the naive expectations of 1861. Marlowe had become worldwise and war-weary. When he first joined the cavalry he bought into the romantic image of the dashing cavalier. "But under the hammer of reality the myth quickly became evident for what it was—in fact, it never had much validity, except in so far as the man on foot had been conditioned to believe in the horseman's natural superiority" (55). Marlowe now knew better. Cavalry worked most effectively as mounted infantry, striking quickly then riding on, not charging in seried ranks, sabers flashing in the sunlight. That much he and other Federal cavalrymen had learned from the example of Nathan Bedford Forrest.

Sinclair laid out the campaign scene before delving into Marlowe's past. He opens *The Horse Soldiers* with Hurlbut, Sooy Smith, and Marlowe in Memphis, plotting the details of the raid. Demonstrating that he had read the official documents carefully, he does not credit any particular individual with the original idea. Though Grant, Hurlbut, and Sooy Smith had all concocted schemes, "none of the three ideas had been precisely alike and now this final, actual plan was something of a synthesis of all of them" (5). Hurlbut's preference that Marlowe turn east into Alabama after cutting the Southern Railroad between Jackson and Meridian, along with Sooy Smith's encouraging Marlowe to choose his own escape route, are also grounded in the historical record. Sinclair's fictional Marlowe experiences misgivings that the real Grierson may have felt but left unsaid. "A ten-year-old could see that with a minimum of luck anybody could get himself into this bear trap," Marlowe says to himself; "the trick would lie in getting out" (10). Knowing that he had been asked to do much, perhaps even too much, and as a colonel when he should have been a brigadier general, Marlowe frets but accepts the call and mentally prepares himself to lead his men into harm's way. "Somewhere in the dark behind them a steamboat whistle bellowed mournfully," wrote Sinclair as the colonel takes his leave of Hurlbut and Sooy Smith. "For an instant Marlowe felt that loneliness of spirit which is the occupational disease of the nonprofessional soldier who fights a war far from the place he thinks of as home" (14).

Sinclair's Marlowe is no larger-than-life military genius. His success comes from a very Grierson-like combination of skill and luck. Nor are his Confederate foes reduced to fools or rubes. Sinclair did not need to change their names because he did not alter their place in real events. For most of the book they hover in the margins, just visible enough to remind readers of the dangers lurking along Marlowe's trail. Nor does Sinclair contrive any great battlefield theatrics. He does not inflate the importance of the skirmishing around Union Church. He uses it, instead, to comment—as had Brown—on the confusion that can occur in any engagement, accentuated here by the rapid Yankee movement and indecisive Rebel response. The fight at Wall's Bridge is the most serious engagement in the book, as it was on the actual raid. Sinclair presents it essentially as it happened, with one notable exception: Grierson is struck by enemy fire. He is lucky; the Rebel bullet is stopped by his watch and he is not injured.

Sinclair writes in skirmishing at Newton Station that did not really occur, but primarily as a backdrop for the interplay of characters, not as a device to make readers fear that Marlowe is about to fail. Marlowe also sends a small detachment composed of men wounded in the fighting at Newton Station and their escort back north up the road to La Grange. They could not stay with the column and were certain to become prisoners if left behind. Marlowe felt that they deserved a chance to escape, however slim it might be. As he understood only too well, "a chance, for that matter, was all any of them had now" (196).

This is not to say that Sinclair's changes are unimportant. On the contrary; his changes, even outright inventions, are what drive the narrative and what readers probably found most engaging. Take, for example, Major Gray, Sinclair's stand-in for Lieutentant Colonel Blackburn of the 7th Illinois, and Colonel Blaney, substituted for Colonel Hatch of the 2d Iowa. Gray is a friend and confidant to Marlowe, as Blackburn was to Grierson. Marlowe often seeks his counsel, and Gray offers sage advice. After Marlowe moved up the chain of command to lead the brigade, Gray became acting commander of the 1st Illinois. He gives the appearance of supreme confidence, but in reality he is unsure of himself and seeking Marlowe's approval.

Gray suffers the same fate as Blackburn: he is mortally wounded at the Tickfaw while leading a wild, ill-advised charge across Wall's Bridge, but he gets there by a different psychological route. The historical Blackburn, the Blackburn of Brown's study, simply exercised poor judgment and paid with his life. Gray is depicted as rushing in because he was in some sense trying to atone for an earlier sin. Marlowe had sent him ahead with two hundred men to scout Hazlehurst. Marlowe told Gray he would delay bringing the rest of the column over the Pearl until he had word from Hazlehurst. If Hazlehurst was too strong to take, then he would move the column in another direction; if Gray secured it, he would bring the column through town. Gray had little trouble seizing Hazlehurst, but he heedlessly delayed sending word to Marlowe to come ahead—"he was weary with a vast weariness that included his mind" (265). Marlowe was left at the Pearl not knowing what was happening so he sent an aide to investigate. Only then did Gray remember his orders. Initially resentful that Marlowe had sent him ahead into the unknown, Gray then turned his anger inward. "Five full hours lost into eternity because he, Dick Gray, was a damned fool who couldn't remember routine procedure. He had been cavorting around Hazlehurst, thinking he was cutting a heroic figure, while the simple truth was that he might, possibly, have put the whole brigade in a hole that even Marlowe's luck couldn't get them out of" (272). The column leaves Hazlehurst behind, rides west toward Union Church, and beats back Rebel troops in a melee. Gray is convinced that Marlowe, who did not reprove him in so many words, is actually furious and that he has to do something to win back the colonel's favor. Anxiety-ridden, he does just the opposite. The colonel thinks the column ought to ride south for Baton Rouge; the major thinks Natchez or even Vicksburg a better choice. Tempers flare; he questions Marlowe's judgment, embarrassing himself in front of the other officers as well as Marlowe. Thus he charges rashly onto the bridge over the Tickfaw (310–12). He was either trying to redeem himself through glorious victory or fall as a martyr who could be redeemed only in death. The reader is left to ponder which fate was uppermost in Gray's troubled mind.

What happens in the transformation of Hatch into Blaney offers more pointed if less dramatic commentary. Brown had told his readers little about Hatch—only that he was a transplanted New Englander who attended a Vermont military academy as a youth, moved west and lived on the frontier for a time, and eventually ran a successful lumber business in Iowa. There was not much else that Brown found germane to his story. The records did not seem to indicate a spiteful Hatch who was jealous of Grierson's command or resentful at being detached and sent back to La Grange early in the raid.

Sinclair, through Blaney, gives freer play to emotions. There is a vague tension in the relationship between the two colonels. One potential but unrealized source is Blaney's technical superiority in rank: he had received his colonel's commission before Marlowe was awarded his and yet Marlowe, not Blaney, commanded the brigade. Marlowe, for his part, finds Blaney irritating because the Iowan seems to be so stolid and unimaginative. "Blaney was ten years older than Marlowe, a reasonably good colonel of regiment who neither merited higher command nor wanted it," writes Sinclair, "the kind of man who actually enjoyed the median position he knew he could manage without too much strain" (37). Simply put, Blaney got on Marlowe's nerves. Marlowe had his reasons for this, and yet he also felt that he was somehow being unfair, even when Blaney offered an innocent enough greeting.

> Marlowe raised a hand to Blaney while he winced at the cheerful clichés, but at the same time he also thought, Why do I always belittle the man in my mind? He had no really valid reason for disliking Blaney, and if he wasn't brilliant he was still a better all-round officer than any number of others Marlowe could name offhand. He spoke to Blaney, then glanced away without allowing his distaste to show. Perhaps that was it. Blaney not only wore a straggly beard that never seemed to grow beyond a certain point but he was also an inveterate tobacco chewer—though this last was certainly no distinction in this army, rather the opposite. But it takes an expert to spit past a beard, especially in any kind of breeze, and Blaney had never bothered to become expert; it nearly always showed. (59)

Blaney was disappointed to be the one whose regiment would turn back early, and he said as much to Marlowe. "Is there some special reason for that?" Blaney demanded to know. "By God, I'd hate to have it suggested that the Second can't stand up alongside anybody—!" he protested (38). Marlowe mollifies him grudgingly, resisting the temptation to bait him verbally as he ponders other concerns. Blaney struck him "as being slightly ridiculous," like an overwrought "mother hen" (39). Marlowe changes his opinion just before the 2d Iowa goes east to return north. He and Blaney were reviewing last-minute details, with Marlowe still unsure of how he felt about Blaney or if the Iowan was up to the task. He commented that Blaney looked exhausted.

> Blaney shrugged indifferently. "Well, why not? This is no dress parade. I'm not an old man yet, Jack, but neither does the juice lubricate like it once did." He looked tired. Oh, not to the point of ex-

haustion, just tired, like a man who has already done a good day's work, looks forward to his rest, but accepts the forced overtime as a matter of course. He kicked an ember back into the fire impatiently, massaged his forehead with a palm. "I don't reckon you know it, Jack—no reason why you should, or give a damn about it if you do—but I've done almost my share of soldierin'. You don't know what I mean? Well, I was with Scott in the shindigs at Cerro Gordo, Molino del Rey, and Chapultepec in '47," he said calmly, impersonally, as though speaking of someone else. "Not that many another man in this army wasn't there too, including nobody less than Grant—also including those Rebel sonsabitches Floyd and Twiggs. Well, none of those shindigs stacked up to Shiloh but they had their points. It was June and July and August, mostly. I was a sergeant in the foot and I walked, not rode, hell's own blistering way from Vera Cruz to Mexico City. We lived, those of us that did, on bad beef, enchiladas, and worse water. Well, that was a long time ago, Jack. It's only after that it catches up with you. Hell, what I am talking about anyway?"

"I didn't know all that," Marlowe said. Suddenly his feeling about Blaney was entirely different from what it had ever been before, though he couldn't have said in exactly what way. (92–93)

Blaney turns out to have the right stuff after all. Though hounded by Barteau, he gets his men back to La Grange and in a fashion consistent with his somewhat plodding nature. More important, he serves as a commentator on the predicament that he, Marlowe, and all of the raiders shared. Marlowe was doing to him what high command had done to Marlowe. Thus the exchange that follows when Marlowe tells Blaney that he needs to destroy as much of the Mobile and Ohio Railroad as possible before angling toward La Grange.

"Is that all?" Blaney didn't try to conceal the sarcasm.

"It's a big order, maybe," Marlowe agreed, "but you can always try. Who knows? With luck you may walk through without a sign of trouble."

"Let us now render 'Praise God, from Whom All Blessings Flow.'"

"All right, damn it! As you said, this is no dress parade, but there's not a Rebel behind every bush either."

"I'll do what the orders say, Jack—within the limits of what *can* be done, but just don't take too much for granted." Blaney got stiffly to his feet. "I'm not strong on this hunch business but this is more than that. I got a feeling. Mostly I'm a practical man and take it as it comes. But this time I'm thinking luck's about run out for the Second."

"Nonsense!" Marlowe said, with a heartiness he couldn't feel. "You're overworking your imagination, Colonel."

"Am I?" Blaney smiled as though at some secret thought. "I'm the goat in this deal, Jack. Oh, it's like everything else in a God-damned war—it's nobody's fault. But it's true all the same. You turn a regiment loose inside enemy territory, a good ninety miles from base in all directions, and what do you expect to happen? No, don't tell me."

"You knew it was this way all the time." Marlowe, in spite of himself and for reasons he couldn't quite fathom, was somehow on the defensive, and he didn't like it.

"I told you I'm a little slow sometimes. Well, I'll say so long and good luck, Jack."

"It ought to be the other way around."

"I reckon we'd just better call this a Mexican standoff. I'll be seeing you—maybe."

Marlowe watched Blaney disappear in the darkness. Then he reached for a saddlebag and extracted a bottle—right now he felt he really needed a drink, perhaps deserved one. He had few il-lusions concerning what—probably—was in store for the Second Iowa. That was one of the prices command exacted. Still, there was such a thing as luck and it didn't necessarily have to be all bad. (95–96)

The oft-repeated maxim that it is lonely at the top, aptly shown in the scene between Marlowe and Blaney, appears even more forcefully in the relationship between Marlowe and Asa Bryce. The colonel and the cap-tain had become close, joined by mutual respect and genuine fondness, with Marlowe playing an avuncular role in the relationship. War had thrust them together, and they did not really know much about each other, though Marlowe did learn that Bryce was a professor of Greek and Roman history at a small college before he joined the cavalry. "The professor as a type was supposed to be impractical, visionary, unaffected by and unable to manage affairs outside his own world," or so said the received wisdom. "Not a particle of all this nonsense applied in Bryce's case" (77). He was as active as he was thoughtful, a naturally resourceful and decisive leader. Sent ahead with his company at the beginning of the march to scout the enemy, they surprised and disarmed a bunch of home guardsmen in northern Mississippi. Tying their captives to the base of a large tree, Bryce and his troopers sat down and enjoyed the barbecue that the Rebels had prepared for themselves. Only after leisurely eating the Rebels' dinner did they return and report to Marlowe.

Marlowe regarded Bryce "as unquestionably the ablest company commander in the First" (77). He wanted Bryce eventually to become a colonel and take command of the regiment, but every time he brought up the subject of advancement Bryce cut him off. The soldier-professor had no interest in promotion, much to his colonel's chagrin. Because Marlowe "was almost too much inclined to call on Bryce and A Company whenever an especially ticklish job turned up," when he decided that he needed a diversion toward Macon and the Mobile and Ohio Railroad he thought of Bryce and no one else. Nevertheless, Marlowe did not relish sending A Company out to face the enemy alone. "He was acutely aware of what he was asking—requiring—of Bryce and A Company. He was aware also— and that's where the fault lay—that Bryce would know. It was at once more than he, Marlowe, had a right (moral at least) to require and no less than he must in the circumstances. These things always got him back to the inherent paradoxes of this war business, one of which was that those who could least be spared must inevitably be most exposed to loss—those who in all logic could least be spared must be offered to preserve the less deserving" (120). Marlowe tries to say as little as possible, hoping that Bryce will volunteer to go and ease the awkwardness by not forcing him to issue an order. Bryce refuses to let him off that easy. He feigns detachment while wielding sarcasm as a sword. "All right, let's boil it down so we understand each other, Colonel," Bryce insists. "I strike the M. & O. As many times as I can—*if* I can. I rejoin the brigade when and *if* I can." Abashed, Marlowe offers Bryce an out by hinting that he could excuse himself for personal reasons and Marlowe would find someone else and some other company. "No, by God!" responds Bryce angrily. "I submit that you put this as an order, Colonel. You can countermand the order if you like but you have no right to put it up to me. I've never refused an order yet and I won't start here" (123–24). So Marlowe issues his order and A Company rides off, with Marlowe wondering if he has done the right thing and Bryce feeling as though he has been made a sacrificial lamb. It does not end there. Only after Bryce departs does Marlowe remember another order he has to give: "Starting tomorrow morning we burn or otherwise tear out every bridge, no matter how small." When Major Gray points out that Bryce will be behind them, he responds tersely, "Certainly—and he'll do like anybody else behind us, manage the best way he can" (126).

Bryce, of course, survives. In addition, with Gray's death at the Tickfaw the command position that he avoided is now his. "Thus it was that Bryce came to the Tickfaw bridge a company commander and crossed it as acting colonel of regiment" (314). Bryce never doubted that Marlowe valued him and did not want to lose him, even while he was on his way to Macon. He "did not question the necessity of the move, not in the circumstances. And if there was any fault it lay in the circumstances, not in the reasoning of Marlowe" (134). But Sinclair is not offering an "all's well that ends well" conclusion here. The rift between Marlowe and Bryce is narrowed but not wholly closed; the exigencies of war make a perfect reconciliation impossible. Not all casualties are left on the battlefield, not all wounds heal quickly if ever, Sinclair is telling the reader.

The escapades of A Company take up all or part of eight chapters, roughly a quarter of the book—paralleling the attention given to Henry Forbes and the real men of B Company in *Grierson's Raid*. Sinclair's A Company rides the same route and on the same time line. Some of what Sinclair includes is simply reworked from actual events; some leaped from his imagination. He turns the moment Stephen Forbes alluded to in his reminiscences when the men of B Company voted to stay together into a very dramatic scene, touching the same emotions in readers who were raised on the heroes of the Alamo and William Travis's line in the sand (237–41). He includes the bluff at Enterprise with almost nothing changed but the names—a real occurrence brought to the aid of the fictive past (232–36). That incident is followed by a chapter-long invented scene, "The Soldier and the Lady," in which Bryce finds himself in an almost surreal situation. He stops A Company at a plantation for food and forage. The mistress of the house is a widow, her husband a Confederate general slain at Shiloh. Grief-stricken, she has lost her mind. When Bryce tries to explain that he is from Illinois and only wants supplies, she twitters, "I had not heard that Illinois had come into our glorious Confederacy, but I have always felt it was merely a matter of time" (247). Saddened, disconcerted by her dementia, Bryce excuses himself as quickly as he can, leaving behind yet another casualty produced by war.

Sinclair did not spend all of his time with the officer corps. Andy Bullen, his answer to Richard Surby, was an enlisted man, but then Bullen and the other scouts—never referred to as Butternut Guerillas—do not figure prominently in Sinclair's tale. Rather, Sinclair invented his own characters and introduced two of them in his second chapter. In an earlier draft he titled this chapter "The Boys from Illinois." He changed it to "The Horse Soldiers," repeating the book's title to emphasize that the heart of his story was in some sense here, among the youngest and least educated, those who took orders instead of those who gave them. The reader meets Sgt. Nate Brown and Pvt. Ed Stumm of A Company. Brown is a veteran, Stumm a new recruit, "a farm boy" who had joined "shortly after that hell on earth at Shiloh" (16). Each has a particular role to play. The veteran would live; the recruit would die.

It was Stumm's fate to be the boy prematurely forced to be a man when he answered duty's call. "With innocent and grave composure he told Captain Bryce that he had come to take the place of his brother Harry," slain at Shiloh. "Nobody doubted his good intentions for a moment—these solemn recruits were often that way in the beginning" (16). Stumm falls victim to "The Sniper" of another chapter's title as A Company tries to find the column. No one ever spots the sniper, despite efforts to flush him. He shadows the Yankees as they ride along, firing unseen through the foliage and rain. The third shot hits Stumm; Brown catches him as he slips out of his saddle. There is nothing to do for the mortally wounded, uncomprehending young trooper as the men of the company gather round. "Perhaps more than anyone else" Bryce "knew how tough Nate Brown had stood like a hard but gentle older brother to Stumm—bawling him out, ragging him, prodding him, and always with an invisible hand under his elbow." Brown finds "a spot a little way back from the road, a low knoll partly surrounded by white dogwood," where Stumm is laid to rest in a grave dug by his tiny knot of friends (227). Bryce tries to find the right words, but they elude him, just as the sniper eludes them all. He escapes; they ride on.

If Stumm is an illustration of the good dying too young and the senseless waste that comes with war, Tom Murphy becomes the caveat about hubris, the man trapped by overconfidence when he should have known better. Murphy dies—in spectacular fashion—outside Newton Station in a chapter called, ironically, "The Hero." One of the locomotives captured in Newton carried powder charges and artillery shells. Marlowe wanted the train destroyed but not in Newton because the resulting explosion would take the town with it. Murphy, a trooper in E Company of

the 2d Illinois, had worked in the rail yards back home in Bloomington—
Sinclair's tongue-in-cheek local allusion—and volunteered to take the train
to the outskirts and destroy it there. Then Murphy had what he thought
was a brilliant idea. He would detach the two cars loaded with munitions
on a trestle, run the locomotive down the track, throw it into reverse with
the throttle wide open, then jump clear at a safe distance. The force of the
explosion would, he was confident, obliterate the locomotive, the munitions, the freight cars, the trestle, and everything else within a few hundred yards. "Private Murphy toured slowly down the track, deliberately
taking his time. He intended to make the most of this. Nothing approaching this in importance had fallen to his lot during the two practically
anonymous years in E Company. This wouldn't make him a national hero
but in the Second he would certainly be pointed out as the man who
singlehandedly had staged the biggest train bust-up in the whole state of
Mississippi" (181).

Murphy drove the locomotive a thousand feet away from the trestle,
did as he had planned, and then disaster struck. He had braced himself for
the locomotive to jerk into sudden motion "but in the wrong direction,
as though the engine would move forward." He was thrown to the floor
of the cab, hitting his head and burning his hands on the firebox. Stunned,
he struggled to rise, tripped over the coal shovel, and fell yet again, knowing in the last few seconds that "this was the end of the line." Fellow raiders waiting for Murphy to jump free felt the blast as "part of Hell rose up
and out from its supposed abode in the nether regions and the sound, so
near, was so vast that none . . . could afterward swear they actually *heard*
it—compression or no compression, the car of powder charges went up
instantaneously with the rest." They "were literally lifted from the earth
and then slammed back, like pins struck by the ball in bowling" (183). And
Private Murphy? He was blown to pieces and never seen again.

One other enlisted man played a leading role in Sinclair's drama.
He enters in the sixth chapter, his own, as "Private Schwartz," and exits
nineteen chapters later in "Private Schwartz's War." The earnest young
trooper, no more than seventeen or eighteen years old, had been Marlowe's neighbor. He was a most unlikely cavalryman—"from boots to hat
his uniform fitted him about like a saddle on a hog" (48). Determined to
prove himself, he had joined the 1st Illinois a few months before. A bout
with malaria would have excused him from the raid, but he wanted none
of that. "This is my first chance to be in anything important," he pled to
Marlowe, and "I don't want to miss it if there's any chance, sir" (49).

Against his better judgment, Marlowe acquiesced, warning Schwartz that
if he got sick he would have to fend for himself. As Marlowe could have
guessed, that only strengthened Schwartz's resolve.

Schwartz does not get sick; he is shot and killed in a case of mistaken
identity. He had volunteered to ride with Andy Bullen as a scout after
the column left Newton Station because he still had not seen any action and wanted "some real soldiering" (214). The scouts, dressed as civilians, stumble onto three Rebel deserters scrounging for food at a small
farm. Thinking the Yankees are local deputies sent out to arrest them, the
deserters start shooting. In the brief firefight that follows two of the deserters are killed and the third is captured, albeit too late for Bernhard
Schwartz. Bullen had yelled for him to find cover.

> But Private Schwartz was caught in a sudden fog of indecision and
> inexperience. At that first rifle shot he had reached for his carbine,
> but when Andy yelled "Get down!" he had stayed his hand and
> instead started to dismount. In fact, he had risen in the saddle, his
> weight on his left leg in the stirrup, when the second shot exploded.
> Balanced in midair, his right leg just coming across the animal's
> hindquarters, a perfect target, the bullet literally knocked him clear
> of the saddle. There was no pain, just a thudding shock, as though
> someone had struck him in the chest with a vigorous but friendly
> fist. He slammed to the ground on his left side, but, strangely, he
> didn't much feel that either. Then he rolled over on his back and
> wondered, but only for a second out of eternity, why the blue spring
> sky had suddenly turned black. (215–16)

Schwartz, then, serves as another example of the senseless waste, the
tragic loss that can accompany war. But Sinclair had something more in
mind. Schwartz was on the raid against doctor's orders. Marlowe had over-
ridden those orders, which brought him into conflict with Major Keller,
1st Illinois regimental surgeon. The relationship between Keller and Marlowe is one of the more interesting in the book, perhaps second in importance only to that of Marlowe and Bryce.

Keller appears intermittently. Sinclair saves him for those moments
when he has a particular point to make. A hint of what will come is offered
at the brigade staff meeting called by Marlowe before the raiders leave
La Grange. Keller is obliged to attend but only in his capacity as a doctor.
Marlowe did not consider him or Dr. Wells, the 2d Illinois surgeon, real

military officers. Like others of their profession, they tended to be in the army "but not too much of it." For Marlowe that was troubling enough. But there was more involved. As Marlowe saw it, "these regimental doctor-surgeons as a group—of course there were exceptions—were inclined to be aloof, cynical, and ungodly, something of a law unto themselves, and they were apt to have little regard for rank as such" (40). On a deeper level, Marlowe resented the presumption that they had unlocked the "supposed mysteries" of life. He did not believe it. His wife's doctors had not been able to save her, despite their assurances. He was not convinced they had truly known what was wrong, so he was inclined to think of them as "skilled mechanics" at best, with no special insight into the human condition. "There wasn't much to be done about Keller—not that he wanted to do anything—and he seemed to be as competent as most of these butchers" (41).

His suspicions about doctors notwithstanding, Marlowe was curious about Keller. Doctors could resign any time they chose. When Marlowe asked Keller why he stayed, he replied, laconically, that "medicine is wherever you find it" (43). But then Keller had his own misgivings about Marlowe. "He had never liked Marlowe particularly—he didn't now; yet neither did he actively dislike him." Marlowe was forthright and fair, insofar "as he saw fairness. Perhaps it was Marlowe's apparently God-almighty cocksuredness that irked him as much as anything" (45).

Marlowe's reinstating Private Schwartz to active duty over Keller's findings—which he had agreed to respect—did not help matters. Still, Keller and Marlowe managed to keep out of each other's way for the first few days of the raid and at one point even engaged in friendly conversation. Marlowe initiated it as a conciliatory gesture. Keller surprised him by putting aside his usual "aloofness." But any personal barriers that had begun to break down rose even higher at Newton Station. The raiders took casualties there, and Marlowe went to check on them. He saw over a dozen laid out in the grass, being tended to by Keller's medical orderly. Keller himself is nowhere in sight. "Where the devil is Major Keller?" the colonel demands. Keller had gone off to assist a woman giving birth, he is told. A fuming Marlowe strode into the house where Keller was at work.

The surgeon straightened up, turned, and faced the colonel. He was in his shirt, his sleeves rolled far up, and his bare arms were bloody to above the elbows. He looked at and apparently through

Marlowe and said abstractedly, "Well, what is it, Colonel?" His manner was that of a man whose mind was concentrated on something else entirely.

"What in God's name do you think you're doing, Keller?"

"Doing? It's obvious, I think. This woman will die if she doesn't get proper attention—maybe even then. You see, the cord—"

"*She'll die!*" Marlowe felt as though about to explode. "What the hell do you think is happening to those men out there in the yard?"

"One man can't do anything. Her need was first."

"It's no business of yours, Keller! Right now it's not your business if ten thousand Rebel brats are born or die!"

"I don't think you mean that, Colonel," Keller said calmly. "It's beside the point in any case. This is simply a matter of a human life. Perhaps two."

"And those ten, fifteen men out there are not?" Fury was building up inside Marlowe all over again.

"Wells will manage to handle it."

"Wells! He's probably got his own hands full, clear over on the other side of town. Hell, I don't even know where he is—it's not my especial business to know. God damn it, Keller! *You're* the surgeon of the First! And moreover you're an officer under oath, in case you'd forgotten."

Keller shrugged. "Possibly a question of which oath, Colonel, a matter of difference in words. In any case, I don't need a brigadier to point out my duty for me—" (173)

Marlowe has had enough. He pulls his pistol on Keller, tells him he is under arrest, and orders him out of the house and back to his official duties. "I think you'll have this on your conscience, Marlowe—if you have one—for a long time," Keller says in parting. "I have arithmetic on my side," counters Marlowe, who is adamant that Keller's first responsibility is to the men of his regiment, not the people of the town (174). This defense—putting the men of the regiment first—will come back to haunt him when Private Schwartz is killed. Keller and Marlowe speak for the first time since Keller had been put under arrest at Newton Station.

"I suppose you recognized the boy?"

"Certainly—why not, Colonel?"

"Of course, I suppose you're thinking—I would in your shoes—that if I hadn't reversed your judgment in La Grange the boy would still be alive?"

Keller shrugged, his face still expressionless. "It had occurred to me, Colonel—but only along with other things. That sort of speculation is futile. You could just as well say that except for certain events at Fort Sumter none of us would be here."

"You might be thinking," Marlowe said as though to himself, "that because I have a certain feeling of responsibility I'm giving the boy as decent a burial as may be, but you're wrong. This is a good excuse to give the men a short rest they wouldn't get otherwise."

"You know your own mind, sir."

Marlowe looked at the sky, the horses and men in the road, and back to the surgeon. His shoulders slumped a little as he said, in an altogether different tone, the bite suddenly gone, "I didn't make this God-damned war, Keller."

The surgeon shook his head slightly. "No, Colonel, I know you didn't," he said softly. "But remember, I didn't either." (220–21)

Keller then disappears from the narrative until the fighting at Wall's Bridge. There he treats the wounded caringly, and Marlowe, finally relenting, drops his arrest order. Marlowe asks Keller what could be done about the most seriously wounded.

"Well, do you have any suggestions?"

"Yes, Colonel. They'll have to have professional care in order to make it at all. With your permission I'll stay and give it to them."

"If you do this," Marlowe said slowly, "you know it's a hundred to one you'll end up in a prison camp."

"I suppose so, but that would be a secondary consideration, Colonel. I think I told you once that medicine is where you find it. Let's leave it at that." (316)

Marlowe promises to send back help once the column reaches Baton Rouge "if it's humanly possible." Keller "smiles faintly" and warns Marlowe not to make any promises he can't keep. Marlowe reminds him, "I said *if*. That's the best anybody could do." To Keller's "I guess we understand each other," Marlowe says, contemplatively, "I wonder" (318). Marlowe offers his hand; Keller shakes it. The man of war rejoins his troops and the man of medicine goes to his patients. They are both honorable soldiers doing their duty, though their allegiances could come into conflict. They had to accept what they could not change and learn to respect what the other felt obliged to do—not exactly a parting of newfound friends but infinitely more satisfying. And thus Sinclair closes an invented relationship that built on the thin foundation laid by Dr. Erastus Yule, real surgeon to the 2d Iowa, who volunteered to remain behind with those wounded at the Tickfaw.[19]

The happy ending that comes soon after is adapted from real events. The Rebels cannot catch the raiders. Bad luck and poor judgment dog them to the last. Marlowe keeps his men moving across the Amite and to the edge of Baton Rouge. In one of many comic scenes inserted in the narrative, a spit-and-polish Union lieutenant stops a bedraggled, exhausted Asa Bryce at the head of the column. The lieutentant's insistence on protocol and inability to grasp what he beheld were his problem, not Bryce's. "Let me give you some friendly advice, Lieutenant. This Colonel Marlowe is a salty sonofabitch," Bryce warns. "He's brought this brigade about six hundred miles without being stopped by all the Rebels in Mississippi. He'll likely take a very dim view of being stopped here by a few feet of headquarters red tape" (329). The troopers ride on, the impromptu parade forms, and Marlowe stands off to the side while his men pass in review.

> As he watched the First go by, file after file of sabers flashing in the hot sunlight, he suddenly remembered that last dew-fresh morning at La Grange, so far away and long ago, felt the same lift of the heart which had nothing to do with the larger issues of the war—and a very great but quite unselfish pride which few men are privileged to know more than once and most men not all.
>
> Far down the tree-bordered street the drums crashed and the band shifted into the warm, lilting melody of "Listen to the Mockingbird." The colonel's throat hurt a little and again he was having trouble seeing clearly. Dust and lack of sleep, he thought. (332)

The end? Almost. Sinclair added a brief epilogue, with a letter from Asa Bryce to his father as the centerpiece. Bryce tells of the "difficult, in a way very foolish operation" carried off successfully because of the "fantastic amount of luck involved." Marlowe, we learn, is finally getting his promotion to brigadier general. Bryce himself is made a lieutenant colonel. Sgt. Nate Brown, farrier to A Company and devoted aide to his former

captain, makes jokes to keep the new regimental commander humble. As
they laugh together, they hear the "faraway notes of Tattoo" signaling
lights out. "Now, as soldiers will, they waited and listened, each lost for
the moment in his own thoughts, until the last long trumpet note died
away" (336). And *there* the story ends.

The Horse Soldiers* worked. Critics liked it; general readers did too.
Earl Schenck Miers, a popular history writer, called it "splendid." True,
it was no *Andersonville,* he added, but then too few books were. Sinclair
had told a good story well without "abusing the historical essentials," all
the while "infusing them with an imaginative depth denied the literary
historian."[20] Sinclair must have been pleased with Miers's assessment.
Dee Brown's foreword had encouraged him to believe that *The Horse Soldiers* would be respected as history as well as enjoyed as fiction. Miers accepted it as both, and so did others. One went so far as to call it a "richly
successful fictional re-enactment" without seeing the pairing of fictional
with reenactment as an oxymoron.[21] Yet another recommended it as "col-
lateral reading for college history courses."[22] Perhaps most gratifying to
Sinclair was Miers's opinion that his book "deserves a place in the first
rank of recent American historical fiction."[23] With these words and those
of other friendly reviewers Sinclair at long last gained the recognition
denied him in years past.

The Horse Soldiers made best-seller lists, putting Sinclair there for
the first and only time in his career. If early success with the *American
Years* had in some sense hurt him later, this newest success had a similar
effect. He made some money, but he did not become rich overnight from
book sales; critics took him seriously, but that only raised expectations for
his next book. Wisely or not, he attempted a sequel that employed similar
plot devices. It was based on another actual event, Gen. Alfred Sully's
1864 campaign against the Sioux in Dakota Territory. This tale also featured a long ride in which cavalrymen press deep into enemy territory
rather than retracing their tracks. After fighting the Sioux at Killdeer
Mountain, they traverse the Badlands to rendezvous with steamboats that
will take them down the Yellowstone River and out to the Missouri. John
Francis Marlowe, now a brigadier general, is once again at the heart of
the tale. Sent off to Indian country on detached duty, he commands the
expedition. Asa Bryce goes with him. *The Cavalryman* has plenty of action and various twists—"Galvanized Yankees" whose loyalty is suspect,
a wagon train of civilians adding to Marlowe's difficulties, and even a love
interest for Marlowe in the form of Ruth Hayes. But the romance does

hist.
novel
strength

not fully bloom; she goes west, he returns to the war in the East. The larger story does not fare much better. Critics were lukewarm; so were sales. It would be Sinclair's last book.[24]

Harold Sinclair died in 1966, never regaining consciousness from an operation to remove a cancerous lung. Weakened by "chronic alcoholism," he ended life, as his son Ward recollected, "dispirited and disillusioned."[25] Stories that he had begun before and returned to after *The Cavalryman* remain unpublished, most of them unfinished. He did write a history of the Illinois home front during the Civil War, but the state centennial commission that had contracted for it turned the text down as unacceptable.[26] At one point, Sinclair became so despondent that he piled manuscripts in his backyard and set them afire. His wife managed to save some but not all. Sadly, a taste of success had not been enough to assuage her husband's bitterness.

Ultimately, Harold Sinclair became famous for a time because he wrote a book that became the basis for a movie. He made more money selling the rights to his book and acting as a consultant to the film than he did from the book itself, and the character that he created for his novel began a whole new life on the silver screen. Sinclair had transformed Benjamin Henry Grierson into John Francis Marlowe. In Hollywood Marlowe would in his turn be transformed, the hero as celebrity, the celebrity as hero.[27]

THE STORY AS FILM

It has been a struggle, but a happy one. We, as screen writers and producers, feel that we have reproduced with realism and feeling one of the little known but gallant moments of the war between the Blue and the Gray. We hope it will be a proud calling card from Hollywood for the world of five hundred million movie fans to see and will augment the renewed interest in the Civil War as we head for the centennial celebration.

We are proud to have produced it, and we hope that the readers of *Civil War History,* as experts, will agree that Hollywood has not violated the memory nor the spirit of the men, who, as General William T. Sherman said, performed "the most brilliant expedition of the Civil War."

—John Lee Mahin and Martin Rackin,
on *The Horse Soldiers*

In 1959 Clyde C. Walton, Illinois state historian and founding editor of the scholarly journal *Civil War History,* did something no editor of that journal has done since. He opened his pages to Hollywood film-makers, inviting John Lee Mahin and Martin Rackin to explain why they were producing *The Horse Soldiers*. In a brief introduction to readers, many of whom were academicians, Walton noted that the soon-to-be-released film was taken from Harold Sinclair's popular novel of the same title. "The following article is a departure from our traditional subject matter," Walton conceded, but he believed that "all Civil War students will be intrigued by the problems involved in telling the story of Grierson's Raid through the medium of the motion picture film."[1]

Mahin and Rackin had met at Warner Brothers, where both worked as studio writers. Mahin was the better known of the two. After he left Harvard he worked as a newspaper reporter and then for a New York advertising agency. Eventually he ended up writing scripts in Hollywood.

He plied his trade at most of the major studios, becoming one of the lead writers at MGM before moving on. With nearly three decades of film experience behind him, he had gained a reputation for being versatile and imaginative, able to write witty repartee for comedy and pithy dialogue for action films. His favorite script was done at Twentieth Century Fox for *Heaven Knows, Mr. Allison,* an engrossing tale of a U.S. Marine and an Irish nun thrown together for survival on a Japanese-held Pacific island during World War II. The film, starring Robert Mitchum and Deborah Kerr, did well at the box office and garnered Mahin his second Oscar nomination. The next year he and Rackin decided to strike out on their own. "Our venture into our first independent motion picture was decided upon when we read Harold Sinclair's novel *The Horse Soldiers,*" they told the readers of *Civil War History.* "To us as writers, it had all the dash and boldness of a commando raid"; moreover, "it had the necessary elements for color and large screen," and "it had reality, which to us is the prime requisite of a great motion picture." They secured the rights to the book from Fox, which had bought the option but not acted on it. They then plunged into their own research, which included reading Dee Brown's *Grierson's Raid,* and they began fleshing out a script in the spring of 1958. Mahin wrote most of the dialogue. He and Rackin were confident that they could use their "motion picture license" to heighten the sense of drama and recreate "the historical raid that made it possible for General Grant to take Vicksburg."[2] Their claim that they were recreating as much as they were creating gave them something in common with Sinclair.

Mahin and Rackin wanted "to spare no expense" in making their film "authentic."[3] They intended to shoot on location with as much realism as possible. They did not, however, have the money to do anything on their own. For financial backing they turned to the Mirisch brothers, who in turn had an arrangement with United Artists. The Mirisches had been putting together film deals for the better part of a decade. United Artists had been around for forty years, founded by D. W. Griffith, Charlie Chaplin, and a few other Hollywood dissidents to sidestep the studio system and stimulate independent filmmakers. *The Horse Soldiers* became part of a twenty-film package deal between the Mirisches and United Artists and would be one of five films released under that agreement in 1959.[4] Generally speaking, the Mirisches saw to actual production; United Artists handled promotion and distribution.

The Mirisches kept their distance, though they offered suggestions. They left the details to Mahin and Rackin and to the one man they were

Director John Ford.
Courtesy of the Lilly
Library, Indiana University,
Bloomington.

confident could actually make the movie the way it needed to be done, legendary director and six-time Oscar winner John Ford. Mahin knew that Ford had a reputation as a "Civil War buff." They had worked together on *Mogambo* with Clark Gable and Ava Gardner six years before. When Mahin and Rackin pitched their idea to Ford, "he fell for it like a ton of bricks."[5] Though Ford had never directed a Civil War film, the war had served as a backdrop, even as a subtext, for his so-called cavalry trilogy, beginning with *Fort Apache* in 1948 and followed in successive years by *She Wore a Yellow Ribbon* and *Rio Grande*. The Civil War also figured in the plot of *The Searchers*, a 1956 film which some consider Ford's finest. Ethan Edwards, as played by John Wayne, is the film's lead character, an unrepentant, embittered Confederate, a social outcast who was a "Rebel" in more than just the obvious sense.

Ford preferred to work from short stories rather than books. His cavalry trilogy, for example, had been adapted from pieces that James Warner Bellah wrote originally for the *Saturday Evening Post*. "I don't like to do books or plays," Ford reportedly said; "I prefer to take a short story and expand it, rather than take a novel and try to condense."[6] Everyone involved understood that if Ford became the director, *The Horse Soldiers* would become his film—in the creative rather than the legal sense. His contract with the Mirisches gave him a salary and a precentage of the gross in exchange for surrendering his rights to the film.[7] His ownership would be more subtle, less formal. He left his mark on everything from the script to the cast selection to the choice of camera angles. "It is certainly a John Ford film," as Dan Ford, the director's grandson put it, in effect giving the film a stamp of authenticity.[8]

Ford was as feared as he was respected, a master of intimidation who brooked no interference. He did not suffer fools gladly, nor would he let any producer's ambition or actor's ego stand in his way. As Harry Carey Jr., a member of Ford's little stock company of players, reminisced, there "was no chain of command with John Ford. There was him, and there was us." As irascible as he was ingenious, Ford inspired ambivalent feelings even among those who knew him best—if indeed anyone in the film industry could be said to have known him well. "He was my nemesis and my hero," all at once, wrote Carey.[9] No doubt others felt the same. John Wayne, who spent much of his career in front of Ford's camera and who suffered the sting of Ford's quick temper and acerbic wit as often as anyone, still stood in awe of the man. Ford, he recalled, read voraciously and "absorbed everything."[10] He was, Wayne concluded, a magnificent artist, who could have been good at anything—*except* public relations.

Ford disliked giving interviews and bristled at the pretensions of critics who thought that they could explain the meaning of his films to others. The deeper they attempted to dig, the more impenetrable he might become. If they tried to take him where he did not want to go, he would deliberately mislead them or cut them off dismissively. Looking for consistency in what he said about himself, his films, and the people he worked with is therefore an exercise in futility. As he put it bluntly to one who probed, "The truth about my life is nobody's damn business but my own."[11] Disinclined to share his deeper feelings, he rarely waxed philosophical on filmmaking. He did, however, tell one interviewer a few years before he shot *The Horse Soldiers* that "it is wrong to liken a director to an author. He is more like an architect, if he is creative. An architect conceives his plans from given premises—the purpose of the building, its size, the terrain. If he is clever, he can do something creative within those limitations."[12] Ford the architect would step in at any point in the production to impose his will, his vision of the grand design. Those who worked with him knew that, writers included. Frank Nugent, a New York film critic who also collaborated with Ford on various scripts, commented that "once the script is finished, the writer had better keep out of his way. The finished picture is always Ford's, never the writer's."[13]

Ford liked to work fast. Filming *The Horse Soldiers* took just over two months, starting at the end of October 1958. It was not done in sequence. On-site work came first, virtually all of it outside Natchitoches, Louisiana, with a brief side trip to Natchez, Mississippi. Ford had no interest in trying to retrace the raiders' route. Rather, he wanted to capture a general Southern flavor and develop what he deemed the proper mood. Oakland, a plantation near Natchitoches owned by the Prudhomme family, served as his primary outdoor set. Production people brought in ties and tracks from Texas to create the illusion of a railroad, with accompanying telegraph poles and lines, and they built a bridge over the Cane River where the film version of the fight at the Tickfaw would be staged. Hills, fields, forests, and a swamp needed for various scenes were close by. Locals who could double as Yankee raiders and pursuing Rebels were hired as extras. Ford and Mahin arrived by train over a week before the shooting started. Rackin flew in, as did those playing the leads. A caravan of twenty trucks hauled equipment all the way from Hollywood. Interior shots were done later at the Samuel Goldwyn studios, and the raid on Newton Station was staged on an MGM back lot. The first scene in the film after the opening—a meeting involving Ulysses Grant and John Marlowe—was not done until New Year's Eve, and apparently work on other scenes continued into the middle of January.[14]

The producers spent some $5 million, the bulk of it to cover the cost of a large cast and crew, horses, construction, and transportation. That was considered a sizable amount in 1959, "a new chapter to the already startling saga of Hollywood production economics."[15] Nearly a third of the total went to pay the salaries of John Wayne and William Holden. Wayne had been cast as Col. John Marlowe, Holden as Major Keller— renamed Curtis by Mahin, altered again to Hank Kendall by Ford. At $750,000 each and a percentage of the profits, Wayne and Holden were expensive, but they were the top box office draws at that time. They had never worked together before. Mahin and Rackin, backed by the Mirisches, were taking a calculated risk. They thought the story appealing in its own right, but they needed a veritable blockbuster to recoup their investment, and big stars were indispensable in courting the public, a variation on the old adage about needing to spend money to make money.

Never mind that Ford's movie was about victorious Yankees; the locals were star-struck. They had anticipated the film crew's arrival ever since

Ford and his son Pat scouted locations. "They say this is Ford's labor of love and so it's bound to be big," reported the *Shreveport Times* in a special section titled "The Movie Makers at Natchitoches." Saying, good-naturedly, that "a sudden appearance of Sherman himself" could not have caused more of a stir, the people of the area were "proud to be host to a big movie."[16] Alexandria joined Shreveport and Natchitoches in putting out the welcome mat. So did Natchez when the film company moved there.[17]

The moviemakers boasted that they used very little of Sinclair's book for the script.[18] Their claim is true only in the narrowest sense. Perhaps they seldom borrowed Sinclair's words, but the story they chose to tell is easily recognizable as his. After all, they could not venture too far without straying away from the historical truths that they professed to be telling. The outlines of Grierson's raid are visible underneath all of the changes made by Hollywood, just as they had been with Sinclair. United Artists promoted the film as fictionalized history, "a robust story of a daring raid that turned the tide for the Union in the Civil War."[19] The filmmakers kept Marlowe's personality essentially as Sinclair had written it—tough but fair, making difficult decisions as best he could. They also left Marlowe a widower suspicious of doctors. Instead of being a successful grain merchant, however, he is converted into a railroad worker, a self-made man who rose from section hand to engineer through hard work and native genius, not formal schooling. Thus they could make the hero even more heroic—a true American everyman—and they could underscore the tragic side of the conflict, as the builder who in peacetime constructs railroads is sent on a wartime mission to destroy them. Furthermore, they added new situations and new characters, including a romantic interest for Marlowe and, in what has turned out to be the most memorable scene, an attack on Marlowe's encamped raiders by boys from a military school.

Not surprisingly, they increased the intensity of the action, with two major battles rather than the skirmishing leading to one decisive confrontation of the smaller budget *Fort Apache* and *Rio Grande*. The first pitched battle is at Newton Station midway through the film, where rail-borne Confederates summoned by telegraph are mown down as they charge up the main street of town. The second comes at the very end. Sinclair's little fight at the Tickfaw, which had been fairly close to the real event, is escalated into a do-or-die engagement. Ford used the creek-sized Cane River as a smallish Amite rather than the Tickfaw and had some of the raiders thunder across the bridge while others outflanked the Rebels, seized their

Marlowe's raiders, from the film's opening sequence.
Museum of Modern Art Collections. Courtesy of MGM/UA.

artillery, and drove them from the field. The route to Baton Rouge now open, the Yankees ride on, blowing up the bridge in their rear to slow the enemy's pursuit.

The Horse Soldiers opens rousingly. Music arranged by the accomplished Hollywood composer David Buttolph provides background to cinematographer William Clothier's sweeping camera vistas. Troopers silhouetted against the sky ride in single file along a rail line, moving past telegraph poles on an earth embankment. Ford had employed variations on this image before—gallant soldiers headed for war—but perhaps never to greater effect than now. Stan Jones wrote the title song, "I Left My Love." Buttolph gave it a contrapuntally jaunty and martial feel, pulsating brass and cadenced strings mixed with strummed banjos, members of a male chorus singing that they would "ride clean down to hell and back for Ulysses Simpson Grant," some of the troopers on the screen seemingly swaying in time to the music. Jones's tune would be repeated when the raiders departed La Grange with the same devil-take-the-hindmost gusto.

It is reprised later by a dying trooper more ironically, as the mission becomes increasingly dangerous, the men exhausted, the outcome uncertain.

Jones's involvement was typical of Ford's approach to moviemaking. Once a ranger in Death Valley, Jones had met Ford when the director was on location there for another film in the late 1940s. Jones wrote songs and sang some of them for Ford. Intrigued, Ford filed the ranger in his vast mental library. When Ford went to Moab, Utah, to film *Wagonmaster* and *Rio Grande,* he remembered Jones, whose "Ghost Riders in the Sky" had recently become a hit. He invited Jones to compose tunes for both films and even put him in front of the camera in *Rio Grande* to sing along with members of the Sons of the Pioneers who serenaded Maureen O'Hara, playing opposite John Wayne. Ford turned to Jones again for *The Searchers.* Jones wrote a title song and had a hand in other pieces as well, his original music being combined with actual period ballads to have the hoped-for emotional impact.[20]

In fact, there was often musical overlap in Ford films. A background orchestration heard in the opening of *The Searchers* includes, hauntingly, a few bars each from "Lorena" and "The Bonnie Blue Flag," tunes from the era depicted in the film. Passages from "Lorena" would be heard again and again in *The Horse Soldiers,* and a full version was recorded as the flipside to the single of Jones's "I Left My Love," released by United Artists, which also did a soundtrack album. (Incidentally, Harold Sinclair had written "Lorena" into his *Horse Soldiers* too.) "The Bonnie Blue Flag," a celebration of the Confederacy, though only hinted at in *The Searchers,* is used repeatedly in *The Horse Soldiers.* Ford intended to squeeze in "The Girl I Left Behind Me," a signature piece in *Fort Apache* and as much a staple in cavalry films as it had been for the real cavalry. It was recorded on the soundtrack even though the scene it must have been intended for is not in the film. The album, like the movie, was marketed as being educational as well as entertaining. The music on it, asserted promotional copy written for the back cover, carried "the stamp of absolute authenticity," making the album, like the film itself, a part of "living history."[21]

Ever ready to cast his favorites, Ford slipped Stan Jones into *The Horse Soldiers,* the musician once again converted into an actor. He appears as Ulysses S. Grant in the all-important first scene. For this opening Ford shifted from Memphis, where Sinclair began his book, to a riverboat anchored on the Mississippi and within sight of Vicksburg. It is a rainy night; big guns boom in the distance. Instead of Hurlbut passing orders to Marlowe, Hurlbut and Marlowe are waiting on Grant. Sherman is present,

Sooy Smith is not; he is not in the film at all. As Mahin wrote it and Ford shot it, Marlowe had never met Grant or Sherman before. Grant is seated, dimly lit behind a desk, with a map of Mississippi off to his side on the wall. The idea for the mission was his. The responsibility for working out the details would be Marlowe's.

> GRANT: Colonel, for your benefit, the war on our side hasn't been goin' well at all.
> SHERMAN: Not in Washington, not in the newspapers, not in the field.
> GRANT: To put it mildly, with less men and less resources, the South has whipped us to a standstill. Now if I could take Vicksburg [he lights his cigar from a lamp as he speaks], the whole picture would change. But I have to do it this summer [thumping the desk with his fist for emphasis].
> SHERMAN: Or sit out here another year, which might cost us a hundred thousand men, might cost us the war.
> GRANT: Which brings all this talk down to their main source of supply, and a thorn in our side, Newton Station.[22]

The strategic imperative of taking Vicksburg established, the importance of Newton Station to Grant's plans identified, the details are hammered out quickly. Marlowe is to take a "short brigade" consisting of his own 1st Illinois, Secord's 1st Michigan—changed from the 2d Illinois in Sinclair's book—and Blaney's 2d Iowa. He is to avoid fighting if possible until he reaches Newton Station. Once there he is to demolish rails, ties, rolling stock, locomotives, and whatever contraband he can lay his hands on. Marlowe wants to destroy "at least enough to keep 'em busy for a couple of months rebuilding, otherwise the raid would just be another horse ride." As the four men savor cigars and whiskey, the danger of what lies ahead for Marlowe and his raiders is emphasized.

> HURLBUT [to Grant]: Sam, even if he should manage to get through to Newton Station he'd be three hundred miles dead center in the Confederacy.
> GRANT [to Marlowe]: Have you thought how you'd get back?
> MARLOWE [wryly]: Have you, sir?
> GRANT: Well, I guess I asked for that. But then I hate to think of you sittin' it out in Andersonville prison. It's a hellhole.

MARLOWE: I'd think about that twice too, sir.
GRANT: Well Colonel, your success [the four share a toast]. (5m)

This scene takes fewer than three minutes. It is indicative of the film-maker's need to simplify where possible for the viewer, keeping the dialogue spartan and using historical figures—Grant and Sherman—whose names should have been recognizable to most filmgoers. Later in the picture Nathan Bedford Forrest replaces Wirt Adams and the other Confederate pursuers for the same reason, the famous man a composite for the more obscure. A Mathew Brady group picture scene of Marlowe and his officers at La Grange serves a similar purpose (9m). Brady was nowhere near southwestern Tennessee in April 1863, but then his is the one name the audience could be expected to link with Civil War photography. The reference to Andersonville, which recurs through the film, is a testament, perhaps, to the popularity of MacKinlay Kantor's critically acclaimed book published just a few years before. That the riverboat meeting never took place and that Andersonville prison did not yet exist were secondary, even incidental issues to Mahin and Ford. Grant had ordered the mission, his concerns were essentially as shown, the real Grierson confronted the same difficulties now facing the fictional Marlowe, and, even if Andersonville did not exist, other prison camps did and the plight of prisoners there was all too real. Interestingly enough, Sinclair had alluded to Andersonville in his original manuscript, an anachronism not caught until MacKinlay Kantor spotted it. Sinclair and his publisher were lucky; it was deleted from the galley proof, with readers none the wiser.[23]

Mahin and Ford kept place names to a minimum. La Grange is the starting point, Newton Station the target, Baton Rouge the destination. Other towns along the route go unnamed, as do rivers, except for a brief allusion to the Amite. Capt. Asa Bryce did not make it into the script, and Colonel Blaney is a mere cipher. Both were casualties of the need to streamline and condense, keeping the viewer's attention focused on Marlowe's column and the interplay of Wayne as Marlowe with the other lead characters. Blaney is at Marlowe's staff meeting in La Grange—the scene that follows the riverboat conference—but only as filler. He and his men return north very early, not, as in Sinclair's fictional rendition or in Brown's historical account of Hatch, to raid the Mobile and Ohio Railroad before swinging toward La Grange. Instead, they are sent straight back to camp because the column chanced upon Rebel pickets in a sharp exchange costing Marlowe a couple of troopers. Marlowe hopes the enemy will be fooled into believing that all the Yankees have retreated, but in the film Blaney's mission is no more complicated than that. The audience watches over Marlowe's shoulder as Blaney's men file back the way they came, to the strains of "When Johnny Comes Marching Home" (23m). The raiders have been discovered within minutes of entering Confederate territory, and Marlowe just reduced their strength by a third. If the audience is now wondering how the mission could possibly succeed, then Hollywood's alteration of the facts served its plot-thickening purpose.

Major Gray is kept in the story, though his role is less important. He is made more dashing, an actor-turned-soldier given to quoting Shakespeare. An earnest but naive romantic, he is anxious "to see some action," as Private Schwartz had been in Sinclair's book. He is gravely wounded rather than killed outright, as he had been in Sinclair's novel. Unhorsed, propping himself up with one hand and stanching the flow of blood from a wound with the other, he urges his bugler "to blow, trumpet, blow!" (1h 55m)

Secord—now Phil instead of Frank—is rewritten as a politico whose driving ambition endangers the entire mission. Sinclair had left Secord in the background as a solid, reliable officer. In Sinclair's version it was Secord who wisely urged Marlowe to ride west and cross the Tickfaw rather than continue south to Osyka. In the Mahin-Ford revision, Secord is incapable of such counsel because he is blinded by delusive dreams of glory, dreams that expand with the column's success. First he aims at Congress, then he ponders becoming governor of Michigan, not stopping until he envisions himself in the White House. Contrastingly, when things do not go well he is too quickly crippled by doubt and fear. He pleads repeatedly with Marlowe to swing north and return to La Grange after Newton Station, contending that to try to ride for Baton Rouge was sheer "suicide" (38m). And when the raiders are apparently caught in a pincer on front and rear he declares there is no disgrace in "honorable surrender" (1h 49m). All along he is out of his element, wanting to attack when it is imprudent and too willing to give up when the going gets tough. Essentially he serves as a counterpoint to Wayne's Marlowe, his bombastic foolishness accentuating Marlowe's understated wisdom.

The ill-fated Ed Stumm, Tom Murphy, and Bernhard Schwartz, all of whom were important to Sinclair's tale, do not make it onto the screen. Like Sinclair, Ford deploys Butternut Guerillas who are identifiable by dress though not by group name. They are referred to simply as scouts or vedettes. Sinclair had made over Richard Surby into Andy Bullen. Bullen is not in the film. Rather, Ford combines his casting preferences with the story line borrowed from Sinclair. Ford's primary scouts are named Wilkie, Dun-

ker, and Deacon Clump, and their personalities are tailored to the actors who played them, two of whom were drawn from Ford's unofficial
film family. Ken Curtis, who had sung with the Sons of the Pioneers and
married Ford's daughter, played Wilkie with the nasal twang he had affected for *Rio Grande* and *The Searchers*. Hank Worden, the film's Deacon
Clump, had also appeared in *The Searchers* and more or less reprised
his oddball role. His moment of glory in *The Horse Soldiers* comes near
the end. Onetime preacher and activist on the Underground Railroad,
he knows southwestern Mississippi well. He guides the column safely
through a swamp and around a regiment of Confederates waiting to intercept them (1h 40m). All of the scouts had donned civilian garb soon
after entering Mississippi. Before then it was Dunker and Wilkie who
figured out where they were going. In camp Marlowe had started a rumor
that the brigade was riding to Nashville for a parade. Dunker and Wilkie,
with the sun on their left in the morning light, knew that could not be
true. "Hey, we've been riding smack dab into Reb territory," a disbeliev-
ing Wilkie exclaims (16m).

Not all of Ford's regulars were on hand—no Ward Bond or Victor
McLaglen, no Ben Johnson or Harry Carey Jr. Ford personally recruited
Hoot Gibson, former Western star and friend from his early Hollywood
days, to come out of retirement and play a small role. Judson Pratt, who
portrayed Sergeant Major Kirby, Marlowe's "topkick," filled the part
once reserved for McLaglen. Pratt was nowhere near McLaglen's size, and
the blustering, brawling character McLaglen perfected in *She Wore a
Yellow Ribbon* is left out. Nevertheless, the standard jokes about drinking written for McLaglen are retained for Pratt. Furthermore, Kirby, by
replacing Sergeant Major Mitchell, Marlowe's trusted aide, gave the new
ranking sergeant a dual role: as comic relief and as an added dimension to
the friction between Colonel Marlowe and Dr. Kendall. Bing Russell, the
actor playing Dunker, was not part of Ford's inner circle either, but his
role was crucial. His death precipitated the clash between Marlowe and
Kendall that was the most marked, though predictably altered, carryover
from the novel.

The film relationship between the soldier and the physician follows the
same general pattern as Sinclair's original: initial verbal clash in La Grange,
arrest connected to a baby's delivery, differences put aside at the end. The
details, however, vary considerably. The mutual antipathy is sharpened on
the screen to exploit what the eye could see and the ear could hear,
whereas Sinclair had to limit himself to what the mind could suggest. Too,
the filmmakers aimed at a larger, more diverse audience, not just readers

of historical fiction who could be expected to know a fair amount about the period. Moreover, the book had one lead character with a supporting cast; the film had two, with Holden's Kendall needing to be on screen almost as much as Wayne's Marlowe.

In Sinclair's story there had never been a question that the doctors would accompany the column. They were, after all, regimental surgeons. The immediate source of friction between Marlowe and Keller was over how to carry Keller's medical supplies on horseback and how many casualties the doctors could reasonably be expected to treat if there were heavy fighting. In the film those nuances are eliminated. Marlowe is upset because he had to take Kendall at all, especially since he would not be able to take fieldpieces or supply wagons. Kendall is not part of his command; the doctor is imposed on him by orders from Grant's headquarters. That that will be a problem is made evident when Marlowe and Kendall meet alone after the final staff meeting at La Grange.

> KENDALL: Colonel, I gather you're not too happy about my going along.
> MARLOWE: I hadn't counted on you, that's all.
> KENDALL: I can understand your reasons for trying to avoid a fight, tactically speaking, but, you're going very deep into enemy territory. Tell me, what did you intend to do about your wounded?
> MARLOWE: I intend to move and move fast. Those too badly shot up to carry on will be left to the clemency of the enemy, civilian or military.
> KENDALL: Including yourself? [put sarcastically, as much statement as question]
> MARLOWE: Naturally. [looking at Kendall irritatedly]
> KENDALL: That's a pretty primitive attitude, medically speaking.
> MARLOWE: Well, Doctor, war isn't exactly a civilized business. 'Course I realize that it gives you fellas a wider field of opportunity. . . .
> KENDALL: For experimenting, Colonel?
> MARLOWE: I didn't say that. [his anger rising] (10m)

Marlowe instructs Kendall to take the troop rosters, examine the men, and, using his "unchallenged opinion," to relieve from duty any who were unfit or who might get sick on the long ride. By his tone Marlowe makes it obvious that he does not want Kendall around and that he thinks little of his supposed expertise. Kendall tries to set him straight. "Look, Colonel, I didn't ask to be assigned to this mission," he points out. "I'm a military doctor. I've been ordered to go and I'm going to do my job. So get off my back" (11m). Kendall strides away; Marlowe silently watches him go. Within moments viewers get to see how this will play out. Kendall starts relieving men of duty, including Marlowe's aide, who suffers from malaria. Marlowe is furious. The absentminded officiousness of Kendall's medical orderly—Otis Hopkins or "Hoppy," as portrayed by O. Z. Whitehead—aggravates him further.

The tensions roiling beneath the surface explode soon enough, as the column enters Confederate territory. Two troopers are shot by concealed Rebel pickets. Kendall examines one, asking Marlowe, sardonically, if he is to be treated or left "to the clemency of the enemy." Marlowe calls a halt and prepares to send Blaney's 2d Iowa back to La Grange. The filmmakers rewrote the scene that Sinclair set at Newton Station in the middle of his story and inserted it here, very early on. Marlowe sees that one man is being buried while the other is resting against a tree. He asks for Kendall; Hoppy tells him that the doctor went into a ramshackle hut just off the road. Marlowe weaves his way past the blacks in homespun clustered around the door and enters. In two more changes from the book Kendall has completed the delivery successfully, and mother and child—black, not white—are fine.

> MARLOWE: We've got a couple of wounded men out there, you know.
> KENDALL: No, one's dead. One's gone; one's born. It's an amazing process, isn't it? As many as I've delivered, it never fails to awe me. [Kendall goes outside to wash his hands; Marlowe follows.]
> MARLOWE: All right, Kendall. Get back and take care of your wounded.
> KENDALL: He'll be all right. Hopkins knows what to do.
> MARLOWE: You're not a country sawbones, you know. You're an officer in the Union army, under oath.
> KENDALL: I took an older oath before that one.
> MARLOWE: They didn't seem to be having any trouble having babies around here, before you arrived.
> KENDALL: I was sent for and I was asked to help and I couldn't turn 'em down. Now come off it, Colonel, even you were born.

MARLOWE: As of right now, you are under officer's arrest. Insubordination.
KENDALL: Do I still carry out my duties, sir? [said in unbowed disbelief]
MARLOWE: From now on you will confine them to the troops.
KENDALL: Very well, sir.
MARLOWE: Don't push me too far, Kendall. [Wayne growls, walking off in his distinctive gait.] (21m)

Marlowe and Kendall find small ways to bother each other for the next hour or so, building toward a confrontation the audience knows must occur. It finally comes when Dunker, the scout, dies. He had injured himself at Newton Station during the destruction of Rebel property when a rusty ax blade ricocheted and sliced open one of his legs. Kendall notices him limping and covers the gash with a poultice to prevent blood poisoning. Marlowe happens upon the scene. "What are you putting on there, dirt?" he asks disgustedly. Kendall responds, "No, tree moss; ordinary green mold. It has some sort of healing agent, I imagine." Marlowe, unimpressed, throws Kendall's words back at him. "You *imagine*," he mocks. "I don't imagine the results," Kendall retorts. "This is an old Cheyenne Indian cure." Marlowe walks off muttering disdainfully, "Cheyenne Indian cure . . . green mold . . . tree moss" (1h 21m).

Though Kendall told Dunker to leave the poultice on, Dunker removed it later because his leg started to itch, the very sign of healing Kendall wanted. Kendall has to operate that night. Too late; Dunker dies the next morning. It is while Kendall is preparing to amputate Dunker's leg that Dunker, drunk from pain-dulling whiskey, slurs a few lines of "I Left My Love." Marlowe observes as Kendall explains to Dunker that only amputation could save him. Dunker asks what would become of a one-legged cavalryman. Kendall can only respond that he would be left with "the closest civilian care." Terrified at his prospects, Dunker rages, "Andersonville! Is that what happens to me Doc, Andersonville?" Downcast, Kendall admits, "quite possibly" (1h 27m). If the column rode on, leaving Dunker behind, an embarrassed Kendall understood that he would then become part of the very thing he scorned in Marlowe at their meeting in La Grange. But in that embarrassment there was also a deeper understanding. He had his duty; so did Marlowe, proving that it could be lonely at the top for both men.

Marlowe demands an accounting the next morning. "You lost us a good man," Marlowe opens accusingly. Kendall cannot really give him an answer because he could not pinpoint the cause of death—perhaps it was blood poisoning, perhaps it was Dunker's heart. "*If . . . if . . . maybe . . . perhaps.* What'sa matter, Medicine Man?" Marlowe barks as he looms over a weary Kendall (1h 34m). Kendall snaps, throwing the cup of whiskey he was nursing in Marlowe's face and challenging him to a fistfight. Marlowe accepts and they ride off to a secluded spot. Their bout is not the donnybrook Ford had staged between Wayne and Victor McLaglen in *The Quiet Man,* but it is enough to prove that each is the other's equal. The eruption of cannon fire stops them mid-fight and they return to duty, with the audience left wondering if anything will change between them.

It does, but the change is not evident until the battle at the bridge. Adding to Sinclair's plot and compounding ironies, Marlowe is wounded in the leg as his men prepare to force open the road to Baton Rouge. He is now dependent on Kendall's surgical skill. The doctor operates on his reluctant, resentful, wide-awake patient. Marlowe grimaces, asking Kendall through clenched teeth if he is "having fun." Ignoring him, Kendall calmly, expertly removes the lead ball and responds, "You may not believe it, Colonel, but I bought you some time" (1h 50m). Bandaged and rebooted, Marlowe is helped into his saddle, leads a charge across the bridge, and returns to Kendall and the final exchange that echoes Sinclair's original dialogue.

MARLOWE: Can those men be moved?
KENDALL: They're all critical.
MARLOWE: May I speak to them?
KENDALL: I'd rather you didn't. They've gotta be quiet. I've given
    them the last laudanum I have.
MARLOWE: A lousy finish for good men. Well, there's bound to be
    a medic with that Reb column. Get your horse.
KENDALL: I can't count on that.
MARLOWE: You mean you're staying? [stunned]
KENDALL: Medicine is where you find it.
MARLOWE: Even in Andersonville?
KENDALL: Even in Andersonville.
MARLOWE: I wouldn't blame you, if you slap it away. Shake hands?
    [he offers his] (1h 58m)

Kendall is agreeable; they shake hands. This time the sarcastic banter they exchange afterward as they part is a sign of mutal respect, not the antipathy they had felt before. Viewers of Ford's film, like readers of Sinclair's book, are being assured that in other circumstances they would have been friends and that what had separated them was their basic similarity, not their differences—yet another irony.

The cannonade that interrupted the fisticuffs between Marlowe and Kendall heralded what has become the best remembered scene in the film: an attack on the raiders by cadets from Jefferson Military Academy. This scene came from Ford, not Mahin. Ford was proud of it; Mahin thought it "one of the best scenes of the piece," ultimately one of the few outstanding moments in the picture.[24] That Ford thought to include it is proof that the claims about his having been a Civil War buff are valid. Though pure invention, it was inspired by an actual event: the succcessful attack of Virginia Military Institute cadets at the Battle of New Market in May 1864. Inserted late in the fighting, they advanced on a Yankee position and took it. To this day the cadets are revered in VMI annals, and those who were slain are listed on an honor roll. They were not, as some would have it, sent out as cannon fodder to be slaughtered or mere children who were "massacred." No such event took place, though Ford believed it had. But Ford, at least, knew that it had not happened at New Market.[25] Most of the boys were sixteen or older, and their casualty rates were in line with those of the regular Confederate army units they fought alongside.

Ford owned a fair number of Civil War histories, among which his favorites were by Douglas Southall Freeman.[26] He could easily have read about New Market in Freeman or run down a more detailed account from one of Freeman's citations. It seems unlikely that he got the idea from James Warner Bellah. True, Bellah had worked with Ford to put the cavalry trilogy on the screen and he authored a book about Stonewall Jackson's 1862 campaign in the Shenandoah Valley that included the activities of VMI cadets.[27] But Bellah wrote about the cadets of that year, not those who fought the campaign two years later, and he and Ford were not especially close.

Ford had the idea in mind back when the script was first being pieced together, long before the production company set up on location. His son Pat found Jefferson Military College outside Natchez, which fit nicely into what he intended.[28] Not only did the college, rechristened the "academy" in the film, predate the Civil War; Jefferson Davis had been a student there

Kids really in war, but not this battle.

for a short time. Ford needed well over one hundred boys so some were brought in from the Chamberlain-Hunt Academy in Port Gibson.[29] Costumers were apparently given an authentic uniform from the period to copy, in contrast to some of the uniforms worn and weapons carried by the men in Marlowe's column—but then, costuming anachronisms were not a major concern if the audience would not know the difference.[30] Jack Pennick, one of Ford's old hands and a former marine, drilled the boys. (Pennick too would have his screen time, as the malaria-infested aide forced to stay behind by Kendall.) The cadets became enthusiastic extras who marched in unison, fired by volley, and shrieked Rebel yells as they broke ranks to chase the raiders.

In the film they were sent into the field at the request of a regular army artillery officer. He had but a handful of men in his two-gun battery and wanted desperately to slow the raiders, who had passed through Newton Station and were riding hard to stay ahead of Bedford Forrest. To the ancient superintendent's protest that none of his boys was over sixteen the officer countered that he had a boy of fourteen and an old man of seventy-two with him. "This is war, sir," he pled. "Just a little show of force" (1h 29m) until their own cavalry could arrive was all he asked. The superintendent, also a preacher, acquiesces and orders the entire contingent to assemble, minus two boys suffering from mumps—a Fordian touch. Then, head bowed, he clasps his Bible in silent prayer.

As the cadets go forth, filmgoers are supposed to feel a combination of exhilaration and dread: exhilaration at the boys in their splendid uniforms, gleaming bayonets fixed, marching to a fife and drum rendition of "Bonnie Blue Flag" behind their superintendent, armed only with his scriptures, but also dread at what might await them. Ford could not resist adding one more touch to the scene: a drummer boy determined to be part of the fighting. "Reverend, my boy Johnny, he's all I got," his mother begs as the column passes her house. His father, his brothers, his uncles—all had perished in the war. "Cadet Buford, you are hereby relieved of duty," says the superintendent as he marches stiffly on at the head of his little column (1h 32m). But Cadet Buford does not want to go home, and his mother, played by Anna Lee, another member of Ford's old stock company, has to drag him kicking and screaming into the house. Not to be denied, he lowers himself out a window and runs to join the column. With his mother's voice in pursuit, pleading for him to come home, Johnny runs off to war. The camaraderie of the corps, the call of duty, and the allure of glory were stronger than any mother's wishes.

The artillery barrage leading up to the early morning assault catches the raiders unaware. Marlowe sees the boys coming and orders his men not to fire, even after the cadets loose a couple of volleys at them. Sergeant Kirby says, "Well, at least that Holy Joe ain't no kid" and draws a bead on the superintendent (1h 36m). Marlowe strikes the barrel of his carbine so that he misses. When Kendall asks what he intends to do, Marlowe says, "I'm gonna get the hell out of here" (1h 38m) The troopers mount and beat a hasty retreat, the boys in pursuit, Marlowe saluting them with a wave of his hat, a lively version of "Dixie" playing in the background. Wilkie had captured the errant drummer boy and asks Marlowe what he should do with his prisoner. "Spank him," Marlowe orders, and Wilkie does, to the protests of the boy, who screams helplessly at the "dirty Yankee" (1h 39m).

Those who have tried to pinpoint Ford's filmmaking intentions naturally scrutinize the cadet scenes closely because they were most clearly his invention, not Mahin or Rackin's, and not Sinclair's. Some say that this scene and the valiant though doomed Rebel charge at Newton Station prove that Ford identified with the lost Southern cause.[31] Possibly, though not likely. The one-armed colonel who leads the charge at Newton Station and, wounded yet again, survives only because his old prewar friend Hank Kendall saves him surgically, is a heroic figure, as Ford intended. But there were heroes and cowards on both sides, North and South. Ford himself was of course no help in sorting through such matters. Besides, it is all but impossible to do justice to a good Ford picture by quoting bits of dialogue or describing a few scenes. His best films did not make the big issues of life seem simpler than they really are, and this is one of those films.

I suspect that his concerns were less about the Civil War than they were with larger, more universal notions of duty and honor. Ford was a World War II veteran and very proud of his service. He had formed a naval reserve outfit, the Field Photographic Unit, before the war and lobbied successfully to have it mobilized after Pearl Harbor. Captain Ford, USNR, now had his own wartime command. Dozens of filmmaking associates served in it. Ford's crew shot footage that was turned into support-the-war documentaries, valued service in itself, but they did more. Ford got them involved in cloak-and-dagger operations run by "Wild Bill" Donovan of the OSS. Ford was at the Battle of Midway in the Pacific, where he was wounded and for which he received a purple heart; he was in Africa for the Allied landings there; he was in the English Channel for the D-Day invasion in June 1944. After the war he bought land in the San

The cadets advance. Courtesy of the Lilly Library and MGM/UA.

Fernando Valley and built the Field Photo Farm. For over a decade Ford and the other veterans of his unit gathered there to reaffirm their patriotism and remember those who gave their lives in service to their country. According to Ford's grandson Dan, a Vietnam veteran, commemorative events at the farm were held reverentially; the farm was "a true community and one of the most unique instititutions ever created in Hollywood."[32] Perhaps the end of the farm reunions, as members of the old war family moved on or died, had as much to do with Ford's supposed growing disillusionment over time as anything else.[33] One of the high points of his life came just months before he died in 1973, when Richard Nixon appeared at a tribute to Ford offered by the American Film Institute to present him with the Presidential Medal of Freedom.[34] Still, he was probably even more thrilled to have been promoted to rear admiral earlier during Nixon's administration, so powerful, so lasting were his impressions of the military and war, so primal his notions of duty and honor.

evident in his film

Ford's *Horse Soldiers* deepened an emphasis on honor and duty already present in Sinclair's *Horse Soldiers,* an important element, lest we forget, in the real history of Grierson's raid. That increased stress is obvious in the relationship between Marlowe and Kendall, in the gallantry of the one-armed Colonel Miles, even in the doggedness of Marlowe's troopers—good Americans all. More important, it permeates the love story inserted in the film that had not been a part of Sinclair's book or the actual raid. Indeed, the military mission is ultimately subsumed within personal odyssey, and by film's end the love story has all but taken over— not because themes revolving around duty and honor are put aside but because the relationship between Col. John Marlowe, Yankee raider, and Hannah Hunter, proud Southern belle, comes to embody them.

All of this unfolds in what is an otherwise fairly conventional boy-meets-girl format, in which intense mutual dislike eventually turns to romance, with all the expected verbal sparring, comedic turns, and dramatic vignettes along the way. Hannah Hunter, proprietress of Greenbriar plantation, was played by Constance Towers in her first starring role. The appearance of Yankee cavalrymen on her northern Mississippi doorstep proves most disconcerting. Even so, she oozes Southern charm and offers a feigned welcome, hoping that she can learn their intentions and send out a warning. She invites Marlowe and his officers to dinner, overplays the ingénue, and gets under Marlowe's skin.

> HANNAH: Major Kendall a doctor, and Colonel Secord almost a congressman, and you [Major Gray] an actor. And now all military men. Such a waste of talent. But of course, Colonel Marlowe, I imagine that you are a professional soldier.
>
> MARLOWE: No. Prior to this insanity I was a railroad engineer. [irritably]
>
> HANNAH: Why, how thrillin'! Why to think of being able to steer one of those huge things, just a-puffin' and a-steamin' and a-ringin' that little bell, ding dong! ding dong! [she says gaily, pretending she is pulling a bell cord]
>
> MARLOWE: Not quite. [agitatedly] My job was in the construction of railroads.
>
> HANNAH: Well, my, such brilliant minds! Well you know, poor little-ole-me just barely squeezed through Miss Longstreet's seminary for young ladies. How did you [to Marlowe again] ever manage to remember all those books in college?

MARLOWE [at his wit's end]: I didn't. I started driving rail spikes at ten cents a day and found. And now, Miss Hunter, I must ask you to leave us. (31m)[35]

Hannah maneuvers her unwelcome guests into another room before leaving. Using a gimmick that Martin Rackin thought up, she opens the doors on an unlit pot belly stove.[36] The piping of that stove is connected to the stove in her upstairs bedroom. With the complicity of her household slave, Lukey, played by tennis star Althea Gibson, she listens in with the intention of reporting what she hears to Confederate forces. She hears that the Yankees are headed for Newton Station and then to Baton Rouge. Kendall, ordered by Marlowe to keep Miss Hunter company and not in the least fooled by her disingenuous warmth, discovers what is afoot and hauls the conspirators before the colonel. Marlowe asks Hannah if she would give her "word of honor" not to disclose what she overheard. "I don't hold honor with any Yankees," she proclaims defiantly. Kendall cannot resist needling the colonel. "I noticed she was getting on your nerves all evening," he comments dryly. "Now's your chance to shoot her." Angry at herself for being caught, frustrated that she may not be able to spread the alarm, she lashes out verbally, only to discover that her time with the Yankees has just started.

HANNAH: Go ahead, shoot us, shoot both of us! But you'll never get away with the rest of your filthy, murderin' plans, Mister Colonel Marlowe. You Yankees and your holy principle about savin' the Union! You're plunderin' pirates, that's what! You think there's no Confederate army where you're goin'? Do you think our boys are asleep down here? Why, they'll catch up with you and cut you to pieces, you nameless, fatherless scum! [now sobbing] I wish I could be there to see it!
MARLOWE: If it happens, Miss Hunter, you will be. [stalking past her] (41m)

Ford uses the historical drama of the raiders' long ride as the backdrop for what happens between Marlowe and Hannah. They learn to separate their personal feelings from their rival causes through Ford's patented combination of humor and pathos. Hannah grudgingly accepts her fate as prisoner, but only after failing to escape by horseback and then, slightly later, failing to signal a passing Rebel column. Marlowe, she slowly begins to see, is an honorable man doing his duty as he sees it. Hannah, Marlowe realizes, is a woman of substance, as dedicated to her cause as he is to his own. Respect leading to affection slowly displaces hostility. Kendall's ironic tendencies and skill at cutting to the quick are often turned to aid that transformation, as Kendall becomes an inadvertent matchmaker. When, on the ride away from Greenbriar, Hannah complains about her dead father's clothes being taken by the raiders, Kendall explains that they would be worn by "scouts"; "spies," she counters, warning, "You'll find out what happens to spies down here." With deft sarcasm he responds, "My personal experience with spies is limited; I've only known one" (44m). She pulls away in a huff, but the point is made.

In another notable instance, just before the column reaches Newton Station, Marlowe pleasantly surprises Hannah. They encounter two Rebel deserters who have taken a county sheriff captive, an older man who had sought to arrest them. Initially, to her disgust, it appears that Marlowe is going to treat them as fellows in arms. Her opinion changes when she sees that he had no intention of letting them go or of harming the sheriff. After he found out what he wanted to know about Newton Station, he had the sheriff untied, gave him a gun, and had the two deserters bound, all "with the compliments of Hannah Hunter of Greenbriar." Confused, Hannah looks at Kendall, who shrugs and says, "Yes Ma'am, a hard man to understand" (58m).

Hannah gets her first real glimpse of Marlowe's vulnerability at the same time that viewers learn that the hard-bitten colonel's disdain for doctors was quite personal. It occurs at Newton Station, where Marlowe has had to fight a bloody engagement he hoped to avoid. Kendall and—significantly—a local doctor team to try to save the lives of men on both sides in a hotel whose first floor has been converted into a field hospital. Marlowe is shown in another room comforting a dying trooper whose last wish is that the colonel write to his mother. Later Marlowe stands at the hotel bar, pouring himself a drink, when he is joined by Hannah, exhausted from her efforts to assist Kendall with the wounded. The groans of one carry through to them from somewhere off-screen.

MARLOWE [caustically]: Go ahead, Kendall, have a field day!
HANNAH [appalled]: What do you mean, "field day?" He's in there fightin' to save men's lives.
MARLOWE: Men's lives or the reputation of his profession? [he downs a glass of whiskey]

HANNAH: Why, you can't be serious, Colonel Marlowe?

MARLOWE: Well, have it your way, ma'am. [pouring himself another glass]

HANNAH: Medicine is the most noble and unselfish. . . .

MARLOWE [cutting her off]: Sure; noble profession, noble oath, lanterns held on high. So high they won't admit they're gropin' for. . . . [he trails off, finishing another glassful]

HANNAH: Why, you're, you're unfair, and. . . .

MARLOWE [again cutting her off, while pouring himself more]: Unfair? There was a girl, not much older than that boy in there. I wasn't unfair then, understand, because they used a lot of fancy words that an ordinary section hand wouldn't understand. So I held her down while two of 'em worked on her. I trusted doctors then. Believed in 'em. Because I was in love and I didn't wanna see her die [downs the glassful; pours another]. A tumor, they said it was, and it had to come out right away. So they stuck a leather strap in her mouth so she could bite off her screams while they cut away to get in there. And what did they find? Nothing! Oh, they were sorry! Sure, they'd made a mistake. They had something to talk about before their next little experiment. But what about me? They left me begging her not to die. I lost my wife. [downs a final glassful] And I didn't kill either one of them. I must have been crazy or too conventional. Quite a speech . . . guess I'm feeling my liquor. [and ends by sliding the nearly empty whiskey bottle down the bar, smashing a stack of double-shot glasses] (1h 14m)

For John Wayne in a John Ford film that actually was a lengthy speech, a veritable soliloquy. Hannah and the audience now know that Marlowe still wrestles with his demons. But he has not become embittered or cynical because of it. He would rather build than destroy; he would rather save lives than take them. He did not want the "insanity" of war, but duty *duty not war* called and he answered. When Lukey is shot and killed by Rebel snipers a few minutes later—her death perhaps the most senseless, most ironic of all—Marlowe sits at Hannah's side, apologizing for all the pain he has caused her (1h 24m).[37] When, awkwardly, he begins to apologize again, this time at the bank of the last river to be crossed, she throws herself into his arms when gunfire erupts (1h 45m). He reluctantly leaves her behind with Kendall after the fight at the bridge, but not before telling her that he

loves her. "Tell her the rest when you get back," interjects Kendall, recall-
ing Marlowe to his duty (1h 58m). She looks at him with tear-filled eyes.
He then takes the kerchief from her head, ties it around his neck as a ban-
danna, lights the powder charge set to destroy the bridge, and gallops
across as it is blown to splinters behind him. Kendall and Hannah watch
him ride off to catch the column. The film ends as they enter a cabin to
tend the wounded, with Bedford Forrest's men passing in the background
and "Lorena" played one last time for effect.

The Mirisches and United Artists wanted a national release on the
Fourth of July, for obvious reasons. They had to be content with merely
getting close in most cases, but *The Horse Soldiers* did open in hundreds of
theaters across the country before the end of the month. Theatrical trail-
ers sent out with other Mirisch/United Artists films touted the picture as
a great visual ride and included action-packed clips. "No adventure in all
the annals of war more daring," stated the voice-over, "no story the screen
has told is more thrilling than this true story of a brigade of brave fighting
men who rode through hell and into military history."[38]

On June 17, before the national release, the Strand theater in Shreveport served as the site for a "gala premiere."[39] Wayne, Holden, and Constance Towers flew in for the festivities, which included a parade, parties, and speeches. A special opening the next day at the Baker Grand in
Natchez followed.[40] Newspapers in both towns used the same promotional ads run nationally, celebrating the "ride to glory" with Wayne and
Holden shown leading "the raiders on horseback who rode like thunder—
and struck like lightning."[41] That they "rode like thunder" through Southern territory did not seem to upset the locals, who were as excited about
the premieres as they had been about the filming. And far away to the
north, in Bloomington, Illinois, Harold Sinclair had his brief moment of
hometown fame, the mayor proclaiming July 16 a day in his honor. The
Pantagraph joined the enthusiasm revolving around the debut there, noting that the film had been taken from "the world-famous historical novel
by Bloomington's own Harold Sinclair."[42]

Once the hoopla died down, *The Horse Soldiers* settled into only modest success. Given Hollywood's incredible output and the pressure of theater bookings, most films did not run very long in any one location. *The
Horse Soldiers* enjoyed respectable one- or two-week engagements, but in
the end the Mirisches and United Artists just about broke even on it. The
byzantine nature of Hollywood accounting makes it hard to say precisely.
They did much better with some of their other less expensive joint proj-

Harold Sinclair receiving the Bloomington "proclamation" honoring him
for writing the book that led to the film, as his wife looks on proudly.
Courtesy of the *Pantagraph*.

ects that year, notably *Some Like It Hot,* made for considerably less and
earning considerably more.[43] *The Horse Soldiers* received no Academy
Award nominations. In 1959 *Ben-Hur* was the top box office draw, whose
eleven Oscars stood unmatched until *Titanic* nearly forty years later.

Reviews were mixed. Those who enjoyed John Ford Westerns tended
to be favorable; those who did not were more critical. Thus some liked the
Fordian feature of long lines of men on horseback; others did not. Some

liked the mix of drama and comedy; others did not. Some liked the film as both history and entertainment; others did not. Most thought the music fine, the cinematography beautiful, Wayne his dependable old self, and Holden a good contrast to him. More than a few thought their rivalry too contrived; even more thought the script in general the weakest link in the film.[44] John Lee Mahin would later concede as much. Looking back years later he told Dan Ford, the director's grandson, "If I had it to do over again, I wouldn't have bothered."[45] John Ford was as dismissive. "I don't think I ever saw it," he responded when Peter Bogdanovich asked him about the picture—probably not true, but that was his standard response to questions about films he would rather not discuss.[46] Interestingly, a later student of Ford's films singled out the closing scene of *The Horse Soldiers* for its dramatic profundity. It was, he felt, "an ending as mysterious and beautiful as Ford ever achieved."[47] Perhaps, but it was not the ending John Lee Mahin had written, and the film became something other than what he had intended. Whether it was what Ford wanted is yet another matter.

5

THE STORY NOT TOLD

When a reader comes to the historical novel he is not, or ought not to be, ignorant of the fact that it is a form of fiction that he is reading, and that history in it is mixed with inventions in a proportion which he cannot be expected to estimate with any precision. The novel does not replace the history-book; it is a splendid thing if it drives us to the history-book, if it provides us with something—some sort of texture—in which the facts of the history-book, when we come to them, can find a context and lively significance and a field that gives them play.

—Herbert Butterfield,
The Historical Novel

I have little faith in history. I read it as I do romance, believing what is probable and rejecting what I must.

—John Adams,
to Jedediah Morse, March 4, 1815

John Ford never did like the script for *The Horse Soldiers*. He liked the idea for the film; it was the way Mahin and Rackin had tried to capture the idea in a story line that bothered him. Mahin recalled an early meeting with Ford aboard the *Araner,* the director's beloved yacht. "You know where we ought to make this picture?" Ford asked Mahin rhetorically. "Lourdes. It's going to take a miracle to pull it off."[1] Even months later, after shooting started on location in Louisiana, he had misgivings. When cinematographer William Clothier commented that he liked the script, Ford huffed, "Well if you think I'm gonna make their goddamned script you are mistaken. Because there are some things in there I don't like."[2]

Ford kept Mahin and Rackin busy on revisions even as scenes were being filmed, dealing with them as writers rather than producers—which

was probably just as well because Ford was notorious for driving producers off a set. The script problems were compounded by casting complica-
tions. Mahin had hoped to get Clark Gable to play the role of Marlowe.
He had written for Gable in a variety of films, including *Mogambo,* where
he first worked with Ford. Gable, it turned out, was unavailable. Up to
that point Mahin and Ford had thought about using John Wayne for Kendall, and they considered casting Gregory Peck—who had expressed an
interest in the film—as Marlowe. They then decided that Wayne would
make a better Marlowe than Kendall. Jimmy Stewart was their next
choice for Kendall, but Stewart was reluctant to play someone so cocky
and seemingly cynical.[3] They eventually settled on Holden, a much better
match for Kendall as written, but nearly did not get him. Paramount
sued—and lost—to prevent him from doing the picture, contending that
he was obligated there. Holden was signed for the part in October, just a
couple of weeks before cast and crew were supposed to be on location.
His negotiations added to an already complex arrangement involving
United Artists, the Mirisches, Mahin and Rackin as producers, Wayne's
"Batjac" company, and Ford's "Argosy," resulting in a contract much
longer than the script. With the two male leads being played by major box
office draws it was decided to go with a relative unknown who could
not command a large salary for the female lead; thus Constance Towers
was chosen only ten days ahead of shooting. Before then they had considered Elizabeth Taylor or someone else with similar star power.[4] But the
Mirisches wanted to keep costs down to $3.5 million if possible, which
it proved not to be. For someone of Ford's temperament, all of these
ancillary issues ran the danger of making the movie more trouble than it
was worth.

The script, still incomplete at the end of June, was expanded here and
there over the next months. The supposedly "final version," dated September 9, was revised three times between September 15 and October 30.[5]
Some of the scenes included in the last revision were either not shot at all
or ended up on the cutting room floor.

Among those not shot was Mahin's preferred ending, written into the
script from the beginning. Mahin followed the lead of Sinclair, who had
followed the actual events in Baton Rouge: an impromptu parade for the
victorious raiders. Nevertheless, the earlier allusions in the film that had
been designed to set up the parade were kept. Hence Marlowe told Hurlbut that he spread the rumor about a parade in Nashville, then Wilkie and
Dunker discovered that they were actually riding south into enemy terri-

tory. The script called for seven more camera shots beyond the battle of the bridge. The first was of a "spick and span Union Major, mounted with white gloves" riding up to a "bedraggled" Marlowe on the outskirts of Baton Rouge—a variation on the scene invented by Sinclair for Asa Bryce, which had been inspired by what actually happened to Grierson. The next few shots show the column coming into town, people scurrying about, the garrison commander ordering an escort for the mud-splattered, exhausted cavalrymen suddenly in their midst. Mahin described the scene he wanted in detail.

> This leading cavalry honor guard, its flags snapping in the breeze, its twelve horses sleek and shiny, heads the parade. Behind them, Marlowe's column, saddle sore, filthy, dead beat, their horses lame, streaked with sweat and coated with caked dust. Here and there are men with bloodstained bandages, no more than able to stay in the saddle. But wounded or not, men with limping horses, walk beside them. Here and there a boot is off, tunics ripped and shredded . . . all in all, as unmilitary a group as rode a soldier's parade. On the street are a few gaping Confederate civilians. Here and there, colored folk are clapping and shouting in time to the music.[6]

The very next camera shot was to be of a grinning Wilkie, who turns to one of the other scouts and says, "Well it ain't Nashville—but we sure got our parade."[7] Marlowe takes his men past the Union officers of Baton Rouge who are mounted to receive them. "Eyes . . . RIGHT," he commands as they ride in review and the "gleaming sabers" of the smartly dressed Baton Rouge contingent "are whipped out and brought to a salute." And then, at last, comes the final shot, of the leading raider. "The weariess seems to drop away from Marlowe as he draws himself more erect. As the music swells"—no doubt the unused "Girl I Left Behind Me"—"we . . . FADE OUT."[8]

Various reasons have been proffered for why Ford did not shoot this ending. The one given most often is that he was despondent over the death of Fred Kennedy, one of the stuntmen on the picture. Kennedy and Ford went back years, at least to the cavalry trilogy. Cast as a Union soldier, Kennedy is seen frequently on-screen as one of the two troopers assigned to guard Hannah Hunter. One proposed scene called for Kendall to take a fall from his horse. Kennedy asked Ford if he could do the routine stunt, one Kennedy had done numerous times. But he was older now and out of shape. Against his better judgment, Ford said yes. Kennedy broke his neck when staging the fall and died from his injuries.[9]

Certainly Kennedy's death devastated Ford. He blamed himself, and he never talked about it publicly. But the fatal accident occurred on December 5, the last day of location shooting outside Natchitoches. Everything else, including the scene where Wayne as Marlowe blows up the bridge, had already been filmed and the entire company was scheduled to leave the next day. The Baton Rouge scenes, along with more fighting for the battle of the bridge, would have been shot on a Hollywood lot, not in Louisiana—as in fact happened with the Newton Station battle sequence.

There were more factors at work here. The Mirisches worried about cost overruns and were not eager to shoot any more back in Hollywood than absolutely necessary. Although Mahin wanted to do both the additional fighting footage and the Baton Rouge parade, Rackin did not push either one. He was convinced that they would "make a fortune" regardless.[10] And John Ford? Odds are that he never intended to do the ending the way Mahin wrote it. He had a reputation as he got older for becoming bored with a film near the end of shooting. By the time of Kennedy's death he may have been detaching himself psychologically from the project. Because he shot so economically, often in one take and using just one camera, there was only so much the editors could do to flesh out material. If there were no parade scene on film it could not be inserted, one reason for Ford not do it at all if he wanted to control the final product. William Clothier, who was working with Ford for the first time, thought it might be simpler still. Perhaps the parade scene struck Ford as too predictable, something he would have been expected to do and therefore decided to leave out.[11] Then too there is the suggestion that *The Horse Soldiers* was a swan song of sorts for Ford, his stock company of players, and the type of film they had come to represent. Audience expectations were changing, and Ford was not sure he wanted to change with the times. That may have depressed him as much as Kennedy's death. But then again perhaps he was just not inclined to end a film as neatly, as unambiguously as he had in the past. He did tell one interviewer a year later that "the old enthusiasm has gone, maybe. But don't quote that—oh, hell, you can quote it."[12]

There is a danger in looking too hard for a deeper meaning in the differences between the script and the finished film, for why Ford did this or did not do that. Take, for example, the claim that *The Horse Soldiers* was indicative of Ford's growing disillusionment with war and the heroic West of his earlier films, a shift supposedly detectable in *The Man Who Shot*

Liberty Valance three years later and *Cheyenne Autumn* two years after that.[13] When a clip from an interview with Peter Bogdonavich was shown at the AFI tribute at which Ford denied having changed his attitudes between *Wagonmaster* and *Liberty Valance,* knowing laughs at his evasiveness rippled through the audience.[14] Ford's evasiveness, ironically, may have encouraged the search for meaning that he found so irksome.

One critic tried to trace an emerging antiwar theme through Wayne's Marlowe, who wanted to avoid any fighting.[15] Thus his being so reluctant to order his men to fire on the Rebels charging up the street in Newton Station, his decision to ride away from the cadets, and his irritation with Major Gray's yearning for action at the battle of the bridge. Indeed, when Gray offered Marlowe a pistol at Newton Station the colonel waved him off, seemingly proof of his desire not to participate in the carnage he was obliged to preside over. There is even more "proof" than this critic noted. To the very end the script had included a scene in Newton Station where Marlowe draws his pistol and shoots a Rebel off a rooftop, thereby saving Sergeant Kirby's life.[16] Apparently it was not filmed. Even so, what this critic did not mention is that in the charge across the bridge Wayne's Marlowe leads the way, pistol in hand (1h 52m). If Ford were so concerned with turning Marlowe into a pacifist, he could have had him lead the attack weaponless or he could have kept him out of it altogether. Physically imposing and famous for playing intimidating men of action, Wayne was hardly a logical choice for a pacifist's role, which John Ford knew perfectly well; so much for critics trying too hard to find symbolism. Wayne's Marlowe actually took the hard-bitten hero of Sinclair's tale even further away from the historical Grierson, a slight, usually soft-spoken man. We also need to remember that avoiding fights was a strategic imperative in the film and in the novel, as it had been in the real raid.

There are certain dynamics common to every movie set. One is that what is said on film is almost never exactly as written, even if Shakespeare was the author. Actors will substitute their own words or give their own inflection to words written by others. Mahin himself was never completely happy with his *Horse Soldiers* script. No matter how many lines or scenes were added or deleted to further explain Marlowe's hostility toward doctors, he never felt that he made it convincing enough. Another commonality is that scenes are altered as the story comes to life in the camera's viewfinder. What happened with *The Horse Soldiers* was therefore fairly typical.[17]

The riverboat meeting scene that opens the film was not added until October 6. Before then the opening scene was at La Grange, without Grant or Sherman. Hurlbut more or less took the lines and played the role later assigned to Grant. The Brady group photograph scene had been inserted a few weeks before. Walter Mirisch thought the film could do without it; Ford retained it.[18] At the same time Ford cut an involved scene showing the raiders in the town of Ripley, possibly in the interest of time, possibly to simplify the viewer's frame of reference and not distract from what was still ahead at Newton Station. Ford also cut a scene with Marlowe outside Newton Station waiting for Major Gray to secure the town and report back—a scene adapted from Sinclair's novel, thereby reducing the role of the actor playing Major Gray.[19] By contrast, the more that Secord was re-shaped into a vile politico, the more lines there were for the actor playing the unsavory colonel.

Ford eliminated material directly connected to the key relationships between Marlowe and Kendall and between Marlowe and Hannah. Through August, Mahin had a scene at La Grange where Kendall (still Curtis in the script) talks to Hurlbut after his run-in with Marlowe. Kendall does not understand Marlowe's prejudice against doctors. Hurlbut does not know what personal hostility, if any, Marlowe might have toward physicians, but he reminds Kendall that prejudice against the profession and superstition about medical practices were still widespread.[20] In September, Mahin wrote a different scene to accomplish the same end. This time it is Marlowe and Hurlbut who talk. Marlowe wants the doctor replaced; Hurlbut refuses. As Marlowe prepares to leave, Hurlbut says, in jest, "Some day I'd enjoy hearing about that doctor who held your tongue and gave you that first dose of castor oil." Marlowe does not see the humor, responding with a flat "No, you wouldn't, sir."[21] This lead-in to Marlowe's scene with Hannah at the hotel bar where he talks about his wife is not shot.

Neither is a rather long talk between Marlowe and Lukey that takes place after Hannah attempts to alert passing Confederate cavalrymen. This discussion was to have come after a scene that is shot and kept for the film where Marlowe throws Hannah on the ground and pins her, his hand over her mouth to silence her. She is willing to let that pass but slaps him after learning he had ordered the two troopers guarding her to watch her every move, even when she was answering nature's call (50m).[22]

LUKEY: Coffee—for *me?*
MARLOWE [sitting down, picking up his cup]: Go ahead. Drink it.
   Now, you and I ought to be friends.

LUKEY: How come?

MARLOWE: Well, after all, we're fighting for the same thing.

LUKEY [guardedly]: We is? Well, ah's on Miss Hannah's side. And ah *know* you and all these other gen'lemen ain't with us. Else why you fetch us away from Greenbriar?

MARLOWE: Look—Lukey—you think a lot of Miss Hannah, don't you?

LUKEY: Ah *loves* her.

MARLOWE: That's good. Now she's given me her word she won't make any more trouble. But she might forget—and then really get hurt. So you just do this for me—*and* for her. If you find out she's planning to get away or something—why, you come and let me know about it, will you?

LUKEY: You mean. . . Ah carries *tales* on Miss Hannah? [shakes her head] Uh-unh! There suthin' you don't understand, Mister Colonel. We's ve'y close. Miss Hannah and me. We's *breast* close.

MARLOWE: Breast close?

LUKEY: Yessuh. You see, when her mammy died—when Miss Hannah was born—why Missy Hannah took her milk from my mammy along with me. And we ain't never been further apart than that. Ah believe, if *you* had commenced with her the same way, *you'd* be. . . .

MARLOWE [trying to stem the tide]: Yes, I know—I see, but . . . Lukey—do you realize that we've come down here to bring you and your people freedom?

LUKEY: Oh. I hears some colored folks shoutin' and explainin' it that way. But ah's just happy stayin' with Missy Hannah. After all, ah's *her* family—and she's mine.

MARLOWE: Don't you understand what freedom means?

LUKEY: What's it mean?

MARLOWE: It means a person's free—free to come and go as you like—to do what you want to do. That's freedom!

LUKEY: [puzzled, thinking]: Oh? [then] *You* got it, hmmmm?

MARLOWE: Of course. Doing what I want to do.

LUKEY: You mean you and all these gen'lemen come down here—killin' and gettin' killed—'cause you *wanted* to?

MARLOWE: No. This is a means to an end. It's. . . .

LUKEY: What end?

MARLOWE [emphatically]: So that you and your people *can be free!*

LUKEY [with a sigh]: Well—I ain't speakin' for other folks, but I just 'splained to you how I felt person'ly 'bout that. No wonder you's in such a fret all the time, Mistah Colonel. It's all mixed up ain't it? [rising] Well, Miss Hannah'll be much obliged to you for this coffee. Thank you, suh.[23]

This scene was most likely doomed from the beginning even though it was left in the script through the end. From Ford's perspective there was too much talk to too little purpose, in a scene that would have been awkward for both John Wayne and Althea Gibson. Wayne could not appear too devious or manipulative; Gibson could not be turned into a simpleton. She already verged on playing a Sambo-like character, and Ford needed to be careful. There is also the possibility that Ford worried Mahin's Marlowe was preaching here, force-feeding a message that the director wanted to deliver more subtly. If Ford intended to tell a tale of national reconciliation, of good people on opposite sides of a vexing dispute, he had to avoid this sort of exchange and find a more indirect way of condemning slavery without condemning the entire white South. Besides, the scene as Mahin wrote it would not have been shot on location anyway because Althea Gibson was never there. Ford did not want her to suffer any indignities in the segregationist South, so all of her scenes were done in Hollywood. The sequence where Lukey is shot and killed as the column rides south after Newton Station was performed by a stunt double.

Even as scenes from the script were shot they were refined. At one point the script called for Hannah and Lukey to be tied to their horses after Hannah's escape attempt.[24] Ford must have disliked the visual image that projected; he got rid of the ropes. He had the escape itself rewritten to make better use of the location and to incorporate at least one element of the deleted conversation between Marlowe and Lukey. As written before the film company arrived in Louisiana, Hannah rides off; troopers catch up with her and bring her back. As filmed she plunges into a bayou, her horse stumbles, and she is soaked. The rewritten scene that followed was more to Ford's liking, one of his trademark pieces. He gets his comic relief and slips in a jab at slavery. Troopers are drying Hannah's underclothes over a fire; she sits, disheveled, wrapped in a blanket. Marlowe and Kendall walk over to her, both of them obviously amused at her predicament, while she is both angry and embarrassed.

[handwritten margin note: so aia commentary]

MARLOWE: Aren't you gettin' a little chilly?

HANNAH: Don't tell me you're concerned about my health?

MARLOWE: If I give you back your clothes, will you promise not to run away again?

KENDALL: I would, Ma'am. There's a point where pride becomes impractical. Actually, if you could get a good look at yourself, I think you'd agree with me.

HANNAH: Very well. I do wish to keep my health. I shall not try to run away again.

MARLOWE [enjoying this]: Your word of honor?

HANNAH: My word of honor.

MARLOWE: To Yankees?

HANNAH: To *Yankees.*

MARLOWE: Cross your heart?

HANNAH [now on her feet]: I gave you my word.

MARLOWE: All right, Lukey. Help Miss Hunter with her clothes. [he ambles off]

KENDALL: I'm glad you're being sensible. You were beginning to worry me, from a medical standpoint.

HANNAH: Thank you, doctor.

KENDALL: I wish I could be of more assistance, but [sarcastically] fortunately you Southern people have your own help. (46m)[25]

To add more intrigue to the relationship between Marlowe and Hannah and to emphasize the risks Marlowe and his raiders ran, Mahin wrote in a brief but potentially crucial scene near the beginning of the Newton Station sequence. When the troopers guarding Hannah are distracted by preparations to stop the Rebels arriving by train she turns to the "proprietor of the hotel" and says, in Mahin's directions: "(sotto voce, urgent) Only way they can get out of town is down to Baton Rouge! I heard them talking! That's why they're holding me!"[26] By disclosing this she breaks the spirit if not the letter of the promise she had given just minutes before not to "cry out for assistance" when Marlowe stopped her from getting the attention of a Rebel force—which Ford increased to a full regiment from Mahin's patrol. She comes to regret betraying Marlowe's trust even though she had acted in defense of her country and her cause. In another brief scene before Marlowe leads his men in their charge across the bridge she confesses and he forgives.[27] Ford cut all of this—again, too much time to too little purpose, in what might confuse and frustrate the audience.

Even the final scene between Marlowe and Hannah had to be re-thought and rewritten. Does Marlowe tell her he loves her? Does he kiss her before he leaves? Ultimately it is yes to the former, no to the latter.[28] Ford, never bound by the script in this or any other film, fell back on the visual conventions that he had mastered over the years, relying on the facial expressions and body language of actors that had served him so well before. Words, he knew, would not carry this most visual of dramatic moments. Mahin had wanted to do more with the final Marlowe-Kendall scene that leads into this one, perhaps to soften Kendall, make him a family man, have him say something about his wife understanding that he had to work "long hours" to lighten the effect of the Andersonville business.[29] But Ford chose not to add anything, keeping the final scene between Marlowe and Kendall, as between Marlowe and Hannah, as brief, as tight as he could. He shot what he wanted and no more.

When Ford altered the ending, he altered the film's entire tone. William Clothier was convinced that *The Horse Soldiers* would have been more of a crowd pleaser if it had had the happy ending in Baton Rouge.[30] That is not necessarily to say it would have been a better film, though it might have attracted more viewers, and it would have reminded the audience about the mission that had been obscured by the romance, John Marlowe and Hannah Hunter becoming more important than the Civil War and the exploits of a Union cavalry brigade.

It is true that films can be an uneasy mix of art and commerce and that even the best intentions to educate can be lost in the desire—and financial need—to entertain. That was no doubt the case in John Ford's *The Horse Soldiers,* an intrinsic tension compounded by the circumstances under which that picture was made. Even so, what happens with films often happens with books, historical works as well as novels. Perhaps Ford's statement about a creative filmmaker being more like an architect than an author is a distinction without a difference. Books too can be reconfigured, the story line being changed even while the grand design or vision remains the same, as the author mimics the architect.

Harold Sinclair, author of *The Horse Soldiers,* spent over a week on Ford's set outside Natchitoches as a consultant. He was astounded by what he saw, by what struck him as the chaos of filmmaking—nearly five hundred people scurrying about in no order that made sense to him. John Wayne told him to think of it as "organized confusion." To Sinclair and to the others on the set, Wayne was "Duke" and Holden was "Bill." But seemingly no one was on a first-name basis with "Mr. Ford," called "the old man" when he was not around. What surprised Sinclair most were the many changes in his story. At first he was taken aback; eventually he became more philosophical. "He figured that they're in the movie business and he's in the writing business," reported the local newspaperman who made the trip from Bloomington to Louisiana with the author.[31] And why would Sinclair complain? He had never been more successful. Flying high at the moment, he talked of a new Civil War novel that he planned to write, one that would have a local connection, and he had been led to believe that *The Cavalryman* was going to be a film as well, with Alan Ladd to play the lead. Neither project came to fruition.

Sinclair vs. Ford

One of Sinclair's biggest surprises was the romance between Marlowe and Hannah, which is nowhere to be found in his published tale. Even so there was a connection. "My most major disappointment is that you didn't get Boy Meets Girl in this," Dee Brown had commented to Sinclair after reading the final draft of his manuscript. "Maybe it would have ruined the story," he added, "but Hollywood would like it better."[32] Brown may have had his own experience in mind here. He had tried and failed to interest Hollywood in *Grierson's Raid*.[33] Sure enough, John Lee Mahin wrote to Harper & Brothers after he and Rackin bought the rights to *The Horse Soldiers* to ask if Sinclair had included any romance in earlier drafts.[34] Unbeknownst to Brown, it turned out that he had. Although Mahin read what Sinclair had done, he decided to go off in his own direction.

Sinclair's romance for Marlowe came near the end of his original manuscript, on the eve of the battle at the Tickfaw. The column, seeking a bivouac for the night and grain for the horses, rode onto the grounds of "Chateaux St. Gervais," the most impressive, most "pretentious" plantation the raiders encountered on their journey. Marlowe had expected to see French place names once he entered Louisiana. He was mildly surprised to stumble across this "chateau" while still in Mississippi. As his horsemen filed onto the plantation grounds, he dismounted and went to the door alone. He was greeted by an older white woman dressed in black with a white apron "and a bit of lace perched on her severely arranged gray hair." She looked at him suspiciously and said simply, "Monsieur?" He inquired about the owner; the woman told him he was on the estate of "Madame Didier." At that moment the mistress of the house made her entrance, in a manner that Mahin adapted for Hannah Hunter at Greenbriar.

Madame Didier came down the broad, curving staircase, holding the voluminous skirt in one hand—Marlowe took for granted it

was she. It is difficult to appraise a woman accurately while she de-
scends a stair, it creates an illusion much like a stage. But when she
stood on his level he had the instant impression, the strongest of
several, that if ever a woman was mistress in her own house this
one was. The girl—well, scarcely that. He guessed her at thirty, perhaps a little more. She was hardly beautiful, certainly not "pretty,"
in the ordinary sense—and yet the kind of face a man of a certain
kind might find overwhelming. She stood like a confident duchess,
completely in command, and quite aware, of her fine body. Her
features seemed oddly assorted, as though they didn't quite belong
to each other, one of those faces which, as between action and re-
pose, might have belonged to two different women. The Colonel
had the impression that her appraisal of him was both candid and
curious. Certainly it was self possessed.[35]

Sinclair's Madame Didier is not much like Mahin's Hannah Hunter.
There is no playful gaiety; she is no pretended ingenue. Her dark features
and sophisticated reserve bespeak a different personality altogether. She
invites Marlowe and his officers to dinner, as Hannah would in the film,
but there is no planned subterfuge, no real interest in the Yankee mission.
Only Secord and Gray join Marlowe and Madame Didier; the doctor—
Sinclair's Keller, not Ford's Kendall—is nowhere in sight. The early verbal sparring has a sexual edge to it that Mahin would transfer into his
script—along with a display of "considerable décolleté," but without the
politics.[36] Nor does Madame Didier accompany the raiders when they
leave. Everything that happens occurs at the "cheateau," an evening of romance followed by a fond but sad parting.

Madame Didier is a widow. Her husband died two years before of
yellow fever—roughly the same time that Marlowe lost his wife. The Di-
diers had come to Mississippi to start over and escape the political turmoil
of their native France. She remained after his death, keeping to herself
on the estate. She breaks through Marlowe's hard shell, charming him at
dinner. He lingers after Secord and Gray excuse themselves. He does not
leave until the next morning. In the meantime, the reader would learn
that the colonel is more worldly than his troopers knew. He had spent a
year in France, most of that in Paris. He still remembers some French;
more important, his tastes are refined. He is a passable pianist who plays
Mozart and Schubert for his hostess and shares her love of opera. That
he plays at all is a hint of what is to come because he had not done so since

his wife died. The colonel and Madame Didier become John and Alix as they drift toward intimacy.

"How can a soldier know there will be any tomorrow, Alix? For some of us there hasn't been, for more of us there will not be." He released her hands and then clasped her warm bare shoulders. "I have not been afraid of dying before now, I think. It was no particular virtue—I just did not have the feeling. But now I *am* afraid—"

She laid a hand softly across his mouth. "Don't say it, don't even think it, please, my darling! I tell you there will be tomorrow—"

Oddly enough these were so far the most intimate physical contacts they had—what? Allowed themselves?

"Yes, I believe it—I must." He laughed without humor, bitterly, and cursed, knowing she would understand. "God damn this war—now! And yet, if it were not for it I would not have found my way here at all? No—!"

"But there would have been something, somewhere."

"Of course—but *this* is what there is. Doesn't that mean we have to take what's thrust into our hands at a given time and place?

Almost invariably the irridescent bubble vanishes into nothing and nowhere when it is touched, but not always, not always.

Gently she took his hands away and stood up. "Come here to me," she said, and it was at once command and invitation. "Now before tommorow comes—"[37]

In the morning he departs with her pendant as a keepsake. "'You will bring it back, my darling,' she said tersely, almost fiercely." He vows that he will; "there was not time for more."[38] But as far as Sinclair's editor at Harper & Brothers, Evan Thomas, was concerned, there was not even time for that. He cut that scene; in fact, he cut everything about Madame Didier, nearly forty pages in all.

Thomas was very taken with Sinclair's tale. He was also sure that it had to be shortened and tightened as it made the transition from manuscript to book. Most of the cuts he urged on Sinclair came after Newton Station and the bulk of those in the last one hundred pages. Thomas worried about readers losing interest, a matter of both length and focus. Therefore his eliminating the "French gal," a major alteration, and numerous minor changes, such as trimming the material on Gray and his death at the Tickfaw. He also eased the tension between Marlowe and Asa Bryce. And it was Thomas's suggestion that Major Keller be strengthened to become a foil to Marlowe. In Sinclair's original text Keller remained with the wounded at Newton Station who were supposed to try to make their way back to La Grange with one company of troopers as an escort. "Keller might in fact volunteer to stay with the wounded men toward the end of the book," Thomas suggested, "and in this way he would be paralleling Marlowe in the sense of duty."[39] Persuaded, Sinclair kept Keller with the column until the battle at the Tickfaw, with the denouement between Marlowe and Keller that follows. Thomas even cleaned up the ending by excising several paragraphs after Bryce and Brown listened "until the last long trumpet note died away," his sense of the dramatic, even of the poetic, coming to Sinclair's aid.[40]

Thomas had shown Sinclair's manuscript to colleagues, including John Fischer, chief editor of *Harper's* magazine. Fischer was a Civil War aficionado. It would be his copy of *Grierson's Raid* that Thomas loaned to Sinclair. For his part Sinclair was flexible. He accepted virtually all of Thomas's emendations. His son Ward typed a fresh draft, and the 504-page manuscript shrank to 453 pages. The original fifty-one chapters were reduced to thirty-three. At Thomas's urging they were also renamed. Originally Sinclair had used time designations—for example, one chapter was headed "5:40 A.M., April 17," another "7:30 P.M., April 17," and so on. Thomas warned that this could become tiresome to the reader and he suggested the simpler, clearer titles Sinclair consequently substituted. It was Thomas who decided to print Dee Brown's endorsement as the foreword and Thomas who got Sinclair to explain more closely in his "Author's Note" how his story differed from actual events.[41]

At least Sinclair had final approval of the editorial changes made at Harper & Brothers. He had no say whatsoever in the London edition that Harper & Brothers authorized for a simultaneous printing. Published by Frederick Muller, that version of *The Horse Soldiers* featured jacket art with Yankee troopers charging at the reader in something akin to the heroic paintings of Royal Scots Greys at Waterloo or the Light Brigade at Balaclava—which of course was precisely the marketing point. "There is a powerful element of suspense in this story which holds the reader's attention to the last page," readers are told on the inside flap, and "Mr. Sinclair's particular achievement is that, given these men in this situation, one feels that is the way they would have acted." Nonetheless, the London editors were apparently concerned about holding the reader's attention "to the last page"; they cut two chapters and Brown's foreword altogether

[handwritten marginalia: novel — & way they would have acted.]

and dropped "The Pursuit" sections in chapters they retained. All totaled they reduced the book's length by about 10 percent.[42]

How Sinclair felt about what went on in London can only be surmised. But it is clear that he willingly allowed Evan Thomas a hand in shaping his tale. Thomas's changes were not merely cosmetic, aimed at improving the book's literary merit. Eliminating Madame Didier and recasting Major Keller in a stronger role were fundamental. In one sense the story was still the same—Yankee raiders riding through Mississippi. In another it was quite different as the book became a collaborative effort between author and editor.

Dee Brown, by contrast, wrote with minimal editorial involvement. He recalls that he was asked to do very little beyond reducing some of his quotations from Richard Surby's account.[43] Other than pushing Brown to go with the more formal "D. Alexander Brown" rather than "Dee Brown," a name by which he was already known, the editor did not have many other changes in mind.[44] Even so, Brown's experience was in some respects similar to Sinclair's. Brown had to edit himself as he went, deciding what to put in and what to leave out, what to emphasize and what to treat in passing. Like Sinclair the novelist and Ford the filmmaker, he could not include everything; and like Sinclair and Ford, the choices he made determined the shape of his story. Just as a film or a novel can be an uneasy blend of art and commerce, so too can a history book be produced with the bottom line in view. Even university presses cannot afford to lose money on every title they publish. Their books need to be kept to a certain length, and overall production cost is an unavoidable consideration. No author can be allowed to give every example or tell every story, both because readers might lose interest—or simply become lost—and because there is a financial point of diminishing returns. If Dee Brown had not written a tight manuscript, editors at Illinois would have sharpened their pencils.

Surby, for example, loaded his account with anecdotes. Brown chose some, not all, for his narrative. One of the longer tales that he left out involved a lawyer named Mosby. Surby rode into Mosby's life near midnight on April 28, as he scouted ahead of the four companies from the 7th Illinois that Grierson detached "to destroy the track" of the New Orleans and Great Northern Railroad at Bahala and "otherwise injure the enemy" while the main column rode on to Union Church.[45] After demolishing the "depot, water-tank, tressle-work, and steam-engine for pumping water and sawing wood" at Bahala, "we rested a short time and began retracing our steps" to rejoin Grierson.[46] At close to midnight Surby came upon "a neat log cabin" owned by a lawyer, "a bachelor living at his ease." He was reading in bed when he heard Surby and a couple of troopers step onto his veranda. When he asked who was there, Surby told him the same lie he had told others all day—that they were Confederate reinforcements trying to link up with Wirt Adams. Invited by the lawyer to come inside, Surby added that he and the two men with him had been ordered "to obtain information about Colonel Adams and the condition of the roads." The lawyer wanted to know more about his late night visitors; Surby was ready with disingenuous details. When the lawyer asked "to whose command do you belong?" he responded earnestly: "To Colonel Faulkner's First Mississippi Cavalry, stationed at Granada, and sent by railroad to Jackson, to assist in intercepting the Yankees at Pearl River, but we arrived too late; the Yankees had crossed, and we were ordered by a dispatch from General Pemberton to pursue the enemy, and, if possible, fall in with Colonel Adams and report to him."[47]

The lawyer probed deeper, asking if Colonel Faulkner was with him. The quick-thinking Surby replied no, he was with an advance party of two hundred under Major Williams—true in that there were two hundred troopers outside, but then they were troopers from the 7th Illinois under Capt. George Trafton. Anticipating a question, Surby explained that some of the men wore blue uniforms captured from the Yankees. The lawyer wanted to know why Surby did not sound like a Southerner. Surby answered that he was originally from Missouri and had come to Mississippi by way of Tennessee after the war started.

Satisfied, the lawyer then told Surby what he wanted to know; namely, that Wirt Adams had passed through around sundown with four hundred men and a six-gun battery and that he intended to attack the Yankees from the rear while other troops would bar their path to the west on the Natchez Road. The lawyer added that he had sent off his horses and mules with his slaves to prevent their falling into the raiders' hands. Otherwise, he said, he would be happy to guide his visitors to Union Church and introduce them to Adams, whom he knew personally. He thought their plan to reinforce Adams a "capital idea" and wanted to help.[48] Surby offered him a horse, and he agreed to go. He rode with the raiders for over four hours, completely unaware that he was aiding and abetting the enemy.

While Mosby rode alongside Captain Trafton—or, as he thought, Major Williams, Surby stayed ahead with George Steadman, the other Butternut Guerrilla with Trafton's command. In the dark Mosby did not see that

Surby and Steadman were playing their masquerade. After they captured three Confederate soldiers and held them off to the side of the road until Mosby passed, the lawyer wanted to know what had transpired. Surby told him the prisoners were Yankee stragglers. Mosby "hoped we would shoot them, that they should not be permitted to live."[49] Surby even apprised Mosby of what the "Yankee" prisoners had told them—that Wirt Adams's men had decided to ride around and ahead of the raiders rather than try to take them from the rear. Mosby offered to act as a courier to Adams; his newfound companions thanked him but said no, they would send one of the troopers. Mosby did not figure out what he had gotten himself into until after he entered Union Church, then occupied by Grierson's full column. He saw acquaintances among some prisoners gathered there. One expressed surprise at seeing Mosby, a civilian, being brought in as a prisoner. "Why, explain; what do you mean? Are these not our troops?" asked the incredulous lawyer.

I could see his face change—color half a dozen times—and turning around he looked "daggers" at me. In a few minutes he returned, and looking me full in the face said, "This is a d———d Yankee trick." I was full of laughter, and laying my hand familiarly on his shoulder said, "Mr. Mosby, you are sold, but it is all fair in war times, and do you not think a 'capital idea?'" He twitched his mouth a little, and at last assuming a contented look said, "Sergeant, you have done well, but for God's sake do not ever mention this to any person." I promised, but it was too good to keep. From that time until he left the place he was very sociable. On inquiring how he was to get back home, he said he could not walk so far, and there would not be a horse or mule left. I told him that I thought I could raise him a horse of some kind, as several had to be left behind. I left him, and finding the Colonel, asked him if there would be any horses left behind, if so, I would like one for Mr. Mosby to return on. The Colonel told me to find one and mount him. I soon found one, and putting on a good saddle called Mr. Mosby, and handing him the reins told him to keep this horse in remembrance of the Yankees. He seemed much pleased, and when I left him he had a very favorable opinion of Yankee hospitality.[50]

Brown did not relate the details of this little escapade, and he passed over Trafton's return to the column rather quickly. If he had included it,

Surby's importance to the overall success of the raid would have appeared that much greater, a matter of page space in a book—the equivalent of screen time for actors in a film, and a matter of emphasis. But Brown was trying to strike a balance. Most of the more interesting details of the raid came from Surby's account, not Grierson's or the Forbes's. If he repeated too many of Surby's tales, readers might have the impression that the scout had somehow assured success single-handedly.

At least one veteran of the raid, Thomas Lippincott, was disappointed that, twenty years after the fact, Surby's book remained the only detailed account of what had happened. Lippincott, who had risen to captain in the 6th Illinois by the end of the war, served as a private in that regiment's Company I at the time of the raid. He entreated Grierson to get something into print. "Sgt. Surby's book poor as it is is about the only thing I have seen except in Harper's Weekly pretending to be an account," he lamented to his old colonel. He had kept a diary—adequate, he felt, for the reflections of a man in the ranks—but he thought the public needed the commander's perspective on "the greatest feat performed by cavalry *in any* war."[51] Lippincott was miffed that the exploits of John S. Mosby and Stuart—men on the *losing* side—were being romanticized while those of Grierson's raiders were nearly forgotten. Indeed, he felt that the western theater in general was overshadowed in the national memory by the campaigns in the East. Earl Van Dorn accomplished as much in Mississippi as Mosby and Stuart did in Virginia, he contended, and Van Dorn had been no match for Grierson.

Lippincott voiced all these opinions in the brief account of the raid he wrote for a Milwaukee newspaper. Although Dee Brown knew of Lippincott's correspondence with Grierson and cited several of those letters, he did not refer readers to the 1889 newspaper piece, possibly because he did not come across it, or perhaps because it did not add materially to the story he chose to tell.[52] Nor did he concern himself with another issue that both Lippincott and Stephen Forbes worried over; namely, who deserved credit for conceiving the raid in the first place. Brown gave the impression that it was all very straightforward: Grant came up with the idea and passed it along to Hurlbut, who then began detailed planning with Grierson.

Actually it was a good deal messier. Surby stated matter-of-factly that Grierson himself came up with the idea three months before the raid.[53] Although Grierson had said in his 1864 affidavit that Surby's account was "correct in every particular," his autobiography suggests that Hurlbut had the idea first.[54] Stephen Forbes tried to find out for himself while he was preparing a paper on the raid that he presented at the Illinois State Historical Society in 1907, which was published soon after in the society's transactions. Forbes, the Company B sergeant who by then had become a respected entomologist, relied on his brother's papers and his own memory for most of what he said. Neither his memory nor his brother's materials could help him on the question of who originated the raid, however. The *Official Records* provided no definitive answer either. Grant and Hurlbut were long dead. Grierson's health and memory were failing, and Grierson had not worked on his autobiography in years. It contained nothing that would have answered Forbes's question anyway. Samuel Woodward, Grierson's adjutant on the raid, was the only man Grierson had confided in before the column left La Grange. He stayed in the army and in 1904 produced a reminiscence for a cavalry journal. Even if Forbes had read it, it would have not brought an end to his quest. Woodward wrote that Grierson had mentioned "some such expedition" to "his superiors sometime before"—a vague statement at best.[55]

Forbes turned to William Sooy Smith, Grierson's immediate superior, in his search for an answer. "The published reports," Forbes grumbled, "are so far inconsistent, that I am at a loss how to reconcile them."[56] Sooy Smith only made matters worse. He claimed that he had originated the idea; "the conception and general plan of the raid were mine," he assured Forbes. If Hurlbut had doctored the record to make it appear as if the idea had been his, Sooy Smith sniffed, he could only feel sorry that his former superior "may have been guilty of such reprehensible conduct."[57] The problem is that Sooy Smith was wrong. He did not even arrive in La Grange until March 1863, at least a month after Grierson, Hurlbut, and Grant had begun their planning.

Ultimately Forbes abandoned his quest. "I shall," he told Sooy Smith resignedly, simply "give the facts as they appear on the record," however incomplete, even inconsistent, that record may have been.[58] Thus his printed essay states noncommittally that Hurlbut "was commander of the district under whose direction the expedition was planned and by whose orders it was set on foot."[59] He even diverted attention away from the point he had wanted to make but could not, emphasizing that Grant, Hurlbut, and Grierson were all Illinoisans; therefore, the raid's success was a proud moment for the entire state.

Even though Forbes gave up, Thomas Lippincott did not want to let the question go unanswered. Lippincott could be obsessive on certain points.

He was convinced, for example, that Grierson was privy to the details of Grant's planned river campaign and that the two men coordinated their movements carefully, even though Grierson told him that that had been impossible. When Forbes sent him a copy of his essay, he responded that he liked it but that he would make two corrections: one, that destroying enemy rails and rolling stock was secondary to diverting Rebel attention away from the Mississippi; and two, that Grant, not Hurlbut, must have planned the raid. "I doubt sometimes if Hurlbut really comprehended Grant[']s object & plan," Lippincott wrote to Forbes.[60] He was convinced that Hurlbut might have sent someone less capable than Grierson if Grant had not asked for him specifically to lead the raid. Furthermore, Hurlbut's recommendation that Grierson strike west of Jackson would have undercut the entire purpose of the raid, concentrating enemy forces in the very area where Grant would be operating. Lippincott added one more observation. When he told the ailing Grierson what Sooy Smith had claimed to Forbes, Grierson shot back "H——we made that raid ourselves, don[']t let anybody steal credit for it that belongs to us."[61]

Dee Brown did not discuss this issue or various others that surfaced in the record. Notably, establishing who came up with the idea for the Butternut Guerillas can be as vexing as determining who originated the plan for the raid. Brown repeated Surby's claim that the idea was his and added "that it is possible that a conversation" Surby had with Lieutenant Colonel Blackburn "led to the organization of the scouts." Brown surmised that Blackburn, the dashing cavalryman fated to fall at the Tickfaw, found in Surby "a kindred spirit."[62] He did not mention that Grierson claimed in his autobiography that the idea was his, not Surby's, not Blackburn's.[63] Nor did Brown choose to explore interregimental tensions between the Illinoisans and Iowans, despite indications that they existed and despite the fairly common presence of state rivalries in the armies on both sides.[64] Likewise, he did not discuss the different attitudes of the two Forbes brothers. Although Henry seemed to take B Company's role as "forlorn hope" in stride, his brother Stephen was more ambivalent—if not exactly bitter toward Grierson, then resentful about the larger circumstances that had exposed the men to such danger.[65]

But then Dee Brown could not tell everything. There was not enough room for everything he knew, he did not know everything there is to know, and there is much that is lost altogether and no longer knowable. He chose those elements from a fragmentary past that fit his intentions, the details that complemented his narrative. His picking and choosing is a

+(lacune—boundlessness (erasures)) unreliability and inaccessibility!

reminder that Brown's storytelling style, one that some historians now dismiss as passé, is no less interpretive than more self-consciously critical approaches. It is just that the interpretation is presented more subtly, masked by the narrative structure.

Early in his career the Cambridge historian Herbert Butterfield expressed a hope that the historical novel and history book would complement each other. Although "the novel does not replace the history-book," he wrote, "it is a splendid thing if it drives us to the history-book." Historical novels, he believed, could provide both "texture" and "context" for the "facts" presented in historical works; they could act as a "field that gives" those facts "play."[66] On the other side of the Atlantic, the historian Carl Becker began writing from another perspective. Whereas Butterfield contended that the key difference between history and fiction is the corpus of "facts" that anchor historical work, Becker cautioned that the so-called facts found in documents are themselves the products of interpretation. They are an inherently shaky foundation on which to build our understanding of the past. Consequently, the historian's conclusion is never truly conclusive, never freed from an element of uncertainty.[67] "The past as it really happened" is much more elusive than Butterfield understood, at least at that point in his career.

A more recent generation of historians has moved beyond Becker, emphasizing that the fact-based distinctions that historians like Butterfield drew between historical writing and fiction may not really exist. "Long ago, as a graduate student in history, I learned to pursue fact and to avoid fiction like the proverbial plague," recalled the noted historian John Demos. But, he confessed, "the boundary itself has grown blurry. It has not vanished entirely, but its meaning and importance seem increasingly hard to grasp."[68] Or, as Hayden White put it, the historian and the novelist both "wish to provide a verbal image of 'reality'" and, when all is said and done, "history is no less a form of fiction than the novel is a form of historical representation."[69] Both literary forms are the result of a creative process in which the writer imposes order on chaos; the historian's efforts are as much an intellectual fabrication as any piece of fiction. Even if a historian is not supposed to create characters, dialogue, or events, what ends up on the printed page is nonetheless an invention, something springing from that writer's imagination. Therefore, some of the same historians who might have raised their eyebrows over Dee Brown's invented dialogue and imagined scenes in *Grierson's Raid* would concur with Brown "that it is impossible to reconstruct the true past from

maybe the distinctions should be blurred in history fiction,

documents."[70] If they are right, then perhaps filmmakers and writers, whether novelists or historians, have much more in common than is normally thought. Yet we need not stop there. Another link could be added to the chain that joins historical works, novels, and films: they are the products of a society whose memory is a collective pastiche, formed as much by one component as another and in a pattern almost impossible to discern, much less control.

The Truth—Ever Elusive

The Centennial Commission welcomes this film as one of the first contributions to its national program, the avowed aims of which are "to pay tribute to the memories of our forefathers who took part in the bitter conflict to determine the exact path our national government should follow" and "to provide Americans with a new understanding of the way in which we built from sacrifice and suffering an enduring nation and a lasting peace."

—Civil War Centennial Commission
on *The Horse Soldiers*

The old friction between writers of historical fiction and writers of formal history has almost been replaced by the high stakes tension between sound, verifiable history, and history that can be rendered filmic, between the emotive medium of film and analytical medium of history. The tension between the history we write and the visual mediums through which it can reach unprecedented mass audiences represents one of the greatest professional challenges of our time. At stake, simply, is the nature and quality of the national and social memory, the vast *public memory* public's knowledge of its past.

—David W. Blight,
"Homer with a Camera," 1997

Congress established the Civil War Centennial Commission in 1957. Over the next eight years that commission did what it could to set the tone for hundreds of commemorative events scattered around the country. The commissioners, a mix of politicians and academicians, hoped that those Civil War observances would "be carried out upon a dignified and elevated plane, free from the stains of commercialism and vulgarity." They encouraged activities that would not "reawaken memories of old sectional antagonisms and political rancors, but instead strengthen the unity of the Nation and popular devotion to the highest purpose of the Republic."[1] In other words, they wanted to perform what on the surface might appear to have been an impossible task: to find something unifying from what had been divisive, something uplifting from what was otherwise our greatest national tragedy, in short, to emphasize the good consensualist traits that Americans had always shared, not disputative tendencies that had once driven them apart.

Significantly, the commissioners sought to honor those who had given their lives in "devotion to a cause"—*a* cause, not *the* cause, meaning that Northerners and Southerners alike could be proud of their ancestors.[2] "That war was America's most tragic experience," intoned President Dwight Eisenhower, and yet "it was a demonstration of heroism and sacrifice by men and women on both sides who valued principle above life itself and whose devotion to duty is a part of our Nation's noblest tradition."[3] Eisenhower said this despite the constitutionally nettlesome notion of states' rights and secession championed by the Confederacy and the growing racial tensions that remained, in part, a legacy of that conflict—which Eisenhower himself had faced in Little Rock, Arkansas. True, Cold War anxiety helped stimulate the perceived need to present a solid front to the supposed Communist menace and show potential enemies that the American people would march as one. Even so, the urge went much deeper, to the most primal levels of national identity.

The Horse Soldiers became a beneficiary of this historical consciousness-raising. John Lee Mahin and Martin Rackin might have decided to make their movie anyway, but their timing was more than a fortuitous coincidence. When Clyde Walton, then editor of *Civil War History*, invited their brief essay on *The Horse Soldiers* as history, they made the connection explicit. Walton, who had acted as a consultant to the Centennial Commission, was presumably gratified that the film received a "special citation." Fittingly, U. S. Grant III, retired army general, Centennial Commission chairman, and namesake of the hero of Vicksburg, made the presentation—not to Mahin and Rackin but to John Wayne and William Holden. The two movie stars, along with their director, John Ford, received top billing on the certificate. They were commended for a film, as yet unseen by commission members, "which retells the story of the famous Grierson Raid—certainly one of the most strategically important, colorful and fascinating stories to come out of the Civil War."[4]

Grant, an Eisenhower appointee, stepped down as chairman of the commission in 1961. John F. Kennedy, Eisenhower's succcessor, appointed the historian Allan Nevins of Columbia University to replace him. Nevins fretted that the centennial was less than it could be. One source of irritation was what he deemed the trivialization of the past through reenactments, where Civil War buffs donned uniforms copied from originals, armed themselves with replicas of period firearms, and fought mock battles. He could not stop what local groups or state committees did, but he swore that "if the National Commission tried to reenact a battle, my dead body will be the first found on the field."[5] It was just as well that he did not go to Manassas, Virginia, where four thousand participants staged a reenactment of the 1861 engagement for an audience approaching one hundred thousand.[6]

For Nevins the problem of proper observance was not restricted to misguided enthusiasts or to those who cared little and knew less. He was disturbed above all by imbalance, by an emphasis on military glory at the expense of exploring deeper issues, a tendency to skirt controversy or ignore the contributions of those like black Americans, free and slave, whose story had yet to be told. Historians themselves did not agree on what should be considered most important, what is most worth studying and what is not. And even if they could agree on what is most important or what is most worth remembering, they did not necessarily agree on why. David Donald, once Nevins's colleague at Columbia, told commissioners of his concern that younger historians were not all that interested in the Civil War, that the best minds in the profession were moving into other periods, leaving the remnant to refight the same old historiographical battles. It was not that he expected Civil War historians to reach a consensus, all giving the same answers to the big questions; rather, he was worried that the big questions might not be asked.[7]

Some disagreements among Civil War historians had more to do with perspective than documentation, the profession's version of the fable about the blind men and the elephant. But some controversies were the result of an incomplete and contradictory record. One hundred years after the event historians were still sifting through Civil War detritus. Part and parcel of that sifting were attempts to set the record straight, to winnow the false or unreliable in a quest to make the "facts" as factual as possible.

Bill Weber, an interested amateur rather than a professional historian, became caught up in that quest, hoping to set the record straight on Grierson's raid. Weber grew up in Bushnell, Illinois, a town where the men of

Company L, 7th Illinois Cavalry, had been recruited. As a boy he heard tales about Grierson. He later read Harold Sinclair's *The Horse Soldiers* and saw John Ford's *The Horse Soldiers* when it came to a local theater. "I think seeing the film prompted me to join the Civil War Round Table that had recently formed in Peoria," he recalled.[8] He also read *Grierson's Raid* and met Dee Brown in 1965 when Brown, at his invitation, spoke to the Peoria group about Grierson's raid and deepened Weber's interest in the subject.

Busy with family and career, it would be another decade before Bill Weber began to pursue Grierson in earnest. It all started innocently enough. He and a colleague at work, a native Mississippian, "shared a common interest in standard-bred horses, and from that our conversations inevitably drifted to cavalry, and thence the raid in his home state."[9] On one of his trips back to Mississippi, Weber's friend took pictures of historical markers, including one in Newton. Weber was alarmed by what he saw in the photo. It was a simple tablet erected in 1963 as part of Mississippi's centennial observance, stating: "Site of Confederate hospital burned on April 24, 1863 by Federals under General Benjamin H. Grierson."[10] By then Weber knew from Brown's book and his reading in various other sources that the inscription on the tablet was wrong. Grierson's band had not burned Newton's hospital. In 1980 Weber went to see the tablet for himself and then launched a fifteen-year campaign to have it changed.

The folks he talked to in Newton were receptive. Sidney Roebuck, a local lawyer, had chaired the state centennial commission at the time the marker was erected. He told Weber that if he could prove to the state's satisfaction that the raiders did not burn the hospital, the chances of getting the marker replaced were very good. Nancy Williams, a columnist for the *Newton Record*, the town's weekly newspaper, also showed an interest. She joined Weber in his crusade, which he pursued for years "to no avail."[11] Apparently these local Mississippians were more interested in helping him correct the record than were fellow Illinoisans. Weber's attempts to enlist the Illinois State Historical Society in his cause failed. On his own, Weber assembled a sheaf of documents drawn from primary and secondary sources, including the *Official Records*, a list of patients in the hospital after the date it was supposedly torched, and *Grierson's Raid*. Far from burning the hospital, he contended, Grierson's men "acted to safeguard it and the welfare of its occupants." The state of Mississippi was persuaded and, at long last, Weber prevailed; Grierson was cleared of the charge. "The text on the old marker did him and his comrades a dishonor," a state official wrote to Weber, who also assured him that the

Changing historical truths: the 1963 marker in Newton (above) and its 1996 replacement (below). Courtesy of Keith Justice, for the *Newton Record*.

marker would be replaced "at our expense" to "redress the wrong."[12] And so in 1996 a new historical marker was substituted for the old one in Newton, Mississippi, and Bill Weber of Bushnell, Illinois, was an honored guest in the festivities leading up to its dedication.[13]

The wording on the original marker had been an honest mistake. Mississippi officials relied on inaccurate or vaguely worded contemporaneous accounts and undocumented popular lore in 1963 when composing those lines. Bill Weber had amassed better evidence and thus caused the "facts" of the event to change. What had been true for over thirty years was discarded as false, displaced by a new truth.

[margin note: pop. memory not always right.]

Mississippi's misleading marker was hardly an anomaly. Questionable truths about the Civil War in general and Grierson's raid in particular abound.[14] Dee Brown accepted Grierson's estimate that his column had ridden six hundred miles. Except for Company B under Captain Henry Forbes, five hundred miles seems more accurate.[15] Brown also attributed the statement that the raid "was the most brilliant expedition of the war" to William Tecumseh Sherman. Sherman may indeed have believed that, but whether he put such a belief into words is unclear. That praise is part of the *Official Records,* but it was offered by Nathaniel Banks, not Sherman.[16] And yet both the six-hundred-mile distance and purported Sherman statement have been repeated countless times by other historians, and of course by Harold Sinclair and John Lee Mahin, who trusted Brown to get the facts right.

Does this mean that Brown's book is undeserving of the plaudits it has received over the years? Hardly. Perfection, as they say, eludes us all. Given the endless dialectic of historical reinterpretation, no doubt another book about Grierson's raid will be written someday. If it does improve on Brown's account, in part that will be because Brown had already cleared a path. Besides, there is no guarantee that the newer account will be the better of the two. Virtually every historian gets something wrong and for any number of reasons: documents that are never found or read, undetected errors in the documents at hand, a phrase or page number miscopied, a name misspelled—the list could go on. And what the historian manages to escape in composition could creep in during production, as the manuscript becomes a book. But the inherent problems run much deeper. It is one thing to correct mistaken "facts" and replace the old and discredited with the new and more credible; it is quite another to alter basic understanding and force a complete reconceptualization of what is historically significant. That next historian of Grierson's raid would prob-

[margin note: errors in history]

ably not make the same mistakes as Brown; most likely Brown's invented scenes and dialogue would be avoided too. Even so, the narrative could be turgid and uninteresting, and the higher truths—whatever they are— might not be told as well.

Of course, the concept of historical "truth" is itself problematical. For some, truth in history is tied to a discredited notion of objectivity, to a "noble dream" that is perhaps more of an illusion when not simply a delusion.[17] With the unavoidably fragmentary nature of the historical record and the inescapability of bias, it is argued, historians cannot tell absolute truths nor can they be objective in any literal sense. But can they tell relative truths instead? "It is normal for there to be more than one true characterization of any event or historical period," contends C. Behan McCullagh, and "the variety of historical interpretations does not exclude the possibility of their truth." Thus, McCullagh continues, "although historical conclusions are fallible, when they are well supported by evidence they deserve to be believed very probably true, that is, telling us something true about the world."[18]

Substitute "facts" for "evidence" and we are back where Carl Becker left an earlier generation of historians. Not everyone will accept the preponderance of "evidence" as establishing a "fact." Our attachments, once formed, can be hard to shake. Ultimately the whole past, as we try to reconstruct it, will be far more than the sum of its vestigial parts. Keith Justice, editor of the *Newton Record,* observed that even after Bill Weber's laborious efforts and the new marker set up by Mississippi officials there were those who were still convinced that Grierson's raiders had set fire to the Newton hospital. They could not cite chapter and verse as proof, and yet in their hearts they knew they were right. "So much for years of dedicated research reviewed by state archives," Justice sighed; "the myth of the terrible/awful Yankees burning the hospital persists."[19] He also confessed that his own weekly twice reprinted a photograph from a Shreveport newspaper whose caption stated that it showed Grierson's men burning a shed in Newton. Actually it was a still taken during the filming of John Ford's *The Horse Soldiers* outside Natchitoches. But trying to persuade local readers that what they had supposed was a photograph of the real event was instead taken from the Hollywood movie version was not easy. Justice commented astutely: "A good story, once freed from the Pandora's Box of imagination, can be irresistible. It takes on a life of its own, and even the razor-sharp sword of truth is powerless in the presence of a good myth. The legend of the photo of the Newton Station burning may persist, but if this happens, it will be in spite of the truth, not because of it."[20]

Harold Sinclair claimed, with Dee Brown's blessing, that he had been "faithful" to the past even though he fictionalized Grierson's raid in *The Horse Soldiers*. John Lee Mahin and Martin Rackin made a similar claim for their film version of Sinclair's novel. The problem lies in the notion that there is a spirit of the past existing apart from human contrivance.[21] What we know as the past, what we include as memory, exists only because of volition; it does not inhere in nature. It is formed over time and across generations, by countless tiny accretions and in an infinite variety of ways. Invoking the spirit of the past is therefore no check on those who stray too far from documentary remnants. That "spirit" is formed by a collective consciousness, some of which may be truly historical, some of which may be more nearly folkloric, and when combined produce chimeralike myths. Those myths become dear to us. To try to eliminate all of them, warns the psychoanalyst Rollo May, might do more social harm than good. He believes that the decline of myth is the reason for the rise of psychoanalysis, as people who search for meaning in life become confused when they are told that myths are falsehoods to be discarded.[22] And yet, it could be countered, if there is no attempt to distinguish the verifiable from the mythical we will become confused in another sense, incapable of discerning what is real and what is not.[23] As Isaiah Berlin cautioned, although historians must have "imaginative insight, without which the bones of the past remain dry and brittle," using that insight "is, and always has been, a risky business."[24]

Historical "facts" may indeed be a shaky foundation for our reconstructed past, but they are better than having no foundation at all. Even if those who use the past without laying that foundation are not guilty of committing "historicide,"[25] they do threaten essential concepts of social responsibility and intellectual honesty. Accepting the premise that historical truth will always elude us does not mean that the ideal must be discarded as somehow delusive. By that reasoning, virtually every ideal ever articulated could be tossed on the junk heap of human frailty.

What historians can and cannot do—or should and should not do—will continue to be subjects for debate. History free of interpretation does not, cannot, exist; similarly, historians cannot avoid drawing inferences. But what inferences can they properly make? And how can a reader know which inference springs from a documentary source and which springs from the historian's preferences and prejudices? Usually only the writer, not the reader, can know, if indeed the writer has stopped to weigh such concerns. The line that separates the factual from the fictive is thin and easily erased by those who do not think as well as those who do not care.

Keeping history, which is ideally precise, from being undercut by memory, which is so often imprecise, has become a concomitant concern. But drawing a distinction between verifiable history and unsubstantiated memory can be like John Ford's characterization of authors versus directors: a distinction without a difference. It would be misleading to say that the participants' trustworthy recollections are lost in the sloppy storytelling of their descendants, and with that history is corrupted by memory.[26] For example, each firsthand account of Grierson's raid does not stand alone as one man's remembrance. Though Surby's account came first, not everything Surby recorded was the result of direct observation, and he added details in a revised version many years later. Had information that he deemed unimportant initially become more important to him with the passage of time? Had he forgotten some incidents and then recollected them long afterward, for this reason or that? We can only surmise. Some of what he recorded he did not see; it had been told to him by others. Grierson's autobiography has numerous passages in it that were obviously paraphrased from Surby.[27] It is possible that Grierson could no longer distinguish between what Surby saw and what he saw. Similarly, Charles Cross, one of the dwindling number of raid survivors, lamented to Stephen Forbes in 1926 that "there are only a few of us left to tell the tale." Then nearly eighty-nine, Cross had worked for a half-century after the war as a railroad man. Apparently he had not kept a journal or, like Grierson, attempted to complete an autobiography. "Whenever" he felt "like reminis[c]ing" he reread Forbes's 1907 essay. "I[t] sure is a *literary gem,* and it reflects my case, *exactly!*" he wrote to his old comrade in B Company.[28] In one sense Cross was wrong; his experience could not be identical to Forbes's. But in another he was probably all too correct. Most of what he remembered came from Forbes as other memories were crowded out or lost. Forbes's essay became for Cross what Surby's account had been for Grierson and no doubt others: a mnemonic device for subconscious learning, a means to create an idealized memory, not simply to recall an actual event. As the historian David Thelen cautioned when discussing history and memory: "The ways that people depend on others to shape their recollections thus create an apparent paradox. People refashion the past to please the people with whom they discuss and interpret it, but they also depend on the accuracy of accounts by others to gain confidence in the accuracy of their own memories. That paradox may explain why people reshape their memories even as they often insist that their memories are vivid, unchanging, accurate."[29]

When we return to the question of who first thought of the raid or who first came up with the idea for the Butternut Guerillas we could say that all those who claimed to know were probably part right and part wrong. Grant, Hurlbut, Sooy Smith, and Grierson had all been involved in planning the raid. Who proposed what is impossible to establish now; it may have been impossible then too, with each man having his own understanding of how decisions were made and his role in that decision making.[30] Likewise for the forming of the Butternut Guerillas. No wonder Simon Schama has decided that, as a historian, he is "left forever chasing shadows."[31]

For some historians, films and historical fiction only make their quarry more elusive. Others are not so sure. Disputes over the historical value of the films *Titanic* and *Amistad* are only the most recent manifestations of an interminable debate. *Titanic* dramatized the sinking of that supposedly unsinkable ocean liner in 1912; *Amistad* dramatized the slave takeover of a vessel off Cuba in 1839, with the subsequent legal issues raised when those slaves were brought ashore in the United States. Like *The Horse Soldiers* nearly forty years before, these films were marketed as being both educational and entertaining. The critical response was likewise reminiscent of that earlier film: some accepted the pairing, some did not. The five million dollars that John Ford spent on his movie seems a pittance compared with the hundreds of millions that director James Cameron invested in *Titanic*. Still, the underlying rationale was the same: start with a dramatic historical event, create fictional characters, add plot twists, sign a major star or two, spend a lot in production, and the audience—if all works as planned—will be lured to the theater. Cameron's gamble paid off better than Ford's, however, and *Titanic* became the first film to gross over one billion dollars.

Amistad did not do as well at the box office, but director Stephen Spielberg did not lose money on it. And if anything, his film provoked even more controversy because Spielberg pushed the historical value and the authenticity of his film even more vigorously than did Cameron.[32] Both could claim that they did research and that they had to choose between conflicting accounts, just as historians do. Cameron had a ship's officer shoot himself, and he depicted musicians playing "Nearer My God to Thee" as the ship plunged into its death throes. Both choices are justifiable on the basis of documentary "evidence," though the "facts" in either case continue to be hotly contested. Screen writers for Spielberg and Cameron invented characters and put words into the mouths of historical figures, not unlike what Mahin and Ford did with Wayne as Marlowe and Stan Jones as Ulysses Grant. Viewers of *Amistad* and *Titanic* therefore run the same risks as those who went to see *The Horse Soldiers*. They might not be able to tell what is history and what is Hollywood. The John Quincy Adams created by actor Anthony Hopkins in *Amistad* swallows the real John Quincy Adams. Benjamin Henry Grierson, it could be contended, suffered an even worse fate, swallowed by Harold Sinclair's John Francis Marlowe, who was in turn swallowed by John Wayne.

Cameron used the *Titanic*'s sinking as a setting for a love story between two wholly fictitious characters, as indeed Grierson's raid had been reduced by Mahin and Ford to a backdrop for the fictitious love story between a Yankee colonel and a Southern belle. Mahin and Rackin nevertheless assured readers of *Civil War History* that they had not done violence to the past. James Cameron echoed them when he talked about his film. "To the best of our knowledge there was no violation of historical truth," he claimed. "We have a great responsibility. Whatever we make will become the truth, the visual reality that a generation will accept."[33]

Cameron may well be right. His version of the past could prevail because films compete very successfully with history books in the marketplace, where memory is bought and sold.[34] As C. Vann Woodward observed, historians must vie with purveyors of popular culture to define an ever-receding past. Often enough it is a competition they lose to the makers of films and television programs. "It is from them more than from historians that the public mainly receives whatever conceptions, impressions, fantasies, and delusions it may entertain about the past," Woodward concluded rather joylessly.[35] That the *American Historical Review* and the *Journal of American History* now have movie review sections is testament to the power of so-called Hollywood history.[36]

Filmmaker Ken Burns, whose PBS documentary on the Civil War first aired in 1990 and enjoyed unparalleled success, is convinced that historians have only themselves to blame if people choose not to read their books. The public appetite for the past is enormous, he contends, but the "academy" is "murdering our history" with tedious, colorless studies. He was not arguing that film is an inherently superior medium for exploring the past, though it can use sight and sound and stimulate the senses in ways the written word cannot. There are bad films just as there are bad books. A good film, like a good book, taps into our deeper emotions, searching for transcendent truths about the human condition. Furthermore, Burns stresses, films can turn people toward, not away from, books. The experience of the author Shelby Foote is proof of his contention. Foote, who worked closely with Burns on his film documentary and appears on-screen as a commentator, wrote a Civil War trilogy that sold well but did not make him wealthy until *after* the documentary aired. In the fifteen years the books were in print before then, thirty thousand copies had been sold. In the six months following, one hundred thousand sets were snatched up by an eager viewing *and* reading audience.[37]

Burns's achievement, though remarkable for a documentary, pales in comparison with the lasting impact of *Gone with the Wind,* David O. Selznick's 1939 screen adaptation of Margaret Mitchell's novel. Mitchell enjoyed brisk sales when *Gone with the Wind* went out to bookstores in 1936, with nearly two hundred thousand copies purchased the first year. A Pulitzer Prize capped the critical acclaim. Then came Clark Gable as Rhett Butler and Vivian Leigh as Scartlett O'Hara on the silver screen, and sales of Mitchell's book increased tenfold following the movie's release. To this day Civil War historians write in Mitchell's shadow.

Mitchell's dominance is hardly unique. Historians in other fields have also struggled to hold their place against the tide of historical fiction on film and in print. "Far more than any professional historian," comments Peter Saccio, "and despite the fact that the professionals have improved upon him in historical accuracy, Shakespeare is responsible for whatever notions most of us possess" of dynastic politics in fifteenth-century England.[38] Doubters need only ask any revisionist historian who has tried to recast Richard III in a more favorable light. Shakespeare's appeal is undiminished, and well over one hundred Shakespeare festivals are held around this country alone each year. The "histories" are as popular as the comedies and tragedies. And the Bard's power carries from text to stage to screen; witness the renewed interest in Shakespeare films sparked by actor/director Kenneth Branagh, then stoked by the Oscar-winning *Shakespeare in Love.*

In an interview with the historian Eric Foner, the filmmaker John Sayles said that "you have to remember that things tend to show up in movies about third." First come historians, "who start working on something and take a look at the record. Their work usually stimulates novelists, and novelists often stimulate movie people."[39] He added that historical subjects could end up on television by the same developmental route. Sayles was not saying that there is some sort of lock-step progression to all of this. Indeed, the order could be reversed. Historians might turn their attention to a subject because of a novel they read or film they saw. Rather than think in terms of linear progression, we ought to see history, fiction, and film as caught in a circular process. There are indeed times when the novel comes directly from the historical work and the film from the novel. John Lee Mahin and Martin Rackin's decision to do *The Horse Soldiers* is an example of the latter: they read Harold Sinclair's book and were inspired to do a film version of it. But Harold Sinclair had apparently not turned to Grierson because he read Dee Brown's historical account. Rather, he arrived at the same point as Brown, but by a different path. And both writers would see their books receive a new literary lease on life, Sinclair when a paperback edition was timed for a simultaneous release with the film, Brown when the popularity of his *Bury My Heart at Wounded Knee* led to the reissue of several of his earlier books, including a new paperback edition of *Grierson's Raid*. In each case the paperback came as a spin-off.[40] That one was the result of a movie, the other a book, is less important than the sameness of the process, as success with one product was turned to try to promote success with another.

Dee Brown watched *The Horse Soldiers* when it was first released and enjoyed it. "I like almost everything John Ford did," Brown confirmed; "he was not pretentious." Nonetheless, Brown would have preferred it if "the script writers had simply followed the historical events."[41] Bill Weber, who struggled so long to change the remembered past in Newton, was disappointed that, at the very least, the film credits did not say something about Brown's book as well as Sinclair's. Whether *The Horse Soldiers* would have been a better film had it stuck closer to the historical record is a moot point.[42]

No doubt there are problems with both fiction and film as history. Someone who reads only Sinclair's book or watches Ford's film to learn about Grierson's raid is half-informed at best. For the novel reader, John Francis Marlowe is probably more real than Benjamin Henry Grierson; for the filmgoer, John Wayne *is* Marlowe. The filmgoer or novel reader who does not care to find out about the actual event, and therefore does not recognize when dramatic license was exercised, can inadvertently become the embodiment of Alexander Pope's dictum about "a *little Learning*" being a "dang'rous Thing."[43] But the danger of a misunderstood past—real enough in all of this—can await the uncritical reader of history books as well. Accuracy and fair-mindedness are not assured simply because certain scholarly conventions were followed.[44]

Rather than bemoan the popularity of films and the preference of many readers for historical fiction over history, we might recall Herbert Butterfield's optimism. Butterfield thought that it would be "splendid" if

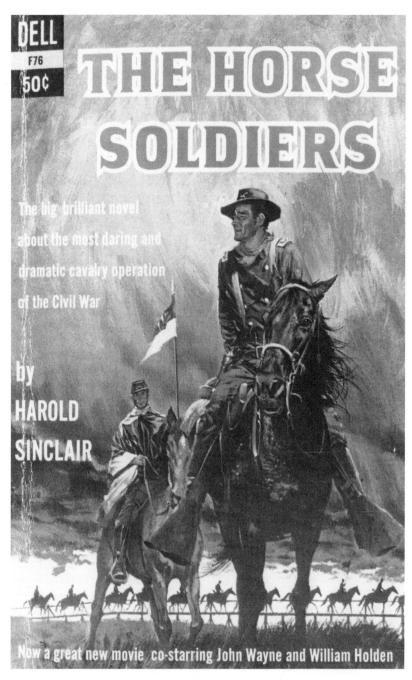

DELL
F76
50¢

THE HORSE SOLDIERS

The big, brilliant novel about the most daring and dramatic cavalry operation of the Civil War

by

HAROLD SINCLAIR

Now a great new movie, co-starring John Wayne and William Holden

The front cover to the American paperback edition.
Courtesy of Dell Books, Random House.

the historical novel drove "readers to the history-book."[45] His was not a hopelessly naive dream. Odds are that Margaret Mitchell stimulated an interest in the Civil War among some of her readers that did indeed turn them toward history. The same could be said of films. Not only did *Amistad* and *Titanic* bring the reissue of out-of-print titles, but there was even coordination of a sort, with publishers—including a university press— marketing their books to cash in on renewed public interest *because* of the films.[46] True, that interest proved fickle and faddish and peaked early as the public moved on to something else. Even so, no matter how fleeting, the interest is undeniable. Films and novels have become an unavoidable, perhaps indispensable, part of the continuous process of historical reinterpretation. *Gone with the Wind* and, more modestly, *The Horse Soldiers,* in both their textual and filmic incarnations, piqued a renewed curiosity about the past. Admittedly, the films and the novels that inspired them replaced old myths with new ones and slipped in new pieces of misinformation even as old, discredited bits were excised. But, again, that happens with historical works as well.

There is, of course, the ever-present danger of politicizing the past. Novelists and filmmakers are not alone here. Historians can have the same tendencies. What one might consider an evenhanded attempt to better inform, another might condemn as an effort to propagandize. Michael Kammen has noted that our national memory tends to be selective, formed all too often for patriotic purposes, and historians have historically been as involved in such efforts as novelists and filmmakers. "The writing of history is commonly affected, even driven by a sense of moral mission or by ideology," he argued persuasively.[47] Recall that the Civil War Centennial Commission was determined to make Americans proud of their past, in part so that they could be ready to defeat Communism. The scholars who sat as commission members understood and implicitly accepted that didactic intent. But then they were hardly unique in wanting to defend heritage as well as promote history. Margaret Mead's classic study of the American character, *And Keep Your Powder Dry,* had been unapologetic in its prescriptive purposes. Mead intended it to be an anthropologist's inquiry into national character formation; she also wrote it so that Americans during World War II would know who they were so they could understand what they were fighting against.[48]

Patriotism, broadly construed, does not refer to just the beliefs of flag-waving traditionalists. Revisionism can be a form of patriotism too, if the aim is to create a substitute image of what the nation should be or should

historians bias in selection

have been all along. Furthermore, even if most historians do not preach their gospel as avowedly as novelists or moviemakers, their interest in certain personality types or behaviors leads them to some people and not others, to some subjects to the exclusion of others, and, consciously or not, to the promotion of some characteristics and condemnation of others. Dee Brown had been as intrigued by the concepts of duty and honor as were Harold Sinclair and John Ford, and Grierson's raid appealed to the sense of adventure in each of them. Highlighting duty and honor helped to perpetuate both attributes, and the general public received reaffirmation of traditional virtues from three different sources.

Sinclair and Ford's trafficking in these symbols was intentional, Brown's perhaps less so. And yet even if the didactic content of Brown's history was less intentional than Sinclair's novel and Ford's film, the message is the same. All of them underscore shared values. Together they serve as a

myth & history

reminder that the mythical and the historical do not necessarily work at cross-purposes. That should not be surprising. The flourishing of Christianity in the Western world not only proves that the spiritual and material can coexist but also that seeming opposites can be reconciled, can even be made mutually reinforcing. Moreover, the interests that linked Brown, Sinclair, and Ford show the persistence of desires to create a morally usable past, desires that reflect a continued attachment to Bolingbroke's dictum

moralize

that history is "philosophy teaching by examples."[49] Perhaps we will never abandon that Plutarchian tendency to moralize, to search the past for archetypes whose lessons are carried into the present.

John Ford, the moviemaker as moralist, taught obvious lessons in his story. His John Marlowe and Hannah Hunter embody the spirit of reconciliation. Their personal tale became a model to emulate, instructing the audience in how it should view the Civil War past and chivalrous codes less locked in time. The point is clear: there are eternal verities of duty and honor, of honesty and integrity; and, though good men and women will disagree, they can learn to respect those differences. They can learn too that even if love does not conquer all, it is hate that poisons. Harold Sinclair's romance between Marlowe and Madame Didier dabbles in the same themes. For both the filmmaker and the novelist there were commonalities, at once universal and national, that could be rediscovered so that American society—albeit a better society freed of slavery—would be reunited. This as the primary lesson to be learned was no mere fictional contrivance. Benjamin Henry Grierson, real soldier in a real war, had sought signs of unionism, hints that there existed a reconciliationist foundation to rebuild on, even as he rode the length of Mississippi on a

Grierson family grave marker in the east cemetery of Jacksonville, Illinois. To the south, far beyond the horizon: Mississippi. Photograph by the author.

mission to tear down and destroy. He subsequently wrote his autobiography for prescriptive purposes, to communicate a message similar to those someday sent by Harold Sinclair and John Ford and even to some extent by Dee Brown.

Grierson had been respected in his lifetime as an exemplar of still-admired traits. Grierson himself will probably continue to drift in and out of our consciousness. Joshua Chamberlain, colonel of the 20th Maine regiment at Gettysburg, has had a similar experience. He was first pulled from relative obscurity in Michael Shaara's Pulitzer Prize–winning novel, *The Killer Angels,* as the hero of Little Round Top.[50] The film *Gettysburg* furthered his reputation, and the soft-spoken former college professor became a heroic figure. What brings Chamberlain, Grierson, and others like them back to living memory is the persistence of our attachment to certain notions of duty and honor.

Moreover, we are drawn to those who do not pursue fame, self-effacing men and women whose modesty makes them just that much more appealing. Here again Benjamin Henry Grierson and his fictional stand-in John Francis Marlowe fit our expectations of how a hero should behave. Grierson had been feted in his adopted hometown of Jacksonville, Illinois, as a local hero in October 1863 because of his successful raid, but he did not seek the acclaim.[51] After the war he did not spend much time in the family home. Having chosen to become a career army officer, he was posted in Texas, where he commanded the 10th Cavalry, one of two black cavalry regiments on western duty. He did not pursue fame there either and had nothing but disdain for the glory-seeking of a George Armstrong Custer. A revival of interest in Grierson a few years ago was more because of his service with the 10th Cavalry than for his Civil War accomplishments. Jacksonville even celebrates annual "Grierson Days," though the man for whom the festivities are named is but a hazy figure to most residents. An obelisk marking his grave in the cemetery on the east end of town has been repaired, not replaced, with the top that had been broken from the base being reset within a metal frame. Still, the inscriptions are so worn that they are difficult to read. Grierson is interred with nine other family members, including his parents and his wife, Alice. The grave marker says nothing about the Yankee raider's military service. Another, smaller marker of more recent vintage a few yards away that notes his military service is in much better shape. The contrast between the two is a reminder of the illusive permanence that gravestones are intended to create. Whether the old family marker will ever be replaced and whether the newer marker for Grierson alone will be better maintained depends on how well Grierson is preserved in memory. Grierson himself made no effort to be remembered as a war hero and carried his modesty to the grave, but then he had waged war to bring peace. Even as he fought, he hoped that North and South would be reconciled, reunited spiritually as well as physically.

Henry Forbes's sentiments mirrored those of his old commander. Many years after the war had ended he wrote an account of his part in the raid, closing, "And so, let it all pass. The past is past. We, who survive, can look back to the old times of struggle and victory and feel we were engirt with noble friends and confronted worthy foes."[52] In 1905, Stephen Forbes, veteran trooper and respected entomologist, echoed his brother Henry. Asked to speak in remembrance of those who fought and died to preserve the Union and end slavery, he honored the soldiers of both armies. The men he served alongside had enlisted bravely "and they were fortunate that the enemies whom they were called upon to face were manly men, much like themselves. . . . Both sides fought unselfishly in the main, partriotically [sic] as each thought, for what each believed to be a national cause."[53]

When Stephen Forbes died in 1930, his family, friends, and colleagues at the University of Illinois gathered to eulogize him. Those who spoke mentioned his wartime service in passing—that he had risen from private to captain, that he had once been a prisoner of war, but not that he had been on Grierson's raid and that he, his brother, and a handful of others rode alone behind enemy lines for five days. He was remembered primarily as a scientist, not as a soldier, which was no doubt the way he wanted it. And the most interesting anecdote that could be told about him was that he loved to drive an automobile and on his eightieth birthday he was, to his glee, given a ticket for speeding.[54]

In a nation whose wartime armies have been composed mostly of citizen-soldiers and whose pride in battlefield prowess is matched by suspicions of a professional military caste, the appeal of a Stephen Forbes runs deep. He and his brother Henry, like Benjamin Henry Grierson, were the consummate volunteers, men who served because they believed in duty and honor.[55] True, much has changed in American life since the Civil War; much has changed even in the years since *The Horse Soldiers*. But not all. The disillusionment accentuated by a failed crusade in Southeast Asia only temporarily dampened national faith in the good man fighting the good war. No doubt new Benjamin Griersons will be discovered and rediscovered, invented and reinvented, as the popularity of Stephen Spielberg's recent film *Saving Private Ryan* suggests. Spielberg built on what many others before him had done and anticipated what others coming after him will continue to do, as each generation finds its own heroes.[56] In the 1950s Grierson was rediscovered because he embodied tendencies that Dee Brown, Harold Sinclair, John Lee Mahin, and John Ford found appealing, values that were in turn passed on to others and once again renewed—in two books and a movie. Those values are with us still.

Serendipity played a part in the rediscovery of Grierson's raid over forty years ago. So too with me more recently. This book began with a trip to a video store. It seems only fitting that it should end with another chance encounter. Visiting my parents just as I was about to finish writing, my wife and I went through old family photograph albums. Questions about this and that prompted my mother to dig a typescript out of a box. It told the story of her great-grandfather John Jacob Kerby, who was born in Pennsylvania in 1840 and ran away from home when he was ten. He worked his way west and was living in Iowa when war erupted in 1861. Like thousands of other young men his age, he volunteered for military service. He fought for four long years—as a private in L Company of the 2d Iowa Cavalry, under Colonel Edward Hatch.[57] Sometimes it really is a small world.

NOTES

PREFACE

1. Peter Stone and Sherman Edwards, *1776: A Musical Play* (New York: Viking Press, 1970), 153.

2. Robert Penn Warren, *The Legacy of the Civil War* (New York: Random House, 1961), 3.

1. THE INSPIRATION: GRIERSON'S RAID

1. U. S. Grant, *Personal Memoirs* (New York: Charles L. Webster, 1894), 250.

2. Sylvanus Cadwallader, *Three Years with Grant* (New York: Knopf, 1955), 38. Also see H. M. Byers, *With Fire and Sword* (New York: Neale, 1911), 40–42; and the account written years later by one of Van Dorn's men in James W. Silver, ed., *Mississippi in the Confederacy as Seen in Retrospect* (Baton Rouge: Louisiana State Univ. Press, 1961), 63–67.

3. Sherman to his wife from a letter of Apr. 10, 1863, in M. A. DeWolfe Howe, ed., *Home Letters of General Sherman* (New York: Charles Scribner's Sons, 1909), 247.

4. From Johnston's report to Jefferson Davis on Dec. 24, 1863, in *The War of the Rebellion: A Compilation of the Official Records of the Union and Confederate Armies*, 128 vols. (Washington, D.C.: GPO, 1880–1901), ser. 1, vol. 24, 1:247 (hereafter cited as *OR*). On April 17, the day that Grierson set out from La Grange, Pemberton repeated his plea to Johnston for more cavalry to protect northern Mississippi—see Pemberton to Johnston, Apr. 17, 1863, *OR*, vol. 24, 3:752.

5. Grierson's activities between January and April 1863 are summarized in reports printed in *OR*, vol. 24, part 1. Sherman's recommendation and reference to "Grierson's Cavalry" are in a letter of February 9, 1863, to the secretary of war, which Grierson included in his unpublished autobiography, "The Lights and Shadows of Life" (1892), 258, Benjamin H. Grierson Papers, Illinois State Historical Library, box 21 (also available on microfilm).

6. Grant to Hurlbut, Feb. 13, 1863, *OR*, vol. 24, 3:50.

7. Hamilton to Hurlbut, Feb. 12, 1863, ibid., 45. Also see Hamilton to Hurlbut, Mar. 12, 1863, ibid., 103–4.

8. Grierson, "Lights and Shadows," 267.

9. Ibid., 288; also R. W. Surby, *Grierson Raids, and Hatch's Sixty-four Days March, with Biographical Sketches, also The Life and Adventures of Chickasaw, the Scout* (Chicago: Rounds and James, 1865), 21. In 1883 Surby reworked his tale, expanding here, con-

tracting there, and had it serialized in the *National Tribune,* a veterans' weekly, for eleven installments, July 12 through September 20, 1883. That version was later combined with an account of John Hunt Morgan's 1863 raid across the Ohio River as *Two Great Raids* (Washington, D.C.: National Tribune, 1897). Whereas in *Grierson Raids,* 20, Surby said that the 2d Iowa had "between six and seven hundred men, rank and file," the 6th Illinois "about five hundred men," and the 7th Illinois "five hundred and forty-two," in the later account (*National Tribune,* July 12, 1883, 1; *Two Great Raids,* 6) he listed the 2d Iowa (more precisely) at 650, the 6th at 500—with the "about" dropped—and the 7th rounded off at 500. Such small differences, taken individually, mean little, but when it is remembered that dozens of these exist, they are a reminder of the caution necessary in retelling the "facts" of the case.

10. Surby, *Grierson Raids,* noted the rations (20) and ammunition (103), but doubled the amount in his revised version printed in *Two Great Raids,* 6. Stephen Forbes, "Grierson's Cavalry Raid," *Transactions of the Illinois State Historical Society* 12 (1907): 199–230, gave the same amount as Surby's original account (on 102). His brother Henry also mentioned the forty rounds of ammunition for each trooper in an unpublished typescript, "Grierson's Raid: An Epic of the Civil War," Stephen Alfred Forbes Collection, 4 D 2.3, Illinois Historical Survey, Univ. of Illinois Library; also page 5 of an earlier version of the same essay, Ms. 66, Univ. of Arizona Library. Grierson's adjutant, Samuel Woodward, wrote in his essay "Grierson's Raid, April 17th to May 2d, 1863," *Journal of the United States Cavalry Association* 15 (Apr. 1904): 686 that each trooper carried "about a hundred rounds" for his Sharps carbine. My guess is that Surby (in his original account) and the Forbes brothers were right about the forty rounds for the Sharps carbines carried by the Illinoisans and that the only men who may have carried one hundred rounds were those in the first and second battalions of the 2d Iowa equipped with Colt repeaters—for which see Lyman B. Pierce, *History of the Second Iowa Cavalry* (Burlington: Hawk-eye Steam Book and Job Printing, 1865), preface. There is nothing unusual about gaps and contradictions in the historical record here, though historians do not always tell readers when they choose one source over another or fill in a blank space with their own inference. Thus what readers might pass over quickly as a simple statement of "fact" is not so simple after all.

11. Hurlbut to John Rawlins, of Grant's staff, Apr. 17, 1863, *OR,* vol. 24, 3:202.

12. Woodward, "Grierson's Raid," 685.

13. Hurlbut to Rawlins, Apr. 17, 1863, *OR,* vol. 24, 3:202.

14. Grierson's official report of May 5, 1863, *OR,* vol. 24, 1:522.

15. Grierson, "Lights and Shadows," 294.

16. See Hatch's report of Apr. 27, 1863 in *OR,* vol. 24, 1:529–31; and Pierce, *History of the Second Iowa,* 47–56.

17. Forbes, "Grierson's Raid," 12.

18. Surby, *Grierson Raids,* 29–30; Surby, *Two Great Raids,* 7–8; and Grierson, "Lights and Shadows," 299–300.

19. See Grierson's official report in *OR,* vol. 24, 1:524–25; his recollections in "Lights and Shadows," 306–9; Surby, *Grierson Raids,* 45–49; and Surby, *Two Great Raids,* 17–20.

20. Grierson, "Lights and Shadows," 310.

21. Hurlbut to Rawlins, Apr. 28, 1863, *OR,* vol. 24, 3:246; and Hurlbut to Halleck, Apr. 27, 1863, ibid., 247. Pierce, *History of the Second Iowa,* 56–58, commented on his regiment's return to northern Mississippi but said nothing about this movement being timed to assist Grierson, who presumably was returning that way. In part, that was because Pierce

was an enlisted man and may not have known anything about Hurlbut's orders, but in part it was the result of his not feeling a special attachment to the 6th and 7th Illinois. Indeed, one could not tell from reading his account that the 2d Iowa had been brigaded with the Illinoisans for several months. Pierce looked to Edward Hatch, not Benjamin Grierson, for leadership.

22. Grierson, "Lights and Shadows," 312–13, which essentially restates what Grierson filed in his report of May 5, 1863, *OR*, vol. 24, 1:525–26.

23. Grierson, "Lights and Shadows," 312, identifies the scout as [George] Steadman; Surby, *Grierson Raids*, 59–61, said it was Samuel Nelson, the former of C Company, the latter of G Company, both of the 7th Illinois. He is not identified in Grierson's official report on May 5 (note 22).

24. Grierson, "Lights and Shadows," 316.

25. Surby, *Grierson Raids*, 67–70, has the most detail; Grierson, "Lights and Shadows," 319–20 adds little to the official report.

26. Grierson, "Lights and Shadows," 321.

27. This map is not among those preserved in Grierson's papers at the Illinois State Historical Library (box 9, folder 6), though there is one hand-drawn rendering of northeastern Mississippi from New Albany down to Okolona. "Colton's pocket map of Mississippi, which though small was very correct, was all I had to guide me," Grierson reminisced in "Lights and Shadows," 343. Presumably, it was a foldable map in the series done by J. H. Colton of New York City rather than one of his pocket guides, which gave mileage distances between some towns but did not include maps. Colton did a Mississippi map in 1856 that was fairly detailed, showing all of the counties, most of the towns, and the rail lines—the Southern running east from Jackson, but without locating Newton Station; the north-south–running Mobile and Ohio; and, to the west, the north-south–running New Orleans, Jackson and Great Northern. Major rivers, most notably the Pearl, are also included, but no roads or mileage distances are shown. Grierson had no doubt seen many maps, though he found it difficult to have maps made for his own use. See his letter to his wife of February 3, 1863, complaining of this in his "Autobiography" (1863), 174, Illinois State Historical Library, almost all of which was later incorporated into his "Lights and Shadows."

28. Grierson, "Lights and Shadows," 322.

29. Surby, *Grierson Raids*, 103.

30. Grierson, "Lights and Shadows," 329.

31. Ibid., 330–32; also Surby, *Grierson Raids*, 103–14.

32. Grierson, "Lights and Shadows," 333–35.

33. Ibid., 338.

34. Ibid., 338–42, quotations from 341, 342.

35. Henry Forbes to his sister Flavilla, May 23, 1863, in the typescript prepared by Forbes's niece (brother Stephen's daughter) Ethel Forbes Scott in 1936 as the "Forbes Family Letters," 217–18, Illinois Historical Survey, Univ. of Illinois Library.

36. Grierson, official report of May 5, 1863, *OR*, vol. 24, 1:528. Grierson said two remained behind at the Tickfaw; Surby, *Grierson Raids*, 112, said it was three and named them.

37. Edward Fontaine, diary entry of Apr. 24, 1863, as taken from John K. Bettersworth, ed., *Mississippi in the Confederacy as They Saw It* (Baton Rouge: Louisiana State Univ. Press, 1961), 112.

38. Adams to Pemberton, May 5, 1863, *OR*, vol. 24, 1:533.

39. Richardson to Pemberton, May 3, 1863, ibid., 550.

40. Hurlbut to Col. J. C. Kelton, May 5, 1863, ibid., 521. Still, the raid very quickly lost its significance in the grand scheme of things. When Hurlbut wrote to Abraham Lincoln just three weeks after the raid ended, he said nothing about Grierson in his review of events beginning with a landing at Bruinsburg on April 30 and victory at Champion's Hill on May 16 leading to Grant's siege of Vicksburg. Thus a letter from one Illinoisan to another let slip an opportunity to tout yet another Illinoisan. See Hurlbut to Lincoln, May 22, 1863, in Roy Basler, ed., *The Collected Works of Abraham Lincoln*, 9 vols. (New Brunswick: Rutgers Univ. Press, 1953–55), 6:226.

41. Banks to Henry Halleck, May 31, 1863, *OR*, vol. 24, 3:367. For Dee Brown's misattribution of this comment to Sherman, see below, chapter 6, n. 16.

42. Grant to Porter, May 1, 1863, in John Y. Simon, ed., *The Papers of Ulysses S. Grant*, 20 vols. (Carbondale: Southern Illinois Univ. Press, 1967–), 8:139.

43. Grant to Halleck, May 3, 1863, *OR*, vol. 24, 1:33, 34. In his final Vicksburg campaign report of July 6, 1863, Grant concluded that the raid "has been one of the most brilliant cavalry exploits of the war, and will be handed down in history as an example to be imitated" (ibid., 58). Also see Grant, *Personal Memoirs*, 289.

44. Halleck to Stanton, Nov. 15, 1863, *OR*, vol. 24, 1:5.

45. Grierson, "Lights and Shadows," 356. George H. Hepworth, serving with the Union forces trying to push north out of Baton Rouge, also believed that the South was "an empty shell." See his *The Whip, Hoe and Sword; The Gulf Department in '63* (Boston: Walker, Wise, 1864), 285–86.

46. *Macon [Ga.] Daily Telegraph*, May 5, 1863, as reported from Jackson, Miss. Getting reliable information from Mississippi was difficult, and this Georgia paper repeated rumors (on April 22) that there were three Yankee columns in northern Mississippi of twenty-five thousand men each, reduced (on April 28) to twenty-five hundred men in each of three columns. Accurate reporting in the Confederate press outside Mississippi did not come until after the fact. Mississippi newspapers caught on sooner and were printing reasonably accurate information about Grierson's troop strength by April 28—after the raiders left Newton Station but well before they were safely within Union lines at Baton Rouge. Still, the publishers of those papers continued to think that Grierson would be caught. See, for example, the *Natchez Daily Courier*, April 28, 1863–May 5, 1863, this last issue reporting that the Yankees "have already received some punishment" and "there is yet some hope of all of them being taken or destroyed." When, by the May 7 issue, it was finally realized that the raiders had escaped, the paper consoled itself that "their motions have been too rapid to commit very extensive depredation."

47. *Macon [Ga.] Daily Telegraph*, May 7, 1863.

48. *New York Times*, May 18, 1863, 1, with earlier notices on May 4 (p. 1), May 6 (p. 1), May 10 (p. 4), and May 11, claiming in the last (on p. 4) that the Confederacy was doomed once its "present armies" were defeated because then "its backbone will be very effectively broken." Also see the *New York Herald*, May 18, 1863, 1–2; and *Frank Leslie's Illustrated Newspaper*, June 6, 1863, 1–2, a story written around an engraved portrait of Grierson.

49. Robert Selph Henry, *"First With the Most": Forrest* (Jackson, Tenn.: McCowat-Mercer Press, 1944), 139–59, dispatched Streight as handily on paper as Forrest bested him in the field.

50. All of this is reviewed in Virgil Carrington Jones, *Eight Hours Before Richmond* (New York: Henry Holt, 1957).

51. See James Pickett Jones, *Yankee Blitzkrieg* (Athens: Univ. of Georgia Press, 1976).

52. For Morgan, see James A. Ramage, *Rebel Raider* (Lexington: Univ. Press of Kentucky, 1986); and Dee Alexander Brown, *The Bold Cavaliers* (Philadelphia: J. B. Lippincott, 1958).

53. Edwin C. Bearss, "Grierson's Winter Raid on the Mobile and Ohio Railroad," *Military Affairs* 24 (1960): 20–37.

54. John S. C. Abbott, "Heroic Deeds of Heroic Men," *Harper's New Monthly Magazine* 30 (Feb. 1865): 273–81; quotation from 273.

55. Francis Grierson, *The Valley of Shadows* (New York: John Lane, 1913), 221.

2. THE STORY AS HISTORY

1. Anne Courtemanche-Ellis, "Meet Dee Brown: Author, Teacher, Librarian," *Wilson Library Bulletin* 52 (Mar. 1978): 553.

2. Robert Dahlin, "PW Interviews: Dee Brown," *Publishers Weekly* 217 (Mar. 1980): 14.

3. Dee Brown, *When the Century Was Young* (Little Rock: August House Publishers, 1993), 189. Paul Andrew Hutton drew on this autobiographical account and added his own insights for an introduction to the reissue of Brown's novel about Davy Crockett, *Wave High the Banner* (Albuquerque: Univ. of New Mexico Press, 1999), first published in 1942.

4. Dee Brown, *The Galvanized Yankees* (Urbana: Univ. of Illinois Press, 1963).

5. Dee Brown, from his foreword to Stan Banash, ed., *Dee Brown's Civil War Anthology* (Santa Fe: Clear Light Publishers, 1998), x.

6. Brown, *When the Century Was Young*, 189.

7. D. Alexander Brown, *Grierson's Raid* (Urbana: Univ. of Illinois Press, 1954), which went through a second printing within months. Brown also told the story more briefly under the same title for a general audience in *Civil War Times Illustrated* 3 (Jan. 1965):4–11, 25–32. His book continues to stand as the most authoritative account of the raid. Virtually everyone who has studied it since cites Brown, from the overviews in Stephen Z. Starr's *The Union Cavalry in the Civil War*, 3 vols. (Baton Rouge: Louisiana State Univ. Press, 1979–85), 3:180–204, and Edwin Cole Bearss, *The Campaign for Vicksburg*, 3 vols. (Dayton: Morningside House, 1985–86), 2:187–236, to Grierson's biographers Bruce J. Dinges, "The Making of a Cavalryman: Benjamin H. Grierson and the Civil War Along the Mississippi, 1861–1865" (Ph.D. dissertation, Rice University, 1978), with a spin-off piece, "Grierson's Raid" *Civil War Times* 34 (Feb. 1996): 50–64; and William H. Leckie and Shirley A. Leckie, *Unlikely Warriors: General Benjamin H. Grierson and His Family* (Norman: Univ. of Oklahoma Press, 1984). Dave Roth, "Grierson's Raid, April 17–May 2, 1863: A Cavalry Raid at Its Best," *Blue & Gray Magazine* 10 (June 1993): 12–24, 48–65, offers a spirited retelling, and on pages 25–27 Roth provides a guide to Grierson's route, though, he admits, much has been "lost to history."

8. Surby, *Grierson Raids*, from the testimonials in the front of the book.

9. Brown, *Grierson's Raid*, 5. Hereafter page numbers are cited in text.

10. Ibid., 106. In *Pemberton: A Biography* (Jackson: Univ. Press of Mississippi, 1991), Michael Ballard paints a similar portrait of a man who became too "tentative, uncertain, and slow to react" (134) with troops "much too scattered among too many unimportant places to be effective" (138).

11. Mississippians did not trust Pemberton, Brown contended. "And although they knew that Pemberton had given up his life's career in the United States Army to join the Confederacy, he was regarded with suspicion. Pemberton might be an ardent believer in states' rights, but he was also a Pennsylvania Yankee, little better than a 'galvanized Confederate'" (35). In a footnote Brown commented that "there were also 'galvanized Yankees' fighting for the North" (35n).

12. Brown's reconstruction of Pemberton's state of mind is based on dispatches for the period covering the raid gathered in *OR*, vol. 24, 3:751–821.

13. Pierce, *History of the Second Iowa*, 50.

14. Brown did not document this particular quotation, possibly because he assumed that readers could find it by going to the previous note, which also dealt with Forbes's party. That note referred readers to page 207 of the collection assembled by Ethel Forbes Scott in the "Forbes Family Letters," Illinois Historical Survey, Univ. of Illinois. The passage cited here is on pages 207–8. Brown altered the wording slightly and gave no hint that some passages had been deleted. Mrs. Scott copied more accurately and did indicate that some passages had been omitted in her excerpts from Henry Forbes's account, "Grierson's Raid," Stephen Alfred Forbes Collection, 4 D. 2.3, also in the Illinois Historical Survey.

15. Brown is quoting again from Mrs. Scott's "Forbes Family Letters," in this case on page 208, which Mrs. Scott had excerpted from Henry Forbes's "Grierson's Raid," 15.

16. As taken from page 208 of Mrs. Scott's account, which in turn had come from Henry Forbes's "Grierson's Raid," 17.

17. Brown adapted this from Forbes's recollections as copied into Mrs. Scott's "Forbes Family Letters," 208–9, which, in turn had come from Henry Forbes, "Grierson's Raid," 18–19. Stephen Forbes, "Grierson's Cavalry Raid," 111, worked from Henry's account. The younger Forbes saw but did not hear the exchange between his brother and the Confederates. Brown's passage *"My informants were either lying or mistaken,"* Captain Forbes was thinking. *"This town is garrisoned,"* which is not in the documents though it could be logically inferred, is the sort of invention that many historians find objectionable, especially when the insertion is made with no warning to the reader.

18. Brown's depiction of a "grinning" Grierson is yet another inference—reasonable enough, perhaps, given the circumstances, and yet too much for historians worried about authors who make too many inferential leaps. Forbes, "Grierson's Cavalry Raid," 113–14, is silent on the matter of Grierson's facial expression. So is Grierson's own "Lights and Shadows," 317–19, where Grierson praised Henry Forbes but said nothing about the somewhat cheeky greeting supposedly delivered by Henry's brother Stephen, which Stephen said he spoke in obedience to his brother's orders.

19. Taken from Scott, "Forbes Family Letters," 212, with Brown italicizing a passage for emphasis. Scott copied from Henry Forbes, "Grierson's Raid," 22–23 (altered slightly from the earlier version at the Univ. of Arizona, Ms. 66, pp. 24–25); so did her father, Stephen, Henry's brother, in "Grierson's Cavalry Raid," 114.

20. Brown cited Surby's tale as printed in the *National Tribune*, July 12, 1883, 1 (also see *Two Great Raids*, 11), but the long version is actually from Surby's original, *Grierson Raids*, 34.

21. Brown referred readers to both the *National Tribune* piece and *Grierson Raids*, 36–38 (the quotation is from p. 37). Also see *Two Great Raids*, 12–13.

22. Brown adapted his account from Surby, *Grierson Raids*, 67–68, with some embellishments added. Also see *Two Great Raids*, 39. Steadman may well have "lifted his hand in a casual greeting" and quite possibly the sheriff pulled up his horse, "his face flushing in

sudden anger," but those are Brown's words based on his inferences, not Surby's account. So too the precise words Brown put in the mouth of the sheriff. Brown deployed but one endnote (the reference to Surby) to cover virtually everything that happened to the scouts in Hazlehurst.

23. Adapted from Surby, *Grierson Raids,* 68.

24. See Brown, *Grierson's Raid,* 192–203, for the Tickfaw fight at Wall's Bridge; and 201–2, for Surby being left behind, though Brown does not refer to any particular source until later in the text, and even then not to Surby's account in *Grierson Raids,* 104–14, from which he obviously drew. Surby noted his change back into uniform, ibid., 152. Also see *Two Great Raids,* 64–70.

25. Brown's reconstruction based on Grierson's 1863 autobiography.

26. Grierson, "Lights and Shadows," 338–39, records this event. Brown worked from the 1863 autobiography later absorbed within the "Light and Shadows."

27. John K. Bettersworth, professor of history at Mississippi State College, from his piece for the *New York Times Book Review,* Dec. 5, 1954, 26.

28. Robert H. Woody of Duke University for the *American Historical Review* 60 (1954–55): 688.

29. Thomas A. Belser Jr. in *Mississippi Valley Historical Review* 41 (1954–55): 718–19; quotation from 718.

30. One more example should suffice. On page 78 Brown referred (without a citation) to the diary of Henry Eby of Company C, 7th Illinois, to describe what it felt like to sleep on fence rails, which apparently some of Grierson's men had done to avoid lying in the muck left by rain. But then Brown had also commented earlier that Eby was on detached service at the time of the raid and was therefore not with Grierson's column (3).

31. Dee Brown, *Yellowhorse* (Boston: Houghton Mifflin, 1956).

32. D. Alexander Brown, "*A Note About* The Horse Soldiers," in Harold Sinclair, *The Horse Soldiers* (New York: Harper & Brothers, 1956), ix, x. That same year another writer, S. E. Whitman, also fictionalized Grierson's expedition. The jacket of his *Cavalry Raid* (Boston: Houghton Mifflin, 1956) had "Colonel Grierson's fantastic sixteen days" under the title, and Whitman acknowledged his intellectual debt to Brown's "fast-paced documentary" on the copyright page. Unlike Sinclair, he kept Grierson as Grierson. Like Sinclair, he used the raid to weave his own tale, in this case about an embittered Mississippian turned Yankee scout who struggles with his resentments.

33. "I believe as strongly or perhaps even more strongly than I did back in the past when I saluted Sinclair's and Underwood's fictionalized versions of history, that a good historical novel can teach history as well or better than straight history" (Dee Brown to the author, July 5, 1997). Brown had written a foreword to Larry D. Underwood's *The Butternut Guerillas* (1981; rpt. Lincoln: Dageforde Publishing, 1994), v, stating that "although he has introduced dialogue and other devices of fiction," Underwood "has held true to the history of the expedition, giving us a realistic narrrative." Underwood in turn thanked Brown, "who gave me the seed for the book" (preface to the second ed., vii). For a very different reaction to a very different book, see the historian Richard N. Current's "Fiction as History: A Review Essay," *Journal of Southern History* 52 (1986): 77–90. Current's distinction between "*historical fiction,*" which he finds more acceptable than "*fictional history,*" was prompted by Gore Vidal's novel *Lincoln* (New York: Random House, 1984). For an appreciation of how difficult it can be to draw distinctions that are mutually satisfying to historians and novelists, see Vidal's response to Current, included in *United States: Essays,*

1952–1992 (New York: Random House, 1993), 669–700, and the letters from Vidal and Don Fehrenbacher in the *American Historical Review* 96 (1991): 324–28.

3. THE STORY AS NOVEL

1. Sinclair wrote an "Author's Note" to his history *The Daily Pantagraph, 1846–1946* (Bloomington: Evergreen Communications, 1976) in September 1946. The newspaper had commissioned Sinclair, but publication came as part of a bicentennial project, ten years after Sinclair died. This book and *The Port of New Orleans* (Garden City: Doubleday, Doran, 1946) were Sinclair's two published nonfiction works. His history of the Illinois home front during the Civil War never got past the manuscript stage (see n. 26 below).

2. Sinclair is discussed most sensitively and perceptively by his son in the foreword (xv–xx) to a fiftieth-anniversary reissue of *The American Years* (1938; rpt. Urbana: Univ. of Illinois Press, 1988), with an introduction by Robert Bray (xxi–xliv). Bray expanded his comments for "The American Years of Harold Sinclair," *Illinois Historical Journal* 82 (1989): 177–94. In an interview with Eleanor Ann Browns, which she included in "Harold Sinclair and the Technique of the Historical Novel" (M.A. thesis, Univ. of Illinois, 1947), Sinclair at midpoint in his career was candid about his frustrations as a writer.

3. Harold Sinclair, *Journey Home* (New York: Doubleday, Doran, 1936), 290.

4. As quoted by Stanley Kunitz and Howard Haycraft, *Twentieth Century Authors: A Biographical Dictionary of Modern Literature* (New York: H. W. Wilson, 1942), 1292.

5. Bray, "American Years of Harold Sinclair," 180.

6. The trilogy, published by Doubleday, Doran, of New York, appeared as *American Years* (1938), *The Years of Growth* (1940), and *Years of Illusion* (1941).

7. Sinclair, *Years of Illusion*, 2.

8. As Sinclair's hometown newspaper, the *Pantagraph*, Mar. 27, 1939, reported proudly.

9. Ward Sinclair in the foreword to the 1988 reissue of *American Years*, xvii.

10. Sinclair, *American Years*, publisher's blurb inside jacket and as prefatory material in the book itself.

11. Harold Sinclair, *Westward the Tide* (New York: Doubleday, Doran, 1940).

12. See Evan Thomas to Dee Brown, Sept. 29, 1955, and to Harold Sinclair, Sept. 30, 1955, in the Harold Sinclair Collection, Milner Library, Illinois State University.

13. Sinclair to Brown, May 11, 1955, ibid. Brown read the galley proof of *The Horse Soldiers* and told Sinclair in a letter of September 26, 1955 (also ibid.), that his "characterizations of Marlowe, Bryce and Gray make the book, and the occasional deviations from fact in the incidents do not matter much."

14. Sinclair, "Author's Note," *Horse Soldiers*, xi.

15. Harold Sinclair, "The Horse Soldiers," original typescript in the Harold Sinclair Collection, from "A Note to the Reader, Necessary but Brief."

16. Sinclair, "Author's Note," *Horse Soldiers*, xii.

17. Ibid., from the promotional blurb on the jacket flaps. Designer Paul Laune put a mounted officer in the foreground of the jacket front who generally resembled the Marlowe who came from Sinclair's pen. At least Laune did not paint the wild charge used for the jacket art of the London edition.

18. Ibid., 103–6, 200–202, 241–42, 296–99, for the "Pursuit" segments; 150–51 for the newspaper excerpt. (Hereafter page numbers are cited in text.)

19. For Yule, whose "services were very valuable," see Surby, *Grierson Raids,* 112; also *Two Great Raids,* 69. In his autobiographical "Lights and Shadows," 332, Grierson states that a "doctor and nurse were left to take charge of the wounded," and in his official report of May 5, 1863, in *OR,* vol. 24, 1:528, says that the "surgeon of the Seventh Illinois" stayed behind, without noting that Dr. Yule had been reassigned from the 2d Iowa. Grierson may have been guilty of slighting Yule's sacrifice, but if he was, there is no indication that it was because of personal animus.

20. Earl Schenck Miers, "Humility in Command," *Saturday Review* 39 (Feb. 18, 1956): 17.

21. Harnett T. Kane, "Yankee Raiders in Deep Dixie," *New York Times Book Review,* Feb. 18, 1956, 4. Of all Sinclair's books, Kane wrote, "this is the best."

22. So wrote Henry James in his review for the *Library Journal* 81 (Mar. 15, 1956): 726. Gene Smedley, who reviewed the book for the *Pantagraph,* Feb. 22, 23, 1956, Sinclair's hometown newspaper, noted that the story Sinclair told might seem too incredible to be true, but "Historian D. Alexander Brown sets the reader straight on this point in an introductory note to the Bloomington author's engaging story." Sinclair had warned readers "that his book is not history. Still, it brings an historical event alive. If history textbooks read like 'The Horse Soldiers' Johnny might forget the television set."

23. Miers, "Humility in Command," 17. Sinclair could have been just as pleased with the reaction of Lincoln biographer Benjamin P. Thomas. "The invented conversation is believable and the characters are lifelike," Thomas wrote approvingly. Sinclair's literary skills lead readers to feel "it must have been that way." That review in the *Chicago Tribune,* Feb. 26, 1956, followed Thomas's earlier praise in the December 12, 1954, issue for Brown's efforts. Thomas called *Grierson's Raid* a book that "pulsates with life" and tells the story "adroitly."

24. Harold Sinclair, *The Cavalryman* (New York: Harper & Brothers, 1958).

25. Ward Sinclair, foreword, to the *American Years,* xv–xvi.

26. Sinclair's manuscript and some of the correspondence concerning it are in the Civil War Centennial Commission Papers, box 16, Illinois State Historical Library. The sad duty of informing Sinclair that his manuscript was unacceptable fell to state historian Clyde Walton, an admirer of *The Horse Soldiers.* As editor of *Civil War History,* Walton had opened his pages to Martin Rackin and John Lee Mahin so that they could promote their movie version of the book.

27. The danger of the real hero being reduced to a mere celebrity is explored in Daniel J. Boorstin, *The Image: A Guide to Pseudo-Events in America* (1961; rpt. New York: Atheneum, 1972), and touched on more recently—and more caustically—in Neal Gabler, *Life: The Movie* (New York: Knopf, 1998). Gabler's warning about the trivialization of life brought by the overvaluing of entertainment, movies included, was also evident, interestingly enough, in screenwriter Andrew Niccol's *The Truman Show* (1998), a satire in which film is both object and subject. Gabler, like Boorstin before him and other writers like Neil Postman, are no mere Cassandras. There is a problem when we entrap ourselves in what Boorstin called a "thicket of unreality," and historical films, viewed uncritically, only add to the undergrowth. Still, the very process of hero-worship brings with it the potential of creating a more puerile celebrity status, evident enough in Homer's epics and Joseph Campbell's discussion in *The Hero with a Thousand Faces* (New York: Pantheon, 1949). Discerning what is *real,* however, was an ontological and epistemological problem long before the advent of film and the birth of the modern consumer society.

4. THE STORY AS FILM

1. Walton in the "Editor's Note" to John Lee Mahin and Martin Rackin, "The Horse Soldiers and Grierson's Raid," *Civil War History* 5 (1959): 183.

2. Mahin and Rackin, ibid., 183–84, 186. They also engaged in a bit of hyperbole, claiming that the stars were joined by "500 of the best horsemen in Louisiana and Mississippi" to ride "in a column of fours as far as the eye could see in the sunset" (186). Actually, the production company hired about one hundred locals to act as both Yankee raiders and Rebel defenders. Including the actors, stuntmen, and professional wranglers, there were perhaps 160 men on horseback, but never more than that. Also, Mahin and Rackin said that they would include "a dramatic rape at Newton Station." There is no such scene in the script or film, nor does it appear that John Ford ever shot it.

3. Ibid., 185.

4. Tino Balio, *United Artists: The Company That Changed the Film Industry* (Madison: Univ. of Wisconsin Press, 1987), 169–80, for *The Horse Soldiers* (mentioned only in passing) as part of the first twenty-picture deal between the Mirisches and United Artists.

5. Or so stated Mahin in an interview with film critic Todd McCarthy and screenwriter Joseph McBride, which they edited as "Bombshell Days in the Golden Age," *Film Comment* 16 (Mar.–Apr. 1980): 58–68; quotations from 68. Also see Mahin's own brief essay, "A Writer Views Directors," *Action* 10 (Jan.–Feb. 1975): 6–9, where Mahin mentions working with John Ford but nothing about *The Horse Soldiers*.

6. Attributed to Ford in Ronald L. Davis, *John Ford: Hollywood's Old Master* (Norman: Univ. of Oklahoma Press, 1995), 92, with no indication of when, where, or to whom Ford made the comment. Still, Davis's study is most insightful and ranks, along with Dan Ford's *Pappy: The Life of John Ford* (Englewood Cliffs, N.J.: Prentice Hall, 1979), as among the best of the Ford biographies. Scott Eyman's *Print The Legend: The Life and Times of John Ford* (New York: Simon & Schuster, 1999), too often tries too hard.

7. A copy of the contract between Ford and the Mirisch Corporation, dated October 17, 1958, is in the John Ford Papers (J. Ford, mss.), box 8, folder 27, Lilly Library, Indiana University.

8. Dan Ford to the author, Oct. 20, 1997. "If I were writing *Pappy* today, I would give 'The Horse Soldiers' a better mention. It's not a great film, but it's not a bad one either," he concluded. Eyman, *Print The Legend,* 471, by contrast, smugly dismisses the film as "a dud, pure and simple." Predictably enough, Eyman touts *The Searchers* as "epic tragedy" (442), yet another critic who makes too much of the latter film, not enough of the former.

9. Harry Carey Jr., *Company of Heroes* (Metuchen, N.J.: Scarecrow Press, 1994), 1.

10. John Ford Papers, tape 79, side 2, from Wayne's interview with Dan Ford. Wayne was also convinced that Ford would get into an argument with a "buff" on a subject just to find out what that person knew.

11. Andrew Sinclair, *John Ford* (New York: Dial Press, 1979), uses this statement, without attribution, as the epigraph to a book that characterizes Ford as an enigmatic genius—a characterization that is fairly typical among Ford biographers. Sinclair uses the troopers in silhouette from the opening scene of *The Horse Soldiers* for his title page. For a taste of Ford at his prickliest, see Bertrand Tavernier, "Notes of a Press Attaché: John Ford in Paris, 1966," *Film Comment* 30 (July–Aug. 1994): 66–75.

12. From Ford's 1955 interview with Jean Mitry, reprinted in Andrew Sarris, ed., *Interviews with Film Directors* (New York: Avon, 1967), 198.

13. As taken from Davis, *John Ford*, 205.

14. The shooting schedule through the end of 1958 is laid out in the John Ford Papers, box 4, folder 35, Mirisch-Batjac Company. Mahin and Rackin wrote in their piece for *Civil War History*, 186, that filming ended on January 17, 1959.

15. See Ford Papers, box 4, folder 35, preliminary Mirisch Company budget as of October 24, 1958—a total of $3,599,447, with nearly half of the total going to the lead actors and John Ford; and the comment on rising film expenses in Thomas Pryor, "Hollywood Costs," *New York Times*, Nov. 9, 1958.

16. *Shreveport Times*, Nov. 16, 1958.

17. The excitement is obvious in both the *Alexandria Daily Town Talk* and the *Natchez Democrat* in various issues from October–November 1958. See, for example, the October 28 and 29 issues of the *Alexandria Daily Town Talk* for the "red carpet" treatment given to the moviemakers by local officials and businesses and the enthusiastic reception at the Jefferson Military College when the film company did some work there, reported in the *Natchez Democrat*, November 21, 22, 1958.

18. "In order that THE HORSE SOLDIERS would prove great entertainment and not just a history lesson filmed in color and wide screen," stated a public relations piece, Mahin and Rackin "used much of the background of the book for research material, but only five pages of the novel as the jumping off place for the screen story." Presumably meaning that the film told a higher truth even as it strayed from the facts, it was claimed that "THE HORSE SOLDIERS faithfully reenacts this daring military raid." From the production notes/news release issued by Rogers & Cowan, in the John Ford Papers, box 6, folder 35, 2, 3.

19. *The Horse Soldiers* (United Artist Pressbook, 1959), p. 13. Author's copy. The marketing effort was impressive, "backed by one of the most intensive pre-release publicity and exploitation programs ever used to promote a motion picture." The overblown budget—now some $6.5 million—was made part of the promotional campaign.

20. Carey, *Company of Heroes*, told of how Ford and Jones first got together (34–36) and also how Jones ran afoul of Ford on the set of *Rio Grande* and was banished for a time (108–9)—not an uncommon occurrence in the tempestuous Ford film family. Carey himself learned this firsthand (120–22), which may explain why he was not in *The Horse Soldiers*.

21. *The Horse Soldiers*, released as an album in 1959 by United Artists (UAL 4035), from the back cover; there are no liner notes. In an example of Civil War Centennial political correctness—that is, finding the good on both sides—it was also noted that the real raiders whose tale the film dramatized "not only helped turn the tide of war by destroying the main Southern rail line into besieged Vicksburg, but" their exploits had "become synonymous with the bravery and daring that both sides so amply displayed during the great conflict between the States." United Artists also produced a companion album, *Constance Towers Sings to the Horse Soldiers* (UAL 3036). The 45-rpm versions of "I Left My Love" and "Lorena" (UA 178 and 179) were performed by Irving Joseph and his orchestra and chorus, not David Buttolph and his orchestra, who performed on the LP album.

22. *The Horse Soldiers* (United Artists, 1959; videocassette format, United Artists/ Metro-Goldwyn-Mayer, MGM Home Entertainment, 1998), dialogue as spoken on screen, not as written in the script, approximately three minutes into the film, which ran, all totaled, just shy of two hours. Hereafter, I have indicated in the text other points in the film where dialogue is to be found—using hours and minutes (e.g., 1h 5m).

23. Evan Thomas to Harold Sinclair, postscript, Dec. 27, 1955, Harold Sinclair Collection. Kantor's *Andersonville* (Cleveland: World, 1955), which won a Pulitzer Prize, is still respected as good historical fiction.

24. Mahin in "Bombshell Days," 68; also Mahin's interview with Dan Ford in the John Ford Papers, tape 63, side 2. For the VMI cadets, read William C. Davis, *The Battle of New Market* (Garden City, N.Y.: Doubleday, 1975). Interestingly enough, when Davis wrote a brief review of James Lee Conrad's *The Young Lions* (Mechanicsburg, Pa.: Stackpole Books, 1997) for members of the History Book Club (*History Book Club Review,* Midsummer 1997, separate flyer), he opened: "There is a memorable scene in John Ford's Civil War film, "The Horse Soldiers," in which John Wayne and a regiment of Yankee cavalrymen are put to flight by the teenage boys of the Jefferson Military Academy in Mississippi. The episode itself is purely mythical." No such thing happened during Grierson's raid, he noted, *but* he knew that many of the club members, a fair percentage of whom are professional historians, had seen the film and might not know that "fact," and it was a good way to open his review of a book about real events. It is also interesting that Captain Henry Forbes's little column sent out as the "forlorn hope" did indeed have a brief encounter with cadets. Residents of Summerville had heard that cavalry was approaching and had no idea the cavalrymen were Yankee raiders. "In the same village was a military school for boys, who also heard the aforesaid report and came rushing through the little town to cheer us on our way. I particularly remember one little fellow in full cadet's uniform, who said that he was a South Carolinian. He was so overjoyed that nothing could express him so well as a series of handsprings which he turned on the grass. He was a quick-witted little chap, however, and all at once he saw through the whole business. The thermometer of his joy fell. Lots of things fell! He strutted away rigid as an icicle, with the rangling consciousness, nevermore to be dismissed, that South Carolina had been turning summersaults of joy in honor of her fell invaders, who, as he slipped behind a hedge, were roaring with irrepressible laughter" (Forbes, "Grierson's Raid," 15–16).

25. Listen to Ford's interview with his grandson Dan in the John Ford Papers, tape 38, side 1.

26. Douglas Southall Freeman, *Lee's Lieutenants,* 3 vols. (New York: Charles Scribner's Sons, 1942–44), 1:708, 3:515, 516n. Sinclair, *John Ford,* 188, claimed that this was Ford's "favorite historical work," but he did not disclose his source.

27. James Warner Bellah, *The Valiant Virginians* (New York: Ballantine, 1953), which appeared originally as "Tales of the Valorous Virginians" in the *Saturday Evening Post* from May 9 through June 10, 1953. Pat Ford urged his father to buy the rights to Bellah's book from C. V. Whitney Pictures, a company about to go under; he hated "to see Bellah's yarn remain buried for lack of interest" (Pat Ford to John Ford, Oct. 14, 1957, John Ford Papers, box 1, Correspondence). Bellah and Dee Brown had been thrown together during the early days of World War II, when Brown underwent army training. As a historian Brown became most famous for revising certain images of the American West, images that Bellah had helped create through his short stories and Ford's film adaptations of them.

28. Pat Ford to John Ford, ca. Sept. 1958, John Ford Papers, box 1, Correspondence.

29. *Natchez Democrat,* Nov. 22, 23, 27, 1958; also see Jefferson Military College superintendent Marcy Dupree to John Ford, July 1, 1959, complimenting the director on his film and reminding him of his promise to make a cash contribution to both schools (John Ford Papers, box 1, Correspondence).

30. Authenticity noted in "Six Days with Horse Soldiers," a brief typescript by Mrs. Stovall, one of the teachers at the college, in the John Ford Papers, box 6, folder 35.

31. J. A. Place, *The Western Films of John Ford* (Secaucus, N.J.: Citadel Press, 1973), devotes a chapter to *The Horse Soldiers,* pages 174–85, and suggests this theme. Tad Gallagher, *John Ford: The Man and His Films* (Berkeley: Univ. of California Press, 1986), 371, feels that Place stretches his point (see 367–73 for Gallagher's own views of the film). Both Lee Pfeiffer, *The John Wayne Scrapbook* (New York: Citadel Press, 1989), 77–82; and William Darby, *John Ford's Westerns* (Jefferson, N.C.: McFarland, 1996), 38–55, admire the film and steer clear of simplified characterizations. Though Darby is virtually alone in comparing Ford's film with Sinclair's book, like the others he worked only from the finished product, not the script in its many incarnations.

32. Ford, *Pappy,* 208.

33. Jeffrey Richards, "John Ford 2: Ford's Lost World," *Focus on Film* 2 (Spring 1971): 20–30; and, more famously, Peter Bogdanovich, *John Ford* (Berkeley: Univ. of California Press, 1968), which includes excerpts from a long 1966 interview with Ford, and Andrew Sarris, *The John Ford Movie Mystery* (Bloomington: Indiana Univ. Press, 1975), attempted to trace a trajectory to Ford's filmmaking. Ford, of course, did not care for such attempts at analysis; neither did his son Pat. When asked if the critics were right—that the great director had become disillusioned with time, so that his later movies told very different stories from his earlier works, Pat responded, "No, I think critics were fools. They're looking for explanations for the most obvious things. The market changed" (from page 31 in the transcript of a 1986 interview with James D'Arc, Archives, ms. 1765, Harold B. Lee Library, Brigham Young University). Some of the best pieces on Ford are actually the shortest, written by those who did not try too hard to explain an enigmatic man and complex medium. See, for example, the brief obituary by Roger Greenspun, "John Ford, 1895–1973," *New York Times,* Sept. 9, 1973.

34. This March 1973 AFI Award program, "A Salute to John Ford," was filmed and made available as a videocassette in 1991 by Worldvision Enterprises. Ford was the first recipient of the AFI's lifetime achievement award. The montage of film excerpts put together to honor Ford included the cadets marching forth to battle in *The Horse Soldiers.*

35. "Found," as Wayne's Marlowe meant it, referred to free food and lodging. Holding a meat platter, Towers as Hunter leans toward Wayne's Marlowe to accentuate her décolletage as she asks the embarrassed colonel if he would prefer more leg or breast. That is just one of several linguistic and behavioral anachronisms in the film—a problem in Sinclair's book too, it should be remembered.

36. So recalled John Lee Mahin, in his interview with Dan Ford, John Ford Papers, tape 63, side 2.

37. Darby, *John Ford's Westerns,* 41, wrote that the "faithful" Lukey looks "mystified when she is accidentally killed by a Confederate sniper near a black church." Perhaps she was indeed shot accidentally by the snipers (two, not one), but if so, that is a conclusion based on inference. Ford left it to the viewer to decide, a mark of his ability to be subtle, even in the midst of his obvious stock comedic and tragic turns. Either way, whether Lukey is slain inadvertently or by design, her death accentuated the senseless waste that can occur even in a "good" war, one of the many ironies that Ford employed in this film as in others.

38. The theatrical trailer was inserted at the beginning of the film by MGM Home Entertainment for the 1998 rerelease of a videocassette version.

39. Covered in the *Shreveport Times,* June 14–18, 1959.

40. See the *Natchez Democrat,* June 17, 18, 1959.

41. See, for example, *Shreveport Times,* June 17, 21, 1959; also *Natchez Democrat,* June 23, 1959, and *Alexandria Daily Town Talk,* June 18, 1959.

42. *Pantagraph,* July 12, 1959; see too the July 17 issue.

43. Balio, *United Artists,* 138, lists the figures. Pfeiffer, *John Wayne Scrapbook,* 237–41, listed Wayne's top ten grossing films and noted that *The Horse Soldiers* was on that list until United Artists reconfigured its movie rental revenue.

44. Overall, *New York Times* film critic Bosley Crowther enjoyed *The Horse Soldiers,* though he thought the script weak. It could, he wrote in his review of June 27, 1959, even act as the "opening gun of Hollywood's coming celebration of the Civil War centenary." Crowther liked the long shots of men on horseback; the anonymous reviewer for *Variety,* June 10, 1959, 6, who thought the film "a whopping big, colorful spectacle in the 'grand' tradition," did not. The unattributed review in *Newsweek,* June 29, 1959, 91, called the film "Ford at his finest"; the unnamed writers for *Time,* July 20, 1959, 63, and *Life,* June 29, 1959, 55–58 (with most of the space taken by publicity stills) were much less impressed. Writing for the *Saturday Review,* June 20, 1959, 28, Arthur Knight wondered if "the same effect might not have been achieved by adhering more closely to the original novel or fact." Paul Hartung in the *Commonweal,* July 3, 1959, 352, was not so concerned. David Robinson in *Sight and Sound* 29 (Winter 1959–60) thought Ford had risen above the middling script to direct a good film and showed that, he too, could be confused on the "facts" of the past, noting that real cadets—"children"—had been "masacred" somewhere on the battlefields of 1863. Finally, *The Horse Soldiers* turns up retrospectively in Donald Chase, "My Favorite Year: 1959," *Film Comment* 30 (Sept.–Oct. 1994): 60–72. Chase did not find the film as engaging then as he had when he first saw it in the theater thirty-five years before. Jack Spears, *The Civil War on the Screen and Other Essays* (New York: A. S. Barnes, 1977), 11–116, referred to *The Horse Soldiers* only in passing. He considered the film too melodramatic. And though he liked the cadet sequence, he called it—erroneously—a sanitized version of a real event where "children" were slaughtered.

45. Ford, *Pappy,* 283. "Ford was wonderful, but that was an unfortunate picture. Bad movie," Mahin lamented in his "Bombshell Days" interview, 68.

46. Bogdanovich, *John Ford,* 97. Ford said the same thing about other movies to other interviewers—just as he led different interviewers, even different members of his film family, to believe one film or another was his favorite.

47. Gallagher, *John Ford,* 373.

5. THE STORY NOT TOLD

1. Ford, *Pappy,* 280.

2. William Clothier interview, John Ford Papers, transcript, box 11, folder 21.

3. For the Gable-Stewart-Peck business, see Mahin and Rackin to Ford, letters of June 24 and 30, 1958, in the John Ford Papers, box 1, Correspondence. Proof of how the script was cobbled together turns up in the June 30 letter. "Enclosed are some additional pages through the goodbye scene between Marlowe and Keller," wrote Mahin and Rackin. "We are undecided yet whether there will be a brief continuance between Hannah and Keller or whether we go directly to the tag and the parade in Baton Rouge. We shall attempt to noodle through this in the next day and will send it along to you so that we can bring a close to this first draft. To be brief, we know it's not right but will only be indicative

of a finish. The result will probably be dictated by the outcome of the battle, which you will brilliantly stage."

4. Rumors about who would play whom moved well beyond Hollywood circles. Harold Sinclair's hometown paper the *Pantagraph,* May 13, 1958, passed along insider information that Clark Gable would portray Marlowe, just as the *Natchez Democrat,* August 26, 1958, reported that Wayne had been set for the Marlowe role and Holden for Kendall, with Elizabeth Taylor—an early possibility—no longer in the running for Hannah. See too ibid., October 15, 1958. That Holden was finally signed to portray Kendall was important news for the *Shreveport Times,* October 16, 1958. Martin Rackin hinted that the female lead had been signed in that same story, but Constance Towers was not identified until two days later (ibid., Oct. 18, 1958).

5. The only script in the John Ford Papers (box 6, folder 34) is dated August 22, 1958, and was dialogue director Meta Stern's copy. The Walter Mirisch Papers, box 4, folder 15, U.S. Mss. 87AN, State Historical Society of Wisconsin, has another typewritten version with "FINAL" and September 9, 1958, on the cover sheet. This was Mirisch's personal copy. Revisions dated September 9, October 6, and October 30 were added later. Inserted in the script (between pages 39–40) are half a dozen changes suggested by Walter Mirisch. Ford, of course, ended up doing what he wanted—something Mirisch knew would happen anyway.

6. *The Horse Soldiers,* Mirisch script copy, 154.

7. Ibid.

8. Ibid., 154–55.

9. The local paper, *Alexandria Daily Town Talk,* December 6, 1958, reported the accident, which happened the day before. Ford, *Pappy,* 282–83, commented on how Kennedy's death saddened the film company. See too Pilar Wayne, *John Wayne: My Life with the Duke* (New York: McGraw-Hill, 1987). "Duke told me that Ford couldn't seem to forget the accident and get on with his work, blaming himself for Kennedy's death," wrote the then Mrs. Wayne. "He began drinking heavily and lost interest in finishing the film" (135). Mahin's comments in his "Bombshell Days" interview (68) and his interview with Dan Ford (John Ford Papers, tape 63, side 2) also leave the impression that everything changed after Kennedy's death. When Dan Ford interviewed his grandfather the director clearly did not want to discuss Kennedy's death—still a painful memory. Dan's mother, the director's daughter, reminded her father that Kennedy's accident came on the last scheduled day of location shooting (John Ford Papers, tape 38, side 1).

10. Mahin in Ford, *Pappy,* 283; interview in the John Ford Papers, tape 63, side 2. In the "Bombshell Days" interview, 68, Mahin remembered that he told Rackin that the big battle scene had to be shot. "I pleaded with the Mirisch Brothers. They said, 'No, we've got Ford, Holden, and Wayne, we'll make a million,'" so they refused to spend the money.

11. Clothier interview, transcript, John Ford Papers, box 11, folder 21; see also the snippets of another Clothier interview in Scott Eyman, *Five American Cinematographers* (Metuchen, N.J.: Scarecrow Press, 1987), 133.

12. Colin Young, "The Old Dependables," *Film Quarterly* 13 (Fall 1959): 9. Young, an editor for the journal, confessed that Ford was difficult. "He is suspicious of the conversation from the start, as if any talk about film-making, especially about his films, was superfluous" (6).

13. See, again, Richards, "John Ford 2," 29–30, and Bogdanovich, *John Ford,* 35. Also see Ford, *Pappy,* 283–93, and Sinclair, *John Ford,* 189–201.

14. AFI Tribute, March 31, 1973, roughly eighteen minutes into the seventy-five-minute program.

15. Place, *Western Films of John Ford,* 176, 182, 183.

16. *The Horse Soldiers* script, Mirisch copy, 92–93.

17. Richard Curtis's film *Notting Hill* is a splendid case in point, as Curtis himself revealed in the printed version of the script, *Notting Hill* (London: Hodder & Stoughton, 1999), which includes scenes written but not filmed, and filmed but not used.

18. See Mirisch's recommendation—"Eliminate Brady taking photo"—in *The Horse Soldiers* script, Mirisch copy, memo from Mirisch inserted between pages 39 and 40.

19. For the cut scene go to ibid., pages 81–83, which included another oppportunity for Holden's Kendall to needle Wayne's Marlowe, this time about drinking from a trough that was probably infested with worms; compare with Sinclair, *Horse Soldiers,* 164–67.

20. *The Horse Soldiers* script, Stern copy, 14–15.

21. *The Horse Soldiers* script, Mirisch copy, 19–20, scene added on September 15, 1958.

22. In an earlier version, Marlowe did not just pull Hannah down; he punched her. See Stern copy of the script, 68.

23. *The Horse Soldiers* script, Mirisch copy, 70–72.

24. *The Horse Soldiers* script, Stern copy, 60.

25. This scene was not added until October 30—see script, Mirisch copy, 62, 62A-B, and even then it was not shot as written.

26. *The Horse Soldiers* script, Mirisch copy, 88, added on October 30.

27. *The Horse Soldiers* script, Mirisch copy, 144–44A.

28. *The Horse Soldiers* script, Mirisch copy, 151–51A; contrast with the Stern copy, 156.

29. John Lee Mahin interview, John Ford Papers, tape 63, side 2.

30. William Clothier interview, transcript, John Ford Papers, box 11, folder 21.

31. Roger Miller, "Novelist on Location," *Pantagraph,* Nov. 11, 1958.

32. Dee Brown to Harold Sinclair, Sept. 26, 1955, Harold Sinclair Collection.

33. See Sally Brown's letter to John Ford of November 3, 1958, John Ford Papers, box 1, Correspondence.

34. John Lee Mahin interview, John Ford Papers, tape 63, side 2.

35. Sinclair, "The Horse Soldiers," original typescript, 410–11.

36. Sinclair, "The Horse Soldiers," original typescript, 427.

37. Sinclair, "The Horse Soldiers," original typescript, 440–41.

38. Sinclair, "The Horse Soldiers," original typescript, 443.

39. Evan Thomas to Harold Sinclair, "EWT's Notes on THE HORSE SOLDIERS," May 19, 1955, quotation from p. 2, Harold Sinclair Collection.

40. Sinclair, "The Horse Soldiers," original typescript, 503–4, with Thomas drawing a line below "trumpet note died away," asking, "end it here?" (503).

41. "EWT's Notes," May 19, 1955, Harold Sinclair Collection. Sinclair made the changes graciously and gratefully—see his letters to Thomas, June 21, and August 15, 1955, ibid. "First let me say that any editorial corrections you make in the book will be all right with me—I doubt that I will want to change them back in the galleys," Sinclair wrote to Thomas on August 23. "Same thing applies in your notions about the chapter titles. Most of my chapter headings were spur-of-the-moment ideas anyway—not too much time for much else. I daresay most of them could be improved."

42. Harold Sinclair, *The Horse Soldiers* (London: Frederick Muller, 1956). Evan Thomas had no role in this edition either—see his letter to Sinclair of December 27, 1955, Harold Sinclair Collection.

43. Dee Brown to the author, Feb. 24, 1998.

44. See the letter from Dee Brown's wife, Sally, to "Messrs. Wayne and Ford," November 3, 1958, John Ford Papers, box 1, Correspondence, where Mrs. Brown offers a wittily sarcastic aside about how Illinois imposed D. Alexander Brown on her husband before she took aim at her bigger target—John Ford—for making a movie based on Sinclair's novel and not her husband's historical account.

45. Surby, *Grierson Raids,* 78.

46. Ibid., 80.

47. Ibid., 86.

48. Ibid., 87.

49. Ibid., 91.

50. Ibid., 95–96. Also see Surby's version of the Mosby business that was printed in *Two Great Raids,* 48–57.

51. Thomas Lippincott to Benjamin Henry Grierson, June 1889, Thomas W. Lippincott Papers, SC-929, Illinois State Historical Library; and, in that same file, "Grierson's Big Raid," *Milwaukee Sunday Telegraph,* no date, with a subtitle stating that the article compared Grierson's accomplishment with J. E. B. Stuart's "cheap affair" in Virginia.

52. The same might be true of the tribute to Grierson written by Squire Epperson, a raider who became part owner and editor of the *Bushnell Weekly Record.* Epperson, captain of L Company in the 7th Illinois at the time of the raid, wrote in the April 26, 1873, issue of his paper that Grierson "is a man of powerful intellect" of a very particular type. "His is that busy practical brain which makes him a man of action, a fine type of the untiring working men, who are making their mark upon the dial plate of this active century. . . . He was bold, energetic, self reliant and persevering. He investigated for himself, he decided for himself, although at a glance, he acted with all his power." He was, like Grant, a great man. "And when the time comes for the historians to chronicle the actions of this age, their names will occupy a bright and proud position in the history of our country."

53. Surby, *Grierson Raids,* 21. It was in La Grange, Surby wrote in *Two Great Raids,* 5, that Grierson "projected his famous raid," which he communicated to Hurlbut, who in turn passed it along to Grant. The other raid was that of John Hunt Morgan, whose exploits would subsequently be the subject of another Dee Brown book.

54. Grierson, "Lights and Shadows," 257. In his *Record of Services Rendered the Government* (n.p., n.d. [1861–66]), however, Grierson wrote that "the expedition, not as it occurred in detail, but in its main scope, had been suggested by Colonel Grierson, months before" (101). He does not carry this passage into the later "Lights and Shadows."

55. Woodward, "Grierson's Raid," 685.

56. Stephen Forbes to William Sooy Smith, Mar. 3, 1907, Forbes Papers, 4 D.1.

57. William Sooy Smith to Stephen Forbes, May 4, 1907, in which Sooy Smith essentially repeated what he had already written to Forbes on November 10, 1905 (Forbes Papers).

58. Stephen Forbes to William Sooy Smith, May 8, 1907, Forbes Papers.

59. Forbes, "Grierson's Cavalry Raid," 99. If Sooy Smith was offended by Forbes's vague language, he did not tell Forbes. See his letter to Forbes of November 25, 1908, Forbes Papers, 4 D.1. "I congratulate you & your brother, if he is still alive, for the extra

hazardous and conspicuous part you took in the historical raid," wrote the onetime general to the former sergeant. "Both you and he must share my great satisfaction, that we were able to render this service for our beloved country when it was so sorely needed." Sooy Smith did not know that Henry Forbes had died in 1903.

60. T. W. Lippincott to Stephen Forbes, Dec. 20, 1908, Forbes Papers, 4 D.1.

61. T. W. Lippincott to Stephen Forbes, Feb. 20, 1909, Forbes Papers.

62. Surby, *Grierson Raids,* 29, recalled that he "suggested to Blackburn that "some scouts" be "dressed in citizen clothes"; in the 1883 version, reprinted as *Two Great Raids,* 7–8, he said nothing about whose idea it had been.

63. Grierson, "Lights and Shadows," 299, which is consistent with what Grierson had written earlier in his *Record of Services Rendered the Government,* 103.

64. Glimpses come through in Pierce's *History of the Second Iowa,* though too much should not be inferred from them; moreover, Surby was lavish in his praise of the 2d Iowa in *Two Great Raids,* 89–96.

65. Henry Forbes, an officer, seemed to take his company's post as "forlorn hope" more in stride than did his younger brother Stephen, a sergeant. In his unpublished essay, "Grierson's Raid," the older Forbes presented the selection of his company for hazardous duty dispassionately (9–10), seemingly accepting his possible fate as sacrifical lamb for the column (see 11). The younger Forbes, by contrast, found it difficult to be so detached in his recollections. He wrote to his sister Nettie on August 2, 1863, from Memphis, "Let me see, I have never written you a word of the 'famous raid,' have I? But I guess that it is just as well; I suppose that you have heard of it in some way, and I am heartily sick of it"; perhaps he eventually told her about it in person (Ethel Forbes Scott, Forbes Family Letters, 224). In his 1907 published essay, genuine admiration for Grierson and pride in what was accomplished notwithstanding, he wrote that the company was "ludicrously inadequate to its purpose" (105) and that after April 26, Grierson, fearful of being caught from behind, "began burning all bridges as he crossed them, thus abandoning to its fate Company B of the Seventh, which he had evidently now given up for lost" (109).

66. Herbert Butterfield, *The Historical Novel,* (Cambridge: Cambridge Univ. Press, 1924), 95.

67. See the essays by Becker collected in Phil L. Snyder, ed., *Detachment and the Writing of History* (Ithaca: Cornell Univ. Press, 1958). A generation of history undergraduates learned the basics of their discipline from Edward Hallett Carr, *What Is History?* (New York: Knopf, 1961). Carr, acknowledging his debt to Becker, warned that "the belief in a hard core of historical facts existing objectively and independently of the interpretation of the historian is a preposterous fallacy, but one which it is very hard to eradicate" (10). Becker's influence permeates William McNeill's December 1985 presidential address to the American Historical Association, printed as "Mythistory, or Truth, Myth, History, and Historians," in McNeill, *Mythistory and Other Essays* (Chicago: Univ. of Chicago Press, 1986), 3–22.

68. John Demos, "The Tenuous Frontier of History and Literature," *Boston Sunday Globe,* Aug. 14, 1994.

69. Hayden White, *Tropics of Discourse* (Baltimore: Johns Hopkins Univ. Press, 1978), 122. Also see White's essays collected in *The Content of the Form* (Baltimore: Johns Hopkins Univ. Press, 1987); and John Lukacs, *Historical Consciousness* (New York: Harper & Row, 1968).

70. Brown, from his "Note" in Sinclair, *The Horse Soldiers,* ix.

6. The Truth — Ever Elusive

1. U.S. Civil War Centennial Commission, *The Civil War Centennial: A Report to the Congress* (Washington, D.C.: GPO, 1968), 3. For the centennial in the context of national celebration, see Michael Kammen, *Mystic Chords of Memory* (New York: Knopf, 1991), 587–610; John Bodnar, *Remaking America: Public Memory, Commemoration, and Patriotism in the Twentieth Century* (Princeton: Princeton Univ. Press, 1992), 206–26; Jim Cullen, *The Civil War in Popular Culture: A Reusable Past* (Washington, D.C.: Smithsonian Institution Press, 1995); and, more acerbically, Edmund Wilson, *Patriotic Gore* (1962; rpt. London: Hogarth Press, 1987).

2. Centennial Commission, *Civil War Centennial,* 3. In allowing dignity to both sides, Eisenhower continued the tradition begun by Abraham Lincoln in his Gettysburg Address, a development treated (too?) imaginatively by Garry Wills in *Lincoln at Gettysburg* (New York: Simon & Schuster, 1992).

3. Centennial Commission, *Civil War Centennial,* 11.

4. From the official citation, a copy of which is in the Harold Sinclair Collection.

5. Centennial Commission, *Civil War Centennial,* 14.

6. Ibid., 44. The report confessed that "public opinion was sharply divided as to the wisdom—even the propriety—of battle renactments." We can only wonder what Allan Nevins would have made of the reenactors and other keepers of the flame who people Tony Horwitz's *Confederates in the Attic* (New York: Pantheon, 1998).

7. See the "Report of the Activities Committee to the Civil War Centennial Commission," *Civil War History* 5 (1959): 374–81; Donald's fears are alluded to on page 377. They were shared by "other" unnamed historians "with whom the Committee conferred."

8. Bill Weber to the author, Jan. 26, 1998.

9. Ibid.

10. Bill Weber photocopied a picture of the old marker and sent it to me in a letter of October 4, 1997. He noted that the June 1993 issue of *Blue & Gray Magazine* devoted to the raid had mentioned the marker. "The editor retraced the route, stopped in Newton, read the erroneous marker, and reported it in this national publication. Although he printed my correction in the next (Aug. '93) issue this was two months later (the damage had already been done). Some communication with General Colin Powell, an admirer of Grierson, and a personal conversation with Gen. John Shalikashvili, who succeeded Gen. Powell as Chairman of the Joint Chiefs of Staff, provided encouragement." Weber pressed on until he won his case. In his travels he also found that the historical marker at La Grange, Tennessee, which identifies La Grange as the starting point for Grierson's raid, has errors. Its states that the "2nd Ind. Cav." rather than the 2d Iowa, went with Grierson and has the raiders arriving in Baton Rouge on May 3 rather than May 2.

11. Bill Weber to the author, Oct. 4, 1997.

12. Michael F. Beard, Civil War Sites Historian for the State of Mississippi, to Bill Weber, Nov. 2, 1994, a letter copied for the author by Bill Weber. The new marker says nothing about the raid; it joins the marker at the railroad depot (burned twice during the war and completely rebuilt in 1905) that states simply: "Here at Newton Station on April 24, 1863, Federals under General Benjamin H. Grierson struck the Vicksburg-Meridian rail route, tore up tracks, & burned depot." Perhaps this marker should be replaced too; Grierson was a colonel, not a general, at the time of the raid.

13. The "Newton Station Celebration" appeared as a special issue of the *Newton Record,* April 24, 1996. The new historical marker for the hospital, replacing the one erected as

part of the centennial, says nothing about the raiders. The *Newton Record,* May 1, 1996, praised Weber's efforts. Bill Weber is also interested in how the raid has been depicted by contemporary artists, notably Mort Künstler and Don Stivers, whose Civil War paintings and prints have become popular. Künstler created a Newton Station scene with Butternut Guerrillas on horseback dashing about to capture a train. He got much of the scene wrong. Stivers painted a scene taken from John Ford's *The Horse Soldiers* that showed John Wayne's Marlowe awaiting the Rebel attack up the main street of Newton Station in a picture called, confusingly, *The Wait at Vicksburg.* Stivers's painting is a fine example of the blurring of fact and fiction.

14. "Fiction—in the form of misinterpretation or the form of outright misrepresentation—is endemic to the history of the Civil War," observed Alan T. Nolan in *Lee Considered* (Chapel Hill: Univ. of North Carolina Press, 1991), 153.

15. Grierson's six-hundred-mile total seems too high; Surby's estimate of eight hundred miles in *Grierson Raids,* 123, repeated in *Two Great Raids,* 76, is way off.

16. Banks to Henry Halleck, May 31, 1863, *OR,* vol. 24, 3:367. Brown, *Grierson's Raid,* 252 n. 4, cited page 483 of Grierson's autobiography without making it clear that he was referring to an early version of the "Lights and Shadows" (box 17, Grierson Papers) and not the 1863 autobiographical segment (in box 16, folder 1) that ended up being printed in Grierson's *Record of Services Rendered the Government.* Grierson included excerpts from a Sherman letter above the praise from Banks, so Brown's mistake is all too understandable. This version of "Lights and Shadows" also differs from the copy (in box 21) that was eventually microfilmed. There the Banks passage is on page 375. Even so, this is not to say that Sherman did not have great respect for Grierson; he did, and it was undiminished with time. In recommending Grierson to Winfield Scott Hancock in a letter of January 25, 1867, Sherman described him as "one of the most willing, ardent, and dashing cavalry officers I ever had—always ready, day or night—against equal and superior foes he handled his men with great skill, doing some of the prettiest work of the war" (Benjamin Henry Grierson Papers, Ayers Ms. 3039, box 4, Newberry Library).

17. Peter Novick, *That Noble Dream* (Cambridge: Cambridge Univ. Press, 1988). Thus, as Richard J. Evans put it in his sprightly *In Defense of History* (1997; rpt. New York: Norton, 1999), an update to Carr's *What Is History?,* the more pertinent question now seems to be "Is It Possible to Do History at All?" (3).

18. C. Behan McCullagh, *The Truth of History* (London: Routledge, 1998), 2, 5. For a different approach to the same problem and a plea for "practical realism" in the pursuit of "truth," even as naive notions of objectivity are put aside, see Joyce Appleby, Lynn Hunt, and Margaret Jacob, *Telling the Truth About History* (New York: Norton, 1994). Whether they intended to or not, Anthony Molho and Gordon S. Wood potentially made themselves part of the debate. As editors explaining what contributors to their *Imagined Histories* (Princeton: Princeton Univ. Press, 1998) had attempted to do in this anthology on historical writing, they commented, "Of course, to imagine the past is not to write fiction, for the histories American historians of the past century imagined were continually measured against an always elusive but still real and objective past" (vii). An unreconstructed or thoroughly deconstructed skeptic may well ask what is "real" and what is "objective"?

19. Keith Justice to the author, Aug. 31, 1997.

20. From Keith Justice, "Newton Station Targeted by Civil War Raid," *Newton Record,* Apr. 24, 1996, 19. For the incorrectly labeled photographs, see ibid., December 4, 1958, and April 13, 1988. In the *History of Newton County, Mississippi, from 1834 to 1894* (Jackson: Clarion-Ledger Co., 1894), local historian A. J. Brown had been quite evenhanded in his

brief treatment of the raiders. He pointed out that they commandeered stock along the route, burned one house outside Newton in retaliation for one of their troopers being slain by a sniper, and burned the depot and "one or two store houses and probably one hospital building" in Newton proper (116), but he did not launch into a diatribe against "damn yankees."

21. The "true to the spirit of the past" net has even been expanded to include the animated film about the Old Testament prophet Moses, *The Prince of Egypt* (1998). Peter Rainier's brief review in *New York,* December 21–28, 1998, 147, alludes to this assertion, which echoes the sort of statement made by Sherman Edwards and Peter Stone for their play *1776.* Rainier called the *The Prince of Egypt* assertion that artistic license could be exercised without distorting historical truth a "disclaimer." Actually it is more claim than disclaimer, an attempt to close the distance between product and past, not increase it.

22. Rollo May, *The Cry for Myth* (New York: Norton, 1991). See also Mircea Eliade, *Myth and Reality* (New York: Harper & Row, 1963). "Somebody has to tell young people what we think is a good person," *Star Wars* creator George Lucas told an interviewer. "I mean, we should be doing it all the time. That's what the Iliad and Odyssey are about—'This is what a good person is; this is who we aspire to be.' You need that in a society. It's the basic job of mythology." In Nick Thorton-Jones, "Master of the Universe," *Sunday (Times) Magazine,* May 16, 1999, 20.

23. A point well made in Michael C. C. Adams, *The Best War Ever* (Baltimore: Johns Hopkins Univ. Press, 1994), though as Adams confessed, the line separating actual experience from memory, even the memory of the participants themselves, can be blurry. What Adams found to be true about Americans and World War II could also be applied to the Civil War, for which see Carol Reardon, *Pickett's Charge in History and Memory* (Chapel Hill: Univ. of North Carolina Press, 1997). For Gettysburg in an even larger context, see Edward T. Linenthal, *Sacred Ground* (Urbana: Univ. of Illinois Press, 1991); and G. Kurt Piehler, *Remembering War the American Way* (Washington, D.C.: Smithsonian Institution Press, 1995).

24. From Berlin's essay on "Giambattista Vico and Cultural History" reprinted in Isaiah Berlin, *The Crooked Timber of Humanity* (London: John Murray, 1990), 69.

25. A word coined by historian Mike Wallace. See Wallace's *Mickey Mouse History and Other Essays on American Memory* (Philadelphia: Temple Univ. Press, 1996), particularly 155n–156n, where Wallace comments on how his addition to the lexicon has been received.

26. It is true that much of our collective memory is devoted to creating a self-conscious sense of heritage, the dangers of which are discussed in David Lowenthal, *Possessed by the Past* (New York: Free Press, 1996). Separating history from heritage can be difficult, however, because participants themselves in the events of the past—and Benjamin Henry Grierson can be included here—were often concerned with leaving behind records that would help form the national memory. Lowenthal explored the difficulties of separating real event from idealized remembrance—history as distinct from memory—in *The Past Is a Foreign Country* (Cambridge: Cambridge Univ. Press, 1987). "'Heritage' as we have known it is not necessarily history, but the *whole* of history, whether we like it or not, is heritage," observed Michael Kammen in "History Is Our Heritage: The Past in Contemporary American Culture," in Kammen, *In the Past Lane* (New York: Oxford Univ. Press, 1997), 224.

27. For example, a passage in Grierson's "Lights and Shadows," 321, is nearly identical to one in Surby, *Grierson Raids,* 75; likewise, two others from "Lights and Shadows," 326, and *Grierson Raids,* 100, 102.

28. Charles E. Cross to Stephen Forbes, Sept. 14, 1926, Forbes Papers, 4 D.I.

29. David Thelen, "Memory and American History," *Journal of American History* 75 (1989): 1123. Patrick H. Hutton, *History as an Art of Memory* (Hanover: Univ. Press of New England, 1993), provides a very thoughtful introduction to "collective mentalities," with Hutton's ideas juxtaposed alongside those of Sigmund Freud, Philippe Ariès, Michel Foucault, and others who have explored the "problem of memory."

30. Michael Kammen, "Some Patterns and Meanings of Memory Distortion in American History," *In the Past Lane,* 199–212, gives various reasons—notably nationalism and partisan politics—as to how and why our collective memory can become distorted. He could have added something more basic still: cognition, the individual's construction of a reality that may be less than real.

31. Simon Schama, *Dead Certainties* (New York: Knopf, 1991), 320.

32. Frederick Dalzall, "Dreamworking *Amistad:* Representing Slavery, Revolt, and Freedom in America, 1839 and 1997," *New England Quarterly* 71 (1998): 127–33, defended the film as "essentially accurate" (131) even though much in it was invented. He explained that Spielberg-Dreamworks reached beyond the historical past in the quest for truth, "compelling the people who made it to cross from historical waters into mythic ones" (133). Eric McKitrick, "JQA: For the Defense," *New York Review of Books,* April 23, 1998, 53–58, was considerably more bothered; likewise Eric Foner in his *New York Times* piece of December 20, 1997. Simon Schama, "Clio at the Multiplex," *New Yorker,* January 19, 1998, 38–43, did not care much for the film either but cautioned that "the academy must take at least some of the blame, for having largely abandoned, until recently, the importance of storytelling as the elementary condition of historical explanation" (39). Stanley Kauffman, "Notes on a Visit," *New Republic,* February 16, 1998, 24–25, found Schama's comments irritating, yet another example of a "let me set your house in order" visit by an outsider not sensitive enough to the film medium.

33. Cameron quoted in *Newsweek* (Dec. 15, 1997): 67.

34. I am more worried about the potential impact of *The Patriot* than I was about that of *Titanic*. Released in the summer of 2000, *The Patriot* attempts to comment on the American Revolution. The problem is not that the screenplay is only loosely based on real people and real events. Films that fictionalize the past routinely create composite characters and contrived situations. But when the fictionalized Banastre Tarleton of *The Patriot* herds men, women, and children into a church, where they are deliberately burned to death, I fear that a line has been crossed. Although the War of Independence, like any war, was brutal, turning Tarleton's "dragoons" into Waffen SS and Revolutionary South Carolina into World War II Poland does little to enlighten and much to confuse. That both film critics and historians complain when they detect the inauthentic where authenticity is claimed is heartening, and a reminder that they can share common ground—that they both expect the filmic past to ring true, whatever that elusive truth is.

35. C. Vann Woodward, *The Future of the Past* (New York: Oxford Univ. Press, 1989), vii.

36. "Historical films help to shape the thinking of millions," wrote Robert Brent Toplin in *History by Hollywood* (Urbana: Univ. of Illinois Press, 1996), vii. Echoing C. Vann Woodward, but more approvingly, he noted that films "are competing effectively with the school teacher, the college professor, and the history book author" (ix). Toplin urged historians to learn how to judge films by their own standards because films, even those that depart from the "facts," can tell "transcendant truths" (12); David Slocum, "Telling Ghost

Stories: Reflections on History and Hollywood," *American Quarterly* 50 (1998): 175–82, suggested that Toplin could do better at heeding his own advice. Not all historians are convinced that films should be given so much attention. "The professional obligation of historians is to write authoritative, accurate history," wrote one, after complaining in the *AHA* (American Historical Association) *Perspectives* 37 (May 1999): 2, about an earlier issue of that newsletter which had focused on film (see n. 56 below).

37. David Thelen, "The Movie Maker as Historian: Conversations with Ken Burns," *Journal of American History* 81 (1994): 1031–50, quotation from 1032, sales figures from 1050, for Shelby Foote, *The Civil War: A Narrative,* 3 vols. (New York: Random House, 1958–1974). Also see Robert Brent Toplin, ed., *Ken Burns's* The Civil War: *Historians Respond* (New York: Oxford Univ. Press, 1996). It is interesting that C. Vann Woodward, his misgivings about how the public learns its history notwithstanding, became an adviser to Burns and contributed to the book by Geoffrey Ward, *The Civil War: An Illustrated History* (New York: Knopf, 1990), that was done to accompany the series. Burns's own research and the expertise of his advisers could not ensure that the final product would be error-free. Ralph Graves, "Who *Are* Those Guys?" *Smithsonian* 29 (Jan. 1999): 110–11, pointed out that Burns and Ward used a famous image of the Richmond Grays improperly, calling them Confederate Volunteers in 1861 when they were actually still just Virginia militia in 1859. Princeton historian Natalie Zemon Davis has offered an interesting commentary on film and history. Her book *The Return of Martin Guerre* (Cambridge, Mass.: Harvard Univ. Press, 1983) complemented a French film on the same subject that was done with her cooperation, an experience she drew on for her discussion "'Any Resemblance to Persons Living or Dead': Film and the Challenge of Authenticity," *Yale Review* 76 (1987): 457–82. Davis's literary inventions and extrapolations raised some of the same questions that could have been asked about *Grierson's Raid.* See the "AHR Forum" on her book—a critique by Robert Finlay followed by Davis's response—in the *American Historical Review* 93 (1988): 553–603.

38. Peter Saccio, *Shakespeare's English Kings* (New York: Oxford Univ. Press, 1977), 4. More ambitiously, Harold Bloom, *Shakespeare: The Invention of the Human* (New York: Riverhead Books, 1998), enshrines the Bard as the psychological father of us all.

39. John Sayles, interview with Eric Foner, in Mark C. Carnes, ed., *Past Imperfect: History According to the Movies* (New York: Henry Holt, 1995), 12. "Like drama and fiction, movies inspire and entertain. They often teach important truths about the human condition," wrote the editor, a professional historian, in his introduction. Still, he cautioned, movie history cannot be "a substitute for history that has been painstakingly assembled from the best available evidence and analysis" (9, 10). I agree, though two considerations ought to be kept in mind. One, an "imperfect past" can flow as easily from a historian's pen as through a filmmaker's camera and perhaps prove even more damaging because most filmgoers understand on some level that what they are seeing cannot be literally true while readers of history books may have their critical guard down. Two, no doubt some professional historians first became interested in studying the past because of what they experienced as children in movie theaters, and those interests may stay with them for life. "Many" of the sixty authors who discussed film and history in Carnes's collection admitted that "movies were what attracted them to history as youngsters" (ibid., 9).

40. Curtis Books of New York did a paperback version of *Grierson's Raid* (no publication date included in the book) *after* and in large part *because of* the success of *Bury My Heart at Wounded Knee,* published in 1970. Illinois had printed a paperback edition in 1962. Morningside Press in Dayton, Ohio, which specializes in Civil War studies, brought

out a new hardback edition in 1981. In 1959 United Artists arranged for a special wrap-around "Streamer" for the hardbound edition of *The Horse Soldiers* in an attempt to boost movie—and book—profits. The 1959 Dell paperback of *The Horse Soldiers* was timed to arrive in bookstores just before the release of Ford's film. In this edition and in the 1959 London edition done by Pan Books, which was taken from the Frederick Muller text, not Harper & Brothers (and thus somewhat misleading in having "unabridged" on the title page), the covers featured John Wayne, not the jacket designs done for the original hardbacks. Both promoted themselves by promoting the film, as Ford's Marlowe came to dominate Sinclair's. Dell Comics printed *The Horse Soldiers* as one title in its "movie classics" series (no. 1048, 1959). The writers worked from the script and inserted scenes not included in the film; they even wrote a few of their own. In one sense, Benjamin Henry Grierson was completely lost in all of this marketing. But in another he might eventually have been found by some (I include myself here) who would never have thought to look for him if not for the movie and the novel. *The Horse Soldiers* enjoyed brief runs in Europe and Latin America. In Italy it was released as *Soldati a Cavallo*. In Argentina it became *Marcha de Valientes*. A promotional poster for the Argentine version, based on one used for the U.S. release, had a mesa in the background, apparently on the assumption that this was yet another John Ford Western.

41. Dee Brown to the author, July 5, 1997.

42. Bill Weber to the author, Jan. 26, 1998.

43. Aubrey Williams, ed., *Poetry and Prose of Alexander Pope* (Boston: Houghton Mifflin, 1969), 44, from Pope's *An Essay on Criticism* (1711), line 215; "Drink deep, or taste not the *Pierian Spring,*" Pope advised, because "There *shallow Draughts* intoxicate the Brain, And drinking *largely* sobers us again" (ibid., lines 216–17).

44. The paperback edition of Whitman's *Cavalry Raid* (New York: Ballantine Books, 1956) included a promotional pitch on the back cover stating that inside was "the story of Grierson's fantastic sixteen days behind the Confederate lines, and of the men who rode and fought with him. Most particularly, it is the story of Scott Hazen, Grierson's chief of scouts, who had seen his father shot and his lands confiscated." Scott Hazen was a figment of Whitman's imagination, as were virtually all of the scenes and dialogue in the book. This blurring of the real and the fictional, also evident in Brown's account of the raid, has its counterpart in so-called living history. For example, Plimoth Plantation is more invention than reconstruction. Well-intentioned though the effort may be, there and on a grander scale in Colonial Williamsburg, the outcome could be ironic, encouraging visitors to think that they are somehow traveling through time and thereby diminishing rather than enhancing their appreciation for the difficulties of doing good history and finding the "real" past. Contrast enthusiast Jay Anderson's *Time Machines* (Nashville: American Association for State and Local History, 1984) with the more skeptical John D. Krugler, "Behind the Public Presentations: Research and Scholarship at Living History Museums of Early America," *William and Mary Quarterly* 3d ser. 48 (1991): 347–85, and Richard Handler and Eric Gable, *The New History in an Old Museum* (Durham: Duke Univ. Press, 1997).

45. Butterfield, *Historical Novel,* 95.

46. See Howard Jones, "A Historian Goes to Hollywood: The Spielberg Touch," *AHA Perspectives* 35 (Dec. 1997): 25–28. Jones, a historian whose book on the *Amistad* affair is widely respected, discussed his reaction to Spielberg's approach and mentioned Oxford University Press's reissuing of his *Mutiny on the* Amistad, first published in 1987.

47. Michael Kammen, "The Problem of American Exceptionalism: A Reconsideration," *American Quarterly* 45 (1993): 27; also Kammen, *Mystic Chords of Memory* and *A*

Season of Youth (New York: Knopf, 1978). The battle over the Enola Gay exhibit at the Smithsonian Institution—detailed in Edward T. Linenthal and Tom Englehardt, eds., *History Wars* (New York: Henry Holt, 1996), and Philip Nobile, ed., *Judgment at the Smithsonian* (New York: Marlowe, 1995), like the battle over proposed national history standards reviewed in Gary Nash, Charlotte Crabtree, and Ross E. Dunn, *History on Trial* (New York: Knopf, 1997), are but two of the more recent examples of the passions raised in the shaping and reshaping of historical memory.

48. Margaret Mead, *And Keep Your Powder Dry* (1942; rpt. New York: William Morrow, 1965).

49. Henry St. John, Viscount Bolingbroke, *Letters on the Study of History,* 2 vols. (London: A. Millar, 1752), 1:15, sentiments that can be traced back to antiquity—to Thucydides and to Dionysius of Halicarnassus.

50. Michael Shaara, *The Killer Angels* (New York: David McKay, 1974).

51. Grierson's triumphal return was reported in the *Illinois State Journal,* Oct. 13, 1863 (copy in the Grierson Papers, box 9, folder 4).

52. Henry Forbes, "Grierson's Raid," 27, Ms. 66, Univ. of Arizona version; p. 24 in the Forbes Papers, 4 D.2.3, version, with "confronted" misspelled as "confromted."

53. Stephen Forbes, May 30, 1905, memorial speech, Forbes Papers, 2 B.11.

54. Memorial service program for Stephen Forbes, Mar. 15, 1930, Forbes 6 B.1. Also see the tribute to Forbes by his University of Illinois colleague Henry Ward in *Science* 41 (Apr. 11, 1930): 378–81, which includes the speeding and ticket anecdote.

55. And as such they exemplified the ideals of "manliness, godliness, duty, honor, and knightliness" that Civil War volunteers carried with them to war, as examined in Gerald F. Linderman, *Embattled Courage: The Experience of Combat in the American Civil War* (NewYork: Free Press, 1987), 16. James M. McPherson paints a somewhat different picture in *For Cause and Comrades: Why Men Fought in the Civil War* (New York: Oxford Univ. Press, 1997). For pride in soldiering but suspicion of the professional military, see Marcus Cunliffe, *Soldiers, and Civilians: The Martial Spirit in America, 1775–1865* (Boston: Little, Brown, 1968).

56. See Ronald Steel, "Who Is Us?" *New Republic,* Sept. 14, 21, 1998, 13–14; Louis Menand, "Jerry Don't Surf," *New York Review of Books,* Sept. 24, 1998, 7–8; Jeanine Basinger, "Translating War: The Combat Film Genre and 'Saving Private Ryan,'" *AHA Perspectives* 36 (Oct. 1998): 1, 43–47; and Tom Carson's bitingly prescient observations in "A Reconsideration of *Saving Private Ryan,*" *Esquire,* (Mar. 1999): 70, 72, 74–75. Linderman, *Embattled Courage,* suggests that the "changing circumstances of combat" in the modern age have altered "notions of a dauntless, assertive soldier courage" and "reduced them from a powerful precept to a fugitive ideal" (19). I am not so sure.

57. He is listed on the muster roll printed in Pierce, *History of the Second Iowa Cavalry,* 229.

BIBLIOGRAPHIC ESSAY

The simple listing of primary and "secondary" sources typical in a scholarly bibliography can be as frustrating as it is helpful. Instead, I will identify materials that I found most useful—or, in a few cases, not as useful as I had thought they would be. Naturally I hope that every reader goes to the endnotes, since what I have included in the discussion here is not just a reshuffling of what appears there.

The unpublished manuscripts and printed records that Dee Brown consulted remain the basic sources for Grierson's raid, with but few additions. These are *The War of the Rebellion: A Compilation of the Official Records of the Union and Confederate Armies,* 128 vols. (Washington, D.C., 1880–1901); R. W. Surby's *Grierson Raids, and Hatch's Sixty-four Days March, with Biographical Sketches; also The Life and Adventures of Chickasaw, the Scout* (Chicago: Rounds and James, 1865), which was revised and serialized in the *National Tribune,* July 12 through September 20, 1883, and reissued as one of *Two Great Raids* (Washington, D.C.: National Tribune, 1887); B. H. Grierson's *Record of Services Rendered the Government* (N.p., n.d.) and Grierson's far more extensive unpublished autobiography, "The Lights and Shadows of Life," circa 1892, both located in Springfield at the Illinois State Historical Library; and, finally, the Stephen Alfred Forbes Collection at the Illinois Historical Survey, University of Illinois Library, in Urbana, which includes an account by Henry Forbes as well as one by his younger brother Stephen, and some very revealing letters.

Supplementing these are Stephen Forbes's published account, "Grierson's Cavalry Raid" *Transactions of the Illinois State Historical Society* 12 (1907): 99–130; S. L. Woodward, "Grierson's Raid, April 17th to May 2d, 1863" *Journal of the United States Cavalry Association* 14 (April 1904): 683–710, 15 (July 1904): 94–103; and Lyman B. Pierce, *History of the Second Iowa Cavalry* (Burlington, Iowa.: Hawk-eye Steam Book and Job Printing, 1865). Pierce included a regimental muster roll. Larry Underwood appended muster rolls for the 6th and 7th Illinois Cavalry to his fictionalized version of Grierson's Raid, *The Butternut Guerillas* (1991; rpt. Lincoln, Neb.: Dageforde Publishing, 1994). And, as Underwood noted, information on those regiments can be found in the *Report of the adjutant general of the state of Illinois, 1861–1866* (Springfield, Ill.: Baker, Bailhache, &

Co., 1867). The 1901 revised edition of that report (published by Journal Company, Printers and Binders, also in Springfield) includes, in volume 8, muster lists for both officers and men in the 6th and 7th Illinois Cavalry, identifying who survived the war and who did not. Information on *some* of the survivors can be gleaned from pension lists at the National Archives and Records Administration in Washington, D.C. Various contemporaneous press reports, such as those in *Harper's Weekly* or *Frank Leslie's Illustrated Newspaper* or the *New York Times* or sundry Southern newspapers, are more valuable as commentary on what people not involved in the raid thought happened rather than as sources for what actually occurred.

That *Grierson's Raid* (Urbana: Univ. of Illinois Press, 1954) remains the standard account has as much to do with Dee Brown's storytelling abilities as his research skills. Seemingly every historian who followed Brown has sent readers to his book, from Stephen Z. Starr's *The Union Cavalry in the Civil War,* 3 vols. (Baton Rouge: Louisiana State Univ. Press, 1979–85) to Edwin Cole Bearss's *The Campaign for Vicksburg,* 3 vols. (Dayton, Ohio: Morningside House, 1985–86) to James R. Arnold's *Grant Wins the War: Decision at Vicksburg* (New York: John Wiley & Sons, 1987) to Grierson biographers Bruce J. Dinges's "The Making of a Cavalryman: Benjamin H. Grierson and the Civil War Along the Mississippi, 1861–1865" (Ph.D. dissertation, Rice University, 1978); and William H. Leckie and Shirlie A. Leckie's *Unlikely Warriors: General Benjamin H. Grierson and His Family* (Norman: Univ. of Oklahoma Press, 1984). Dee Brown has given many published interviews over the years, but none discuss Grierson's raid or the making of his book in detail. Neither is there much on the raid or the book in Brown's reminiscences, *When the Century Was Young* (Little Rock, Ark.: August House Publishers, 1993).

Dee Brown will no doubt inspire at least one full-length biography; Harold Sinclair has not to this point, and, sadly, may never do so. Interestingly enough, both Brown and Sinclair became great admirers of Mark Twain and his ability to make fiction ring true to life. The best introduction to Sinclair and his books can be found in Robert Bray's "The American Years of Harold Sinclair" *Illinois Historical Journal* 82 (1989):177–94. Eleanor Ann Browns's "Harold Sinclair and the Technique of the Historical Novel" (M.A. thesis, University of Illinois, 1947) caught Sinclair at mid-career. *The Horse Soldiers* (New York: Harper & Brothers, 1956) received the usual reviews and virtually nothing more. The same is true for the rest of Sinclair's books, with the exception of *The American Years* (New York: Doubleday, Doran, 1938), which was reissued in 1988. The Harold Sinclair Collection is housed at the Milner Library, Illinois State University, Normal, Ilinois. It was catalogued in 1968, not long after the papers were deposited there. That catalog hardly does the collection justice, as I found to my great surprise when librarian Teresa Thomason brought out files that had not been listed in the collection description. Dee Brown has always emphasized the indispensable role of serendipitous discoveries in research and they have occurred time and again in my own work; what happened in Bloomington is just one example.

The Walter Mirisch Papers, U.S. Mss. 87AN, State Historical Society of Wisconsin, Madison, have production materials from *The Horse Soldiers*—soundtrack, poster, pressbook—and Walter Mirisch's copy of the script, but little else. Tino Balio's *United Artists: The Company That Changed the Film Industry* (Madison: Univ. of Wisconsin Press, 1987) deals with *The Horse Soldiers* only in passing but is essential for larger context. Dialogue director Meta Stern's script copy is among the John Ford papers housed in the Lilly Library, Indiana University, Bloomington. Although the general correspondence files are rather slim and materials for *The Horse Soldiers* (aside from still photographs) are scant, the taped interviews (and transcripts) done by Dan Ford, John Ford's grandson, are thick and rich. Dan Ford's biography, *Pappy: The Life of John Ford* (Englewood Cliffs, N.J.: Prentice Hall, 1979) remains the best starting point and serves as a reminder of how difficult it is to reconstruct a life working in archives alone. Much of what Dan Ford recounted he knows from personal experience that will escape any documentary record. Andrew Sinclair did not have Dan Ford's advantages when writing *John Ford: A Biography* (New York: Dial Press, 1978) but he was able to interview many film industry veterans. So, too, with Ronald Davis in his briefer *John Ford: Hollywood's Old Master* (Norman: Univ. of Oklahoma Press, 1995). Scott Eyman's *Print The Legend: The Life and Times of John Ford* (New York: Simon & Schuster, 1999) is the most self-consciously ambitious effort to date. Bill Levy's *John Ford: A Bio-Bibliography* (Westport, Conn.: Greenwood, 1998) is a handy guide, with a small section on *The Horse Soldiers* (184–85) that includes cross-references to various reviews, essays, and general works on Ford and his films.

The better specialized studies on Ford's films, with at least some discussion of *The Horse Soldiers*, are William Darby, *John Ford's Westerns* (Jefferson, N.C.: McFarland, 1996); Tad Gallagher's *John Ford: The Man and His Films* (Berkeley: Univ. of California Press, 1986); and J. A. Place's *The Western Films of John Ford* (Secacus, N.J.: Citadel Press, 1973). The leading John Wayne biographies—Randy Roberts and James S. Olson's detailed *John Wayne: American* (New York: Free Press, 1995); Ronald Davis's concise *Duke: The Life and Image of John Wayne* (Norman: Univ. of Oklahoma Press, 1998); and Garry Wills's idiosyncratic *John Wayne's America* (New York: Simon & Schuster, 1997)—have comparatively little on *The Horse Soldiers*.

Film is taken more seriously by mainstream professional historians than it used to be, though there are still those who feel that the profession should concern itself with other, supposedly higher, matters. Because old prejudices die hard, some historians would rather that the *American Historical Review* and the *Journal of American History* drop their film review sections. But Robert Brent Toplin's *History by Hollywood* (Urbana: Univ. of Illinois Press, 1996) marked a trail that others will no doubt follow. Intellectual historians interested in the social context of ideas had independently been moving in that direction anyway. Steven Watts's *The Magic Kingdom: Walt Disney and the American Way of Life* (Boston: Houghton Mifflin, 1997) and Karal Ann Marling's *George Washington Slept Here* (Cambridge: Harvard Univ. Press, 1988) are fine examples of intellectual history set within a popular culture framework, and Michael Kammen's *A Season of Youth* (New York: Knopf, 1978) and *Mystic Chords of Memory* (New York: Knopf, 1991) are excellent models for those looking to combine what were once considered distinct fields. In some sense, all are building on the foundation laid by an earlier generations of scholars, such as Henry Nash Smith, in *Virgin Land* (Cambridge: Harvard Univ. Press, 1950) and John William Ward, in *Andrew Jackson: Symbol for an Age* (New York: Oxford Univ. Press, 1955). The so-called myth and symbol approach that Smith and Ward pioneered has its limits, but it has been indispensable in breaking down barriers that once artificially separated fields of inquiry. Thus our understanding of the Civil War has already been enhanced by Jim Cullen's *The Civil War in Popular Culture: A Reusable Past* (Washington, D.C.: Smithsonian Institution Press, 1995); and Carol Reardon's *Pickett's Charge in History and Memory* (Chapel Hill: Univ. of North Carolina Press, 1997). No doubt other studies on the Civil War in popular culture and national memory will appear soon, as the historian's net is cast ever wider.

INDEX

Abbott, John, praises raid, 22

Adams, John, on history, 105

Adams, John Quincy, as portrayed in *Amistad,* 136

Adams, Wirt, 14, 16, 22, 30, 47, 56, 120, 121; characterized, 31; in film, 87, in novel, 56; on Grierson, 18

Amistad (film), 135–136

Amite River, 16, 47, 75, 87

Andersonville, anachronistic allusions to, 87, 92, 93

Banks, Nathaniel, praises Grierson, 18, 132

Barteau, Clark, as depicted by Brown, 32–34

Baton Rouge, La.: as raiders' destination, xii, 15, 26; as raiders' destination in film, 87, 99, 113; as raiders' destination in novel, 63; raiders' arrival in, 16–17, 17, 28, 30; raiders' arrival in, in film, 106–7, 108, 114; raiders' arrival in, in novel, 75

Becker, Carl, on historical "facts," xii, 125, 132

Bellah, James Warner, 80, 94

Belser, Thomas, review of *Grierson's Raid,* 48

Berlin, Isaiah, on imagination in history, 134

Blackburn, William, 11, 15, 45, 124; in novel, 62–63; in film, 88, 110; blacks: assist raiders, 34, 43; follow them, 12, 16–17

Blight, David, on history and film, 127

Bogdanovich, Peter, interviews John Ford, 104, 109

Bolingbroke, Henry St. John, on history, 142

Brady, Mathew, fictionalized in film cameo, 87, 110

Bragg, Braxton, 2, 5

Branagh, Kenneth, and popularity of Shakespeare, 138

Bray, Robert, 53

Brown, Dee: 24; account of the raid, 27–48; background, 25–27; critical reaction to, 48, 50; errors by, 132–33; on fiction and history, 50–51, 134, 145, 152n.33; likes Ford film, 139; real events left out by, 119–22, 124–25; rediscovers Grierson's raid, xiii, and Sinclair, 50–51, 55, 115

Buffington, William, 37

Burns, Ken, on film and history, 137–38

Butterfield, Herbert, on history and novels, 105, 125, 139–41

Butternut Guerillas: exploits of, 11, 13, 15, 22, 37, 41–45, 119–22; formed, 10, 124; in novel, 69, 71; film version, 88; questions surrounding, 122–23, 124, 136

Buttolph, David, music for film, 84

Cameron, James, 136

Carnes, Mark, on film and history, 168n.39

Carey, Harry, Jr., 81, 89

Chamberlain, Joshua, 143

Chamberlain-Hunt Academy cadets in film, 95

Civil War Centennial Commission, 127–28, 141

Clothier, William, 84, 105, 108, 114

Corinth, Miss., 2, 6

Cross, Charles, 135

Current, Richard N., on fiction and history, 152n.33

Curtis, Ken, in film, 89, 96, 106–7

Custer, George Armstrong, 144

Dahlgren, Ulric, failed cavalry raid of, 20–21

Davis, Jefferson, 4, 21, 30, 94

Davis, Natalie Zemon, on film and history, 168n.37

Demos, John, on fiction and history, 125

Dodge, Grenville, diversion for raid, 7, 8

Donald, David, 129

Early, Jubal, 21

Edwards, Sherman, and play *1776,* xii

Eisenhower, Dwight, on Civil War centennial, 128

Enterprise, Miss.: in novel, 68; raid incident outside, 38–39, 41; facts, questionable, about raid, 129, 132–33, 146n.9, 147n.10, 148n.23, 149n. 46. *See also* fiction and history

Fehrenbacher, Don, fiction and history, 152n.33

Fiction and history, xiii, 50–51, 57, 119, 125–26, 132–45, 152n.33

Field Photo Farm, and John Ford, 97

1st Illinois Artillery, 7; not in novel, 59

Fischer, John, 118

Foner, Eric, 138

Foote, Shelby, Burns documentary and success of books, 138

Forbes, Henry, 10, 124, 144; account of raid, 17, 26, 27; Brown on exploits of, 34–41; in novel, 50, 66–68, 75–76; not in film, 87

Forbes, Stephen, 28, 124, 144; account of raid, 26, 27, 123, 135; Brown on exploits of, 34–41

Ford, Dan, 104; on John Ford, 81, 97

Ford, John, 80–83, 135; didactic intent of, 142–43, 145; dislike of *The Horse Soldiers,* 104, 105, 108–9; patriotism of, 96–97; synopsis of film by, 84–102; tinkering with film, 108–14

Ford, Pat, 83; on film critics, 158n.33

Forrest, Nathan Bedford, 3, 5, 31, 61; defeated by Wilson, 21; defeats Streight, 20; as fictionalized composite for film, 87, 95, 102

Freeman, Douglas Southall, John Ford's favorite historian, 94

Gable, Clark, 138; considered for film, 106

Gibson, Althea, 99; death as Lukey in film, 101; rewritten scene, 110–12

Gibson, Hoot, in film, 89

Gone with the Wind, impact of, 138, 141

Grant, Ulysses S., 22, 32, 79, 123, 136; admires Grierson, 6, 18, 19; attempts to take Vicksburg, 2–5, 7, 14–15; depiction by Brown, 29; depiction in film, 82, 84, 86–87; pressure on to take Vicksburg, 2, 29, 86

Grant, U. S., III, and Civil War centennial, 128

Grierson, Benjamin Henry: Brown on, 45–48; character of, 162n.52; command of, 5–6, 26; on disputed history of raid, 124, 135–36; fictionalized in film, 83, 86–87, 89–102; fictionalized in novel, 50, 56, 59–61, 75, 77; lasting appeal of, 142–44; love story in film, 98–102, 108–14; raid by, 7–24

Halleck, Henry, 19

Hamilton, Charles, Grierson dislikes, 6

Hatch, Edward, 6, 7, 28, 30, 32, 145; fictionalized in novel, 59, 62, 63–66; marginalized in film, 87–88; successful ruse by, 9, 32–34

Hazlehurst, Miss., 12, 14, 30, 31; actual incident in, 43–45; scene in novel in, 62–63

Herodotus, xi

Holden, William, in film, 82, 89–94, 100, 106, 112–13, 128

Holly Springs, Miss., 4, 5

Hopkins, Anthony, in *Amistad*, 137

Horse Soldiers, The (Sinclair novel): xii; as history, 50–51; critical reaction to, 76; material cut from, 115–19; role in shaping values, 139–45; synopsis of, 55–76

Horse Soldiers, The (Ford film): xii; changes while filming, 108–14; critical reaction to, 102–4; role in shaping values, 139–45; synopsis of, 84–102

Hurlbut, Stephen, 6, 7–8, 123–24, 135, 149n.40; in novel, 56, 61; in film, 85–87, 106, 110

Jackson, Miss., 6, 7, 14, 18, 30, 61, 124

Jacksonville, Ill., as Grierson home, 7, 45, 143–44

Jefferson Military College, fictionalized in film, 94–96, 157n.24

Johnston, Joseph E., 4, 30

Jones, Stan, and film, 84–87, 137

Justice, Keith, on persistence of fable, 133

Kammen, Michael, on selective historical memory, 141

Kantor, MacKinlay, 87

Kelly, Lycurgus, 43–44

Kennedy, Fred, death of, 107–8

Kennedy, John F., 129

Kerby, John Jacob, 145

Kilpatrick, Judson, failed cavalry raid of, 20–21

La Capra, Dominick, xii

La Grange, Tennessee: Grierson's cavalry based in, 5; raid launched from, 6, 8, 22, 28; some raiders return to, 9, 33, 65, 88

Lee, Anna, in film, 95

Lincoln, Abraham, 20, 45, 53, 149n.40

Lippincott, Thomas, account of, 122, 123–24

Lukacs, John, xii

Mahin, John Lee, 78–79, 128, 138, 145; deal with Mirisch brothers, 79–80, 82,

108, 160n.10; disappointed in film, 104, 109; and *The Horse Soldiers* as history, 79, 133–34, 136–37; preferred ending, 104, 106–8; working with Ford, 80, 94, 96, 105–6, 110, 112–15; writing *The Horse Soldiers* script, 79, 83–84, 86–88, 115–16, 159n.3

Martin, Charles, 37

May, Rollo, 134

McClernand, John, 4

McCullagh, C. Brendan, on historical truths, 133

McLaglen, Victor, 89

Mead, Margaret, 141

Meade, George G., 21

Memphis, Tennessee, 2, 6, 61, 82

Meridian, Miss., 6, 30, 61

Michener, James, on history, 25

Miers, Earl Schenck, on novel, 76

Mirisch brothers, 79–80, 82, 102, 106, 108

Mississippi Central Railroad, 2

Mitchell, Margaret, 138, 141

Mobile and Ohio Railroad: Confederate attempts to protect, 30, 32; damage to, 22; plans to disrupt service on, 6, 9, 10, 35, 65, 67, 87

Morgan, Edmund S., on fiction, 52

Morgan, John Hunt, 5, 19; defeat and capture, 21–22

Mosby, John S., 122

Natchez, Miss., 18, 30, 63; filming at, 82, 83, 102

Natchitoches, La., filming at, 82, 83, 108, 133

Nevins, Allan, Civil War centennial worries, 129

New Orleans, Jackson and Great Northern Railroad, 12, 14, 119

Newton Station, Miss.: historical markers in, 130–32; raid in film, 82, 83, 86, 108, 109; raiders in, 9, 10–12, 14, 43, raiders' destination after, 12, 30, 35, 37

Nixon, Richard, 97

Nugent, Frank, writer, 81–82

Patriot, The (film), as bad history,
167n.34
Pearl River, 10, 13, 42–43, 63
Peck, Gregory, 106
Pemberton, John C., 2, 5, 18, 32, 56;
characterized, 29–31, 150n.10
Pennick, Jack, 95
Pierce, Lyman, raid account by, 33
Plimoth Plantation, and invented past,
169n.44
Pope, Alexander, 139
Port Gibson, Miss., 12, 14, 18
Porter, David, 4, 7, 18
Pratt, Judson, 89
Prince, Edward, 13, 35, 43, 44;
fictionalized in novel, 59; further
changed in film, 88

Rackin, Martin, 115, 128, 139; *The Horse
Soldiers* as history, 79, 134; working
with Ford on film, 96, 105–6, 106;
writing the script, 78–79, 99, 159n.3
Richardson, Robert, 47; fails to stop
Grierson, 18; assessed, 31–32
Robinson, Isaac, 37
Roebuck, Sidney, 130
Rosecrans, William S., 2
Russell, Bing, 89, 106

Saccio, Peter, on Shakespeare, 138
Saving Private Ryan (film), 145
Sayles, John, 138
Schama, Simon, 136, 167n.32
Schmitt, Martin, 26
2d Iowa Cavalry, 5, 8, 9; in film, 86; in
novel, 63; success on raid, 33–34
1776 (Broadway musical), xii
7th Illinois Cavalry, 5–11, 13, 16;
Company B of as "forlorn hope,"
34–41; in film, 86; in novel, 66–68. *See
also* Forbes, Henry; Forbes, Stephen;
Surby, Richard
Shakespeare, William, 138
Shaara, Michael, 143
Sherman, William Tecumseh, 4, 22, 24,
32, 83; admires Grierson, 5–6;

compliment misattributed to, 27, 78,
132; in film 86, 110
Shreveport, La., and film, 83, 102
Sinclair, Harold, xiii, 50; background of,
52–55; and film, 102, 103, 114–15; last
years of, 76–77. *See also Horse Soldiers,
The* (novel)
Sinclair, Ward, 55, 77
6th Illinois Cavalry, 5–8, 13, 16. *See also*
7th Illinois Cavalry
Smith, William Sooy, 6, 7, 8; in novel, 56,
61; faulty memory of, 123, 136
Southern Railroad, 6, 9, 61
Spielberg, Stephen, 136, 145
Stanton, Edwin, 20
Steadman, George, 43–44
Stewart, Jimmy, 106
Stone, Peter, xii
Streight, Abel, failed raid of, 20
Stuart, J. E. B., 19, 21, 22, 122
Sully, Alfred, campaign fictionalized, 76
Surby, Richard: displaced in film, 88;
exploits of, 10, 15, 41–45, 119–22; in
novel, 50; raid account by, 22, 27, 135.
See also Butternut Guerillas

Taylor, Elizabeth, 106
Thelen, David, on history and memory, 135
Thomas, Benjamin, 154n.23
Thomas, Evan, 55; changes to novel,
117–19, 161n.41
Thucydides, xi
Titanic (film), 103, 136
Toplin, Robert Brent, on film and history,
167n.36
Towers, Constance, in film, 98–102, 106,
112–14
Trafton, George, 120, 121
Truth, problem of historical, xi, 132–45.
See also fiction and history

United Artists, 79, 83, 102, 106

Van Dorn, Earl, 4, 5, 11, 30, 122
Vicksburg, Miss., 63; Grant's victory at,
22, 29, 79, 128; importance of railway

to, 15, 30; strategic importance of 2,
85–86; Union attempts to take, 2–5
Vidal, Gore, on fiction as history debate,
152n.33
Virginia Military Institute cadets, 94,
157n.24

Wall's Bridge, battle of, 15, 45; in novel,
55, 62–63; in film, 83–84
Walton, Clyde, 78, 128, 154n.26
Wayne, John, as fictionalized Grierson, xii,
81, 82, 84–102; altered scenes with,
108–14; fictional character over
historical figure, 128, 137, 139

Weber, Bill, quest for historical truth,
129–32, 133
White, Hayden, on history and fiction, xii,
125
Whitman, S. E., novel about Grierson's
raid, 152n.32, 169n.44
Williams, Nancy, 130
Wilson, James, cavalry raid of, 21
Woodward, C. Vann, 137, 168n.37
Woodward, Samuel L., 7
Worden, Hank, 89

Yule, Dr. Erastus: 15; in film, 89–94, 110;
in novel, 71–75

Fiction as Fact

was designed

by Will Underwood;

composed in 10/13$\frac{1}{2}$ Sabon

by The Book Page, Inc., on an

Apple system using QuarkXPress;

Printed by sheet-fed offset lithography

on 60-pound Supple Opaque stock (an

acid-free paper with recycled content),

notch bound with paper covers and

Smyth sewn over binder's boards,

with dust jackets and covers

printed in three colors by

Thomson-Shore, Inc.;

and published by

The Kent State University Press

KENT, OHIO 44242